Start Your Own

IMPORT/ EXPORT BUSINESS

Additional titles in *Entrepreneur's **Startup Series***

Start Your Own

Bar or Club

Bed & Breakfast

Business on eBay

Business Support Service

Car Wash

Child Care Service

Cleaning Service

Clothing Store

Coin-Operated Laundry

Consulting

Crafts Business

e-Business

e-Learning Business

Event Planning Business

Executive Recruiting Service

Freight Brokerage Business

Gift Basket Service

Growing and Selling Herbs and Herbal Products

Home Inspection Service

Information Consultant Business

Law Practice

Lawn Care or Landscaping Business

Mail Order Business

Medical Claims Billing Service

Personal Concierge Service

Personal Training Business

Pet-Sitting Business

Restaurant and Five Other Food Businesses

Retail Business and More

Self-Publishing Business

Seminar Production Business

Specialty Travel & Tour Business

Staffing Service

Vending Business

Wedding Consultant Business

Wholesale Distribution Business

Entrepreneur MAGAZINE'S

start*up*

2ND EDITION

Start Your Own

IMPORT/
EXPORT
BUSINESS

*Your Step-by-Step
Guide to Success*

Entrepreneur Press and Jennifer Dorsey

Ep
Entrepreneur
Press

Editorial Director: Jere L. Calmes
Managing Editor: Marla Markman
Cover Design: Beth Hansen-Winter
Production and Composition: Eliot House Productions

This publication is designed to provide accurate and authoritative information in regard to the subject matter covered. It is sold with the understanding that the publisher is not engaged in rendering legal, accounting or other professional services. If legal advice or other expert assistance is required, the services of a competent professional person should be sought.

Library of Congress Cataloging-in-Publication Data
    Dorsey, Jennifer.
        Start your own import/export business/by by Entrepreneur Press and Jennifer Dorsey.—2nd ed.
            p.   cm.
        Includes index.
        ISBN-13: 978-1-59918-108-0 (alk. paper)
        ISBN-10: 1-59918-108-8 (alk. paper)
            1. Trading companies—Management. 2. New business enterprises—Management.
    II. Title.

HF1416.D66 2007
658.1'1—dc22   2007011665

Printed in the United States of America
12 11 10 09 08   10 9 8 7 6 5 4 3

Contents

▲

Preface

You're holding this book either in your hands, on your lap, or on your desk—probably dangerously near a spill-able cup of coffee—because you're one of those people who likes to live on the edge. You're contemplating starting your own business.

This is one of the most exhilarating things you can do for yourself and your family. It's also one of the scariest.

Owning your own business means you're the boss, the big cheese, the head honcho. You make the rules. You lay down the law. It also means you can't call in sick (especially when you are also the only employee), you can't let somebody else worry about making enough to cover payroll and expenses, and you can't defer that cranky client or intimidating IRS letter to a higher authority. You're it.

We're assuming you've picked up this particular book on starting and running an import/export business for one or more of the following reasons:

- You have a background in the import/export field.
- You're an avid fan of the Travel Channel, your passport is close at hand even when you're just going to the supermarket, and you think international trade is a glamorous and exciting business.
- You have a background in sales or distribution and feel that sales is sales, no matter where in the world you are.
- You have no background or interest in any of the above but believe import/export is a hot opportunity and are willing to take a chance.

Which did you choose? (Didn't know it was a test, did you?)

Well, you can relax, because there is no wrong answer. Any of these responses is entirely correct so long as you realize that they all involve a lot of learning and a lot of hard work. They can also involve a heck of a lot of fun, as well as a tremendous amount of personal and professional satisfaction.

Our goal here is to tell you everything you need to know to decide whether an import/export business is the right business for you, and then, assuming it is, to:

- get your business started successfully,
- keep your business running successfully, and
- make friends and influence people. (That's actually part of Chapter 12, which is about advertising and marketing.)

We've attempted to make this book as user-friendly as possible. We've interviewed lots of people out there on the front lines of the industry—all around the world—to find out how the import/export business really works and what makes it tick. And we've set aside lots of places for them to tell their own stories and share their own hard-won advice and suggestions, which creates a sort of round-table discussion group with you right in the thick of things. (For a listing of these successful business owners, see the Appendix.) We've broken our chapters into manageable sections on every aspect of start-up and operations. And we've left some space for your creativity to soar.

We've packed our pages with helpful addresses, phone numbers, and web site addresses so that you can get up and running on your new venture as quickly as possible. And we've provided a resource section crammed with even more contacts and sources. (Here's a tip: You'll find a complete listing of the sources mentioned throughout the book in the Appendix.)

So sit back—don't spill that coffee!—get reading, and get ready to become an import/export pro.

For Will

International Trade
Passport to Success

International trade is one of the hot industries of the millennium. But it's not new. Think Marco Polo. Think the great caravans of the biblical age with their cargoes of silks and spices. Think even further back to prehistoric man trading shells and salt with distant tribes. Trade exists because one group or country has a supply of some commodity or merchandise that is in demand by another. And as the world becomes more and more technologically advanced, as we shift in subtle and not so subtle ways toward one-world modes of thought, international trade becomes more and more rewarding, both in terms of profit and personal satisfaction.

This chapter explores the flourishing business of international trade from both the import and export sides of the fence. Think of this chapter as an investigative report—like those TV news magazine shows, but without the commercials. We'll delve into the steadily rising economic success of the field and dip into the secrets of America's, and the world's, import/export industry.

The International Adventurer

The quintessential importer is Trader Sam in his battered fedora, bargaining for esoteric goods in exotic markets amid a crescendo of foreign tongues. Or maybe that's Indiana Jones. If that's your idea of an international trader, you're absolutely right. You're also dead wrong.

Importing is not just for those lone footloose adventurer types who survive by their wits and the skin of their teeth. It's big business these days—to the tune of an annual $1.2 trillion in goods, according to the U.S. Department of Commerce. Exporting is just as big. In one year alone, American companies exported $772 billion in merchandise to more than 150 foreign countries. Everything from beverages to commodes—and a staggering list of other products you might never imagine as global merchandise—are fair game for the savvy trader. And these products are bought, sold, represented, and distributed somewhere in the world on a daily basis.

But the import/export field is not the sole purview of the conglomerate corporate trader. While large companies exported 70 percent of the value of all exports, according to the U.S. Department of Commerce, the big guys make up only about 4 percent of all exporters. Which means that the other 96 percent of exporters—the lion's share—are small outfits like yours will be—when you're new, at least.

Champagne and Caviar

Why are imports such big business in the United States and around the world? There are lots of reasons, but the three main ones boil down to:

Stat Fact

According to the U.S. Department of Commerce, America's recent annual exports to Europe exceeded $163 billion. American exports to Western Hemisphere nations totaled more than $323 billion.

- *Availability*. There are some things you just can't grow or make in your home country. Bananas in Alaska, for example, mahogany lumber in Maine, or Ball Park franks in France.
- *Cachet*. A lot of things, like caviar and champagne, pack more cachet, more of an "image," if they're imported rather than home-grown. Think Scandinavian furniture, German beer, French perfume, Egyptian cotton. Even when you can make it at home, it all seems classier when it comes from distant shores.
- *Price*. Some products are cheaper when brought in from out of the country. Korean toys, Taiwanese electronics, and Mexican clothing, to rattle off a few, can often be manufactured or assembled in foreign factories for far less money than if they were made on the domestic front.

Aside from cachet items, countries typically export goods and services that they can produce inexpensively and import those that are produced more efficiently somewhere else. What makes one product less expensive for a nation to manufacture than another? Two factors: resources and technology. Resources are natural products, such as timber and minerals, as well as human ones, like low-cost labor and highly skilled workers. Technology is the knowledge and tools to process raw resources into finished products. A country with extensive oil resources and the technology of a refinery, for example, will export oil but may need to import clothing.

To Boldly Go

Because the United States covers a wide geographic region with a large population, we haven't really felt the need to travel abroad to sell products. But exports represent a vast, virtually untapped field of endeavor—one into which few companies have boldly gone.

Surprisingly, most of those daring exporters are smaller firms. According to a recent report from the U.S. Census Bureau, companies with fewer than 100 employees accounted for about 90 percent of all exporters, while almost 96 percent of the total exporters were small or medium-sized companies (meaning they employ fewer than 500 people). Small companies account for 19 percent of total known export value.

Also surprisingly, most exporters—to the tune of 91 percent—shipped goods to fewer than 10 countries. The top export destinations, in order of preference, were Canada, Mexico, Japan, China, the United Kingdom, and, last but not least, Germany.

Import/Export—The Prequel

OK, you may be thinking, sounds good. But what exactly does an international trader do? In the simplest terms, he or she is a salesperson. Instead of peddling domestically manufactured products on his or her home turf, a trader deals in more exotic merchandise, materials that are foreign to somebody on some far shore. The importer/exporter also acts as a sort of international matchmaker, pairing up buyers and sellers of products in different countries. He can operate as a middleman, purchasing merchandise directly from the manufacturer and selling to retailers or wholesalers in another country. Or he may have his own network of retail distribution representatives selling on commission. As a third permutation, he might hire an outside company to find sales for him. And as a fourth version, he might serve as a consultant for foreign countries that want to export their products but don't know how.

Let's back up a little and take this one step at a time. When you're wearing your import hat, you'll be bringing goods into the United States. When you've got on your export cap, you'll be shipping things out of the country, into foreign markets.

Let's say, for example, that you've decided to import Guatemalan handcrafts. You might have spotted them at an outdoor market while you were traveling through Central America, or maybe you became involved by answering a trade lead, a "want ad" placed by a local artisan group desperately seeking U.S. representation. In either case, you swing into action. You get hold of a price list and some samples and then, here in America, you ferry the samples around to wholesalers or retailers, generate interest through your top-notch salesmanship, and book orders. Once you've made a predetermined number of sales, you purchase the handcrafts from the artisans, have them shipped to your buyers, and then those buyers pay you.

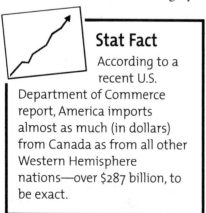

This may sound complicated, with you busily purchasing merchandise and having it sent on to third parties who haven't yet coughed up a dime, but there are ways to protect yourself that you'll learn as we go along in this book. And this won't be the only way you'll structure deals. You might, for example, work off a commission as a representative, negotiating payments directly between artisans and buyers, so that you don't put up any money yourself. But we'll discuss all this later, too. For now, let's say that you'll learn how to make it work.

Ice Chests to Siberia

You'll also learn how to export merchandise. You might, for example, decide to sell ice chests in Siberia. (Well, why not? It isn't icy there all the time.) You may have seen the manufacturer's advertisement seeking a sales or distribution representative. But in this instance, let's say you came up with this idea on your own after spotting the sporty items in a local store and figuring that the really American-looking country-western decals on the product would give it a certain "imported" cachet in the target country. You approach the manufacturer, who may very well be astounded by the idea of exporting her product—this is still a novel idea to most companies. But you explain why you think she has a hot ticket for a cold climate, and you offer to purchase the ice chests at her factory price and she can leave the selling to you. All you need from her is a price list, some samples and figures on what quantities you can order, and how long it will take her to fill your Siberian orders.

The manufacturer agrees and you're off and running, with your first tasks being to determine just how to generate sales in Siberia and how to price the ice chests to cover expenses (including shipping costs, taxes, and tariffs) and still make a profit. Next, you find a foreign partner to distribute your product in Siberia. You send him some samples and a price list, and he gets busy selling.

As you predicted, the American ice chests are a smash hit. Your sales representative generates oodles of sales from Siberian retailers and sends the orders to you along with letters of credit from the buyers. (A letter of credit is an agreement from the buyer's bank to release the buyer's funds into your local bank account. More on this later.) So with your orders and letter of credit in hand, you purchase enough ice chests to fill the orders and have them picked up by the shipping company directly from the manufacturer. Then you take the shipping documents—showing that you've fulfilled your part of the deal by sending out the merchandise—and the letters of credit to your bank and—bingo! The money goes into your account. As a final step, you send your Siberian sales representative his commission.

And that's—in a very basic way—how the international trade business works. It can appear daunting, with convoluted components like customs, trade barriers and tariffs, currency fluctuations, exclusive/nonexclusive distribution rights, and packing and shipping plights—not to mention cultural and communication twists—but it can also be exciting, rewarding, and profitable. And not at all daunting once you've done your homework.

Back to the Future

It's no wonder that international trade is a hot field today. We're living in a brave new world. The enthusiastic emergence of free market ideas around the globe has created an unprecedented bounty of international trade opportunities. Markets that didn't even exist a few short years ago now devour imported goods with startlingly voracious appetites.

If you picture the globe as a world market map and the international trader as a jet-setting country-hopper (like in those old movies where a dotted line shows the trail of the hero's plane), you'd be hard-pressed to find a spot where you couldn't deal in imports or exports. The "Asian Tigers" and other nations of the Asian Pacific Rim are booming, with China representing the single largest market opportunity in the world. On the other side of the International Date Line, Mexico has emerged as one of the United States' biggest trading partners. The passage of the North American Free Trade Agreement, otherwise known as NAFTA, offers a historic opportunity to create a single, unified market from Cambridge Bay in northern Canada to Tapachula at the southern tip of Mexico. Across the Atlantic, Europe is experiencing a new era of economic expansion. Former Soviet countries—the "stans"—are developing quickly and eager to trade with wealthy nations. And in Africa, traditionally isolated countries are beginning to follow South Africa's successful example in using economic development to facilitate social and political reform.

As a budding import/export entrepreneur, you couldn't wish for a better setup. The world is your oyster, the globe your market. Opportunities abound whether you want to import foreign goods into America or export our own products to outsiders.

Counting Your Coconuts

What can you expect to make as an international trader? The amount's entirely up to you, depending only on how serious you are and how willing you are to expand. Annual gross revenues for the industry range from $40,000 to $300,000 and beyond, with an average of about $85,000. Some traders work from home, supplementing nine-to-five incomes with their trading expertise. Others have launched thriving full-time businesses that demand constant care and feeding.

Dan S., an exporter in New Jersey, runs his trading business on his own. Farther down the East Coast in Maryland, Wahib W. heads an export company that, with a staff of five, oversees multimillion-dollar contracts.

"There are tons and tons of opportunity for [export] trade," says Wahib W. "U.S. manufacturers are at least ten years behind the clock in exporting." So the potential for growth is entirely up to you—as long as you're willing to put in the time.

"Be prepared to work long hours!" advises Jan H., a trader in Belgium.

"You have to try with all your energy," says Bruno C., an export manager in France.

And Wahib echoes this sentiment. "Just keep doing your job," he counsels. "Work on it all the time."

> **Fun Fact**
>
> According to the U.S. Department of Commerce, United Arab Emirates, Norway, and Israel rank among the top 50 suppliers of imports to the United States. Canada, Mexico, and Japan are at the top of the list. At the bottom? Tuvalu, Western Sahara, and Mayotte.

"Do not expect immediate or short-term success," adds Lloyd D., an export manager in Florida. "Be willing to work around the international clock, if you will; accept discourtesies, both foreign and domestic, in stride; maintain the highest standard of personal and business ethics in dealing with your principal and buyer, learn from your mistakes, and keep a supply of antidepressants nearby."

Crank-Up Costs

One of the catch-22s of being in business for yourself is that you need money to make money—in other words, you need start-up funds. These costs range from less than $5,000 to more than $25,000 for the import/export business. You can start out homebased, which means you won't need to worry about leasing office space. You don't need to purchase a lot of inventory and you probably won't need employees.

> **Tip...**
>
> **Smart Tip**
>
> What is a BEM? It's what the U.S. Department of Commerce's International Trade Administration calls a Big Emerging Market, or in other words, a country with rapidly expanding trade opportunities. Current BEMs include Egypt, Mexico, Poland, South Africa, South Korea, and Turkey.

Your basic necessities will be a computer, printer, fax machine, and internet service. If you already have these items, then you're off and running. Several of the traders we talked with started from ground zero. "We started from nothing," says Wahib W., "but once they got a large project, that was all it took."

Peter P. started a trading company from a similar financial position. "We had very little money in the bank," he says. What they did have was a carefully built relationship with suppliers, and with this valuable asset the company was able to get up and running.

The Rock of Gibraltar

In addition to profits and start-up costs, two other important aspects to consider are risk and stability. You want a business that, like the Rock of Gibraltar, is here to stay. In import/export, the stability factors are as strong as you are. The world isn't going anywhere (we hope), and neither is the need and desire for international trade.

The key to longevity in import/export, Peter P. feels, is in maintaining a consistent performance. "There are a lot of opportunists who have come into this business," he says. "They've got a fax [machine] in their house; they make a couple thousand dollars and disappear. They're here today, gone tomorrow. To prove yourself as a consistent [trader] who can keep the clients and businesses alive on a day-in, day-out basis, that's very important."

The risk factor is relatively low, providing you're willing to work for your rewards. Michael R., an international trade consultant in Daugendorf, Germany, advises: "Look at the markets, the pricing, the trends. Look to your customers' wishes, target your market, and you will never, ever fail, so long as you do all this thoroughly and earnestly."

The Right Stuff

So you've decided that running an import/export business is potentially profitable for you. You're willing to invest not only the money but also the time to learn the ropes and become established as a pro. What else should you consider? Personality.

Not everybody is cut out to be an international trader. This is not, for example, a career for the sales-phobic. If you're one of those people who would rather work on a chain gang than sell Girl Scout cookies, or if you blanch at the thought of making a sales pitch, then you don't want to be in import/export. This is also not a career for the organizationally challenged. If you're one of those let-the-devil-handle-the-details types whose idea of follow-up is waiting to see what happens next, you should think twice about international trading.

If, on the other hand, you're an enthusiastic salesperson, a dynamo at tracking things like invoices and shipping receipts, and your idea of heaven is seeing where new ideas and new products will take you and then getting them there, and if, to top it off, you love the excitement of dealing with people from different cultures, then this is the career for you.

> ### Bright Idea
> Cruise the world on the internet. Meet international businesspeople, get an idea of what global small business is like, even ask advice. For starters, check out the International Small Business Consortium, which boasts more than 30,000 members from more than 130 countries at www.isbc.com. You can get help from, and develop business connections with, people all over the world.

Traits of the Trade

Hey, kids! Take this fun quiz and find out if you've got what it takes to become an ace international trader.

1. *My idea of a fun evening is:*
   a. Watching James Bond movies on television. He's my idea of an agent!
   b. Kicking back with a piña colada, a copy of *Export Today* magazine, and a Spanish for Gringos tape on my headset.
   c. Cruising around town singing "American Pie."

2. *When I send Christmas gifts to relatives who live out of state, I usually:*
   a. Wait until December 24, stuff the gifts into old grocery bags with the addresses scribbled in crayon, then rush to the post office and stand in a huge, snaky line with all the other procrastinators and hope my gifts arrive on time and intact.
   b. Wrap my gifts carefully in specially selected packaging no later than December 10, call my predesignated FedEx or UPS courier (I've already checked to see which is cheaper and faster), then follow up to make sure the gifts arrive on time and intact.
   c. Hope no one notices I forgot to send gifts.

3. *I consider myself to be a "people" person because:*
   a. Even though I have to force myself, I'm able to interact with people so long as it's not more than once a day.
   b. I love working with all kinds of folks!
   c. I know all the words to the Barbra Streisand song "People."

4. *If I could spend one week a month in a foreign country, I would:*
   a. Go to the nearest McDonald's and stay there until it's time to go home.
   b. Try to meet all kinds of people so I could see the world from different perspectives and learn about other cultures.
   c. Try not to breathe in case I picked up some sort of weird foreign germs.

Scoring: If you chose "b" for each answer, you passed with flying colors! You've got what it takes to become an international trader. You're self-motivated, detail-oriented, and eager to work with people all over the world on their own terms.

Move Over, Trader Sam

It also helps if you already have a background in import/export. Most of the traders we talked with were well-versed in the industry before launching their own businesses. Peter P., who founded a Russian trading company, segued directly from his college major in international business to an operations position with an international frozen meat trading company in Atlanta, which landed him in the right place at the right time.

Tip...

Smart Tip
The former Soviet Union countries are thriving centers for international trade. According to a recent U.S. Department of Commerce report, American exports to the region have jumped almost a billion dollars in one year.

"I speak both Russian and Ukrainian fluently," Peter says. "I'm of Ukrainian descent. I took Russian as a minor in college, initially as an easy grade. Little did I know when I graduated back in '89 that Russia would open up to the West shortly thereafter."

Lucky for Peter. After he'd worked up to a senior trading position with the Atlanta company, a top food trading and distribution company in Russia hired him as its procurement director. "After two years with them, a group of executives from the firm [and I] decided to strike out on our own and form a new company," Peter says. "We felt we could run a business as effectively if not more effectively."

It's No Secret

Should you forget a career in import/export if you're not already steeped in the industry? No. It's entirely possible to start from scratch. You simply offset your deficit in international trade with your assets in a business you already know. If you're a computer whiz, start out importing or exporting computers. If your turf is landscape materials, go green. Launch your import/export business with those same materials. Go with what you already understand.

And don't let the mechanics of international trade—like letters of credit—scare you away. "You have to know what you're doing," advises Wahib W. "Otherwise, you may send a shipment and never get your money just because you spell a name wrong."

For your first few forays, the native Egyptian suggests, hire a customs broker or freight forwarder to handle the paperwork for you. After that, you can do it on your own. "It's no secret at all," Wahib says. "It's just a trick."

The Trade Bug

Michael R., the German trade consultant, let his enchantment with the world be his entrée into the industry. "I was simply interested in the worldwide markets and their cultural and personal relationships," he explains, "and I started from being an apprentice—right from the beginning—mostly in investment and construction goods and projects." Now, over 35 years later, Michael is still in the business—and still enjoying it.

For Jan H., an importer/exporter in Belgium, just living in Western Europe was enough to open the door to international trade. So how did he get started? "I don't really know," he says. "It's an instinct. Belgium is such a small country that one has to look around. And I love to travel the world, especially warm countries."

> **Tip...**
>
> ### Smart Tip
> International business discussion groups are full of information for the SME. Just what is this entity? What you're about to become—a small or medium enterprise.

Dan S., who lives and works in New Jersey, fell in love with the world of international trade on the assembly line at a plant where Chanel cosmetics were packaged for export. Fueled by a goal to deal in import/export, he worked his way up various corporate ladders to a job with AT&T, exporting connectors and fiber cable to Asia. From there he moved on to his present position in Lucent Technology's wireless division.

Dan's new company sells products he knows intimately—cables of every description, as well as software solutions. "I have more than ten years of experience in import/export and technology," Dan says. "I caught the [international trade] bug and decided to venture off on my own."

Overnight from Nothing

Wahib W., a native of Egypt, started out as a mechanical engineer for Caterpillar, the world's leading manufacturer of construction and mining equipment, working overseas. In 1985, he arrived in the United States, where he promptly started in on both an MBA degree and a position with a company that sold runway lights and navigational aids for airports. When the company became too heavily involved in domestic sales to handle the international work, Wahib formed a company to take up the slack. The new company also began selling other types of construction projects, from wooden telephone pole installation to railroads, supplying materials, construction services, or both. Soon business was so good that Wahib was able to buy out his former employer.

Wahib stresses that his success developed from his prior experience in the field. "Nobody becomes an exporter overnight from nothing," Wahib says. "You have to be coming from somewhere."

Take John L., an international business services provider in São Paulo, Brazil. John learned the ins and outs of import/export as an international purchasing manager for a large company before striking out on his own in 1994.

And in Florida, Lloyd D. worked in the operations sector of international banking before making the move to his own company. "I decided to expand into export management and export trading," he explains, "relying on my previous experience in an international environment to support my new endeavors."

Here You Are

Bruno C., who makes his home in Derchigny Graincourt, France, studied international trade at universities in France and Spain and completed his schooling in South America by teaching import and export strategy and techniques to others. He then went on to the college of real life. "One of my first jobs after my studies was in one of the first three major French supermarket groups as an import assistant," Bruno says. "I can say that in four months [there], I learned much more than in four years of studies."

But that wasn't enough to get him a job in international trade. Despite a year of teaching in Ecuador and his supermarket job, he lacked hands-on training. "Therefore," Bruno continues, "because I was not considered to have enough experience to work in the [international trade] department of a medium-sized company, I decided to create my own business. And here I am."

Here, too, are you—on the brink of an exciting new course of action, starting your own import/export business. As you can see, there are many paths you can take toward your own niche in the field, many roads that lead to success. Keep in mind, however, that they all require dedication, hard work, and, especially for those who are newbies in the field, a great deal of learning.

Future Forecast

Perhaps the import/export business looks like the perfect fit for you—at least, on paper. There is, however, one more thing to take into consideration: the industry prognosis. Will international trading be around for the next 100 years and beyond?

The answer is optimistic. There is a great big beautiful tomorrow for the import/export industry. Unless aliens from another planet land on the White House lawn and either enslave us all or show us how to live on love alone, thereby eliminating the need to earn a living, the industry outlook is healthy. On the other hand, if aliens landed on the White House lawn, they would probably bring with them greater opportunities for trade—of the intergalactic kind.

It is always possible, of course, that world events will discourage even the hardiest international traders. We do, after all, live in "interesting" times. Perhaps the faces of our economic allies will fade and no others will take their place, or natural disasters

Trader's View

Wahib W. advises the newbie trader to focus on a country in which he or she already has direct experience. "I see a lot of [traders] who were in the American military overseas," Wahib says, "or who have an ethnic background from another country and have family or contacts overseas. Personal contact is a very strong [asset]."

will occur on a more regular basis due to the evolution of the planet's climate. But the world has already experienced many of these events, from world wars to ravaging hurricanes, and the future of international trade remains brighter than ever.

So fasten your seatbelt, hang on tightly, and let's start your learning curve.

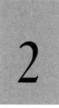

2

Import/Export
101

It's a wide world out there with trade opportunities around every bend. Of course, as with any business that features governmental guidance, there are also reels of red tape. So where on this big blue marble do you start? At the beginning!

Most international traders use freight forwarders or customs brokers to handle all the details of shipping and documentation. These people earn their living by sorting out government rules, regulations, forms, and assorted red tape—both foreign and domestic—but they're also excellent sources of advice on freight costs, port charges, consular fees, and insurance.

Even if you use their services and leave the form filling to them, you should have a working knowledge of what goes on behind the scenes. This chapter, therefore, takes you on a whirlwind tour of the import/export world.

The Players

First off, let's take a look at the players. While you've got your importers and your exporters, there are many variations on the main theme:

- *Export management company (EMC).* An EMC handles export operations for a domestic company that wants to sell its product overseas but doesn't know how (and perhaps doesn't want to know how). The EMC does it all—hiring dealers, distributors, and representatives; handling advertising, marketing, and promotions; overseeing marking and packaging; arranging shipping; and sometimes arranging financing. In some cases, the EMC even takes title to (purchases) the goods, in essence becoming its own distributor. EMCs usually specialize by product, foreign market, or both, and—unless they've taken title—are paid by commission, salary, or retainer plus commission.

- *Export trading company (ETC).* While an EMC has merchandise to sell and is using its energies to seek out buyers, an ETC attacks the other side of the trading coin. It identifies what foreign buyers want to spend their money on and then hunts down domestic sources willing to export, thus becoming a pseudo-EMC. An ETC sometimes takes title to the goods and sometimes works on a commission basis.

- *Import/export merchant.* This international entrepreneur is a sort of free agent. He has no specific client base, and he doesn't specialize in any one industry or line of products. Instead, he purchases goods directly from a domestic or foreign manufacturer and then packs, ships, and resells the goods on his own. This means, of course, that unlike his compatriot, the EMC, he assumes all the risks (as well as all the profits).

The Big Boys

There are, of course, more players than just the importers, exporters, and their cast of distributors and representatives. You'll also be dealing with the big boys (or girls) in the game: the government entities.

Who You Gonna Call?

So you're an exporter with a really hot product to sell. Who you gonna call? A buyer, otherwise known as an importer. Here's the rundown on the various types:

○ *Commission agents.* These are intermediaries commissioned by foreign firms searching for domestic products to purchase.

○ *Commission representatives.* Similar to independent sales reps in the United States, these folks usually work on a commission basis and, since they don't purchase (take title to) the product, they don't assume any risk or responsibility.

○ *Country-controlled buying agents.* These foreign government agencies or quasi-government firms are charged with the responsibility of locating and purchasing desired products.

○ *Foreign distributors.* Similar to wholesale distributors in the United States, these merchants buy for their own account, taking title to, and responsibility for, the merchandise.

○ *State-controlled trading companies.* Some countries have government-sanctioned and controlled trading entities. These agencies often deal in raw materials, agricultural machinery, manufacturing equipment, and technical instruments.

I've Grown Accustomed

You may already know the U.S. Customs officers as those people who fix you and your luggage with a beady eye as you trudge through the airport on your way home from a foreign vacation. But customs takes on many more tasks than just checking for contraband souvenirs. According to their web site, they also:

• assess and collect customs duties, excise taxes, fees, and penalties due on imported merchandise

• intercept and seize contraband, including narcotics and other illegal drugs

• process people, baggage, cargo, and mail

• administer certain navigation laws

• protect American business, labor, and intellectual property rights by enforcing U.S. laws designed to prevent illegal trade practices, including provisions related to quotas, and the marking of imported goods

• enforce the Anti-Dumping Act

• provide customs recordations for copyrights, patents, and trademarks

- enforce import and export restrictions and prohibitions, including the export of technology used to make weapons of mass destruction
- protect against money laundering (and you thought this was just a job for Elliott Ness!)
- collect import/export data to translate into international trade statistics

Lend Me Your EAR

The Bureau of Industry and Security, also known as BIS, is another entity that governs the exportation of sensitive materials—the Dr. No. stuff, like defense systems, plutonium, and encrypted software. BIS administers export controls, coordinates Department of Commerce security activities and oversees defense trade. BIS manages the export of most merchandise through the Export Administration Regulations, also known as EAR.

Say Cheese

Of course, since the federal government is involved, it's not quite that simple. Beyond the U.S. Customs Service and the BIS and the Department of Commerce (which oversees the BIS), various agencies regulate the importation of sundry products, some of which even a Trivial Pursuit champ couldn't guess. If you're planning on importing, for example, Cleopatra's magic milk bath, lucky Chinese crickets, cereals, fur coats, or parrots, you'd better check with the agency in charge. Here is a sampling of what you can expect:

1. *Cheese, milk, and other dairy products.* Cheese and cheese products are subject to the vagaries of the Food and Drug Administration (FDA) and the Department of Agriculture. You must have an import license to bring in most cheeses, which are usually subject to quotas administered by the Department of Agriculture's Foreign Agricultural

Service. Milk and cream fall under the aegis of the Food, Drug, and Cosmetic Act (maybe milk baths make milk a cosmetic!) and the Federal Import Milk Act, and cannot be imported unless you have a permit from the Department of Agriculture, the FDA's Office of Food Labeling, and other agencies.

2. *Fruits, vegetables, and nuts.* Some fresh produce items (including fresh tomatoes, avocados, mangoes, limes, oranges, grapefruit, green peppers, Irish potatoes, cucumbers, eggplants, dry onions, walnuts, filberts, processed dates, prunes, raisins, and olives in tins) must meet import requirements relating to size, quality, and maturity. All these tidbits must have an inspection certificate indicating importation compliance issued by the Agricultural Marketing Service of the Department of Agriculture. For questions, contact the Agricultural Marketing Service. You may also have to deal with additional restrictions imposed by the department's Animal and Plant Health Inspection Service, otherwise known as APHIS, or by the FDA's Division of Import Operations and Policy.

Fun Fact

Everything you ever wanted to know about export controls is available on the BIS' web site at www.bis.doc.gov/licensing/ex portingbasics.htm. It's not exactly hot-and-steamy, read it in the bubble bath on a Friday night material, but it's just as therapeutic if you're losing sleep over your exporting questions.

The Importer's Pal

The customs broker (sometimes called a customhouse broker) is the importer's pal. It's his or her job to know the ins and outs of importing in intimate detail and to handle them for you. Some brokers are small outfits consisting of a single owner-operator at a single port of entry; others are corporate types with lots of employees and offices in many ports. The Treasury Department licenses them all.

When you hire a customs broker, she acts as your agent during the entry process. She prepares and files the entry documents, acquires any necessary bonds, deposits any required duties, gets the merchandise released into her custody or yours, arranges delivery to the site you've chosen, and obtains any drawback refunds.

A customs broker is not a legal necessity, but you'll find that a good one will make your life considerably easier.

3. *Plant and plant products.* If you've got a green thumb and want to import garden goodies, be sure you check with the Department of Agriculture first. The agency regulates plants and plant products (including nursery stock, bulbs, roots, and seeds), certain materials (including cotton and lumber), and soil.

4. *Radio frequency devices.* Radios, stereos, tape recorders, televisions, CB radios, and other radio frequency devices are subject to the radio emission standards of the Federal Communications Commission (FCC). If you import these little sound blasters, you'll need to make sure they comply with FCC standards.

> ### Fun Fact
> To read up on everything you could possibly hope to know about bamboo, including economic plans for distribution of the variety indigenous to the Americas, check out Bamboo of the Americas at www.bamboo oftheamericas.org.

5. *Foods and cosmetics.* Before you import that European miracle fat-melting pill or the Asian wonder longevity lozenge, you'd best check with the FDA to make sure you're not unintentionally bringing in articles that can be considered "misbranded," i.e., making false or misleading claims.

That's APHIS, Not Aphids

Other products that fall under some agency's thumb are as follows:

- *Insects.* Animal and Plant Health Inspection Service (APHIS, not to be confused with aphids), Department of Agriculture
- *Livestock and animals.* APHIS
- *Meat and meat products.* APHIS
- *Poultry and poultry products.* APHIS
- *Arms, ammunition, explosives, and implements of war.* In a word: no, except with the express permission of the Bureau of Alcohol, Tobacco, and Firearms, which falls under the Treasury Department.
- *Radioactive materials and nuclear reactors.* In another word: nope, unless you have a permission slip from the Nuclear Regulatory Commission.
- *Household appliances (including refrigerators, dishwashers, clothes dryers, room air conditioners, and kitchen ranges and ovens).* Department of Energy, Office of Codes and Standards, and/or the Federal Trade Commission (FTC), Division of Enforcement
- *Flammable fabrics.* Consumer Product Safety Commission
- *Radiation-producing products (including those that produce sonic radiation, i.e., TV receivers, microwave ovens, X-ray equipment, laser products, ultrasound equipment, and sunlamps).* FDA's Center for Devices and Radiological Health

- *Seafood.* FDA and the National Marine Fisheries Service
- *Biological drugs.* FDA

Don't stop reading! You're halfway through the list.

- *Biological materials and vectors.* Think "Andromeda Strain." Think killer bees. Prohibited except with special license from the Secretary of the Department of Health and Human Services, and then with a sample of the licensed product forwarded by the port director of customs to the FDA's Center for Biologics Evaluation and Research in Rockville, Maryland. Plus, you must obtain a permit from the Centers for Disease Control in Atlanta to import any insect, animal, or plant capable of being a vector of human disease.

- *Narcotic drugs and derivatives.* Need we say NO?!!! Unless you're trying for something like hospital-use morphine, in which case you need to get the OK from the Drug Enforcement Administration, which falls under the Department of Justice.

- *Drug paraphernalia.* Another major no.

- *Gold and silver.* To ensure that precious metals meet quality standards, talk with U.S. Customs and the FBI.

- *Caustic or corrosive substances for household use.* Office of Hazardous Materials Transportation, which falls under the Department of Transportation

- *Furs.* FTC

- *Textiles.* FTC

- *Wildlife and pets.* U.S. Fish and Wildlife Service, Assistant Regional Director for Law Enforcement, for the state in which you're located. For birds, cats, dogs, monkeys, and turtles, check with the Centers for Disease Control in Atlanta as well as APHIS.

- *Petroleum and petroleum products.* Department of Energy

- *Alcoholic beverages.* Bureau of Alcohol, Tobacco, and Firearms and the Treasury Department

Don't let this list keep you from treading into international trade waters. Chances are that you're not going to be dealing in most of

Fun Fact
The original killer bees were bred from stock exported from Africa to Brazil in the 1950s.

Smart Tip
Tip...
Hop onto www.customs.ustreas.gov and search under "Trade Publications" for a copy of *Importing Into the United States.* Although it's not what you'd call a fun read, it's (surprisingly) clear, understandable, and chock-full of import rules, regulations, and tidbits. And it's free! You can also check www.cbp.gov for all the latest rules and regulations concerning customs information.

this merchandise anyway. But if any of these goods are where your particular interests lie, you'll know who to call for more detailed information. And remember, as the Customs Service people like to say, "Know before you go." If you have any questions at all, ask! There's no charge for asking, and answers are free.

Swimming the Trade Channel

Now that you're familiar with the players, you'll need to take a swim in the trade channel, the means by which the merchandise travels from manufacturer to end user. A manufacturer who uses a middleman who resells to the consumer is paddling around in a three-level channel of distribution. The middleman can be a merchant who purchases the goods and then resells them, or he can be an agent who acts as a broker but doesn't take title to the stuff.

Who your fellow swimmers are will depend on how you configure your trade channel. We'll discuss this more in Chapter 12, but for now, let's just get acquainted with the group:

- *Manufacturer's representative.* This is a salesperson who specializes in a type of product or line of complementary products; for example, home electronics:

Forward Ho!

While the customs broker is the importer's best friend, the freight forwarder is the exporter's pal. Acting as the exporter's agent, the international freight forwarder uses his expertise with foreign import rules and regulations as well as domestic export laws to move cargo to overseas destinations.

Freight forwarders can assist with an order from the get-go by advising you of freight costs, port charges, consular fees, special documentation charges, and insurance costs. They can recommend the proper type of packing to protect your merchandise in transit, arrange to have the goods packed at the port or containerized, quote shipping rates, and then book your merchandise onto a plane, train, truck, or cargo ship. Like a concierge in a really good hotel, they can get anything you've got anywhere you want it to go. "There's nothing we say 'no' to," says Ray Tobia, president of Air Sea International Forwarding. "We try to offer everybody everything, provided it's legal."

Like customs brokers, freight forwarders are licensed, but in this case, by the Federal Maritime Commission. You don't have to use the freight forwarder's services to transport your goods, and not all exporters rely on such services, but they're a definite plus.

---

televisions, radios, CD players, and sound systems. He often provides additional product assistance, such as warehousing and technical service.

- *Distributor or wholesale distributor.* A company that buys the product you have imported and sells it to a retailer or other agent for further distribution until it gets to the end user.

- *Representative.* A savvy salesperson who pitches your product to wholesale or retail buyers, then passes the sale on to you; differs from the manufacturer's rep in that he doesn't necessarily specialize in a particular product or group of products.

⚠ Beware!

Many people use the term "agent" interchangeably with the term "representative." An agent is technically a rep who has the legal authority to make commitments on behalf of the firm she represents. The United States and other developed countries have stopped using the word "agent" because its implications can lead to legal mishaps.

- *Retailer.* This is the tail end of the trade channel where the merchandise smacks into the consumer; as yet another variation on a theme, if the end user is not Joan Q. Public but an original equipment manufacturer (OEM), then you don't need to worry about the retailer because the OEM becomes your end of the line. (Think Dell purchasing a software program to pass along to its personal computer buyer as part of the goodie package.)

Building Bridges

Within these pages, we're talking mainly about importing and exporting products. But some international traders do very well importing or exporting services—which can mean a variety of things. As a contractor, you export services and sometimes equipment when your company builds bridges, airports, or telecommunications facilities in a foreign country. As a consultant, you're exporting a service when you supply your knowledge to a foreign firm. And you're importing a service when you purchase the licensing to open your own pub franchise that started in England.

You negotiate terms the same way you develop any international trade transaction. And—as you'll read repeatedly in the pages of this book—when dealing with any goods, you take care to check the details with your customs broker or freight forwarder and, when dealing with goods or services, with your international banker before signing on the dotted line.

The Rules

Now that you know all the players and their channels, let's look at some of the rules of the import/export game. As you already know, countries typically export goods and services that they can produce inexpensively and import those that are produced more efficiently somewhere else. But, as usual, when governments are involved, it's not quite that simple. Countries also have a tendency to block and counter-block sundry items of each other's products in a sort of giant, industrial-sized game of Risk.

Those Tetchy Trade Barriers

Trade barriers are set up by national governments to protect certain domestic industries from hefty foreign competition. If the shoe industry in the Land of Oz, for example, makes ruby slippers for $2 a pair, and the Land of Nod manufactures them for only $1 a pair, then Oz might put a tariff trade barrier on any ruby slippers brought in-country from Nod, charging, say, $1.50 per pair in import tax, or duty. Since this extra charge will have to be passed on to the consumer for the Nod people to make a profit, the Oz government figures it can keep its native slippers competitive in the marketplace.

Beware!

Before you decide whether you can trade profitably with a particular country, you need to know what tariffs or other barriers might stand in your way. For imports, check with the U.S. Customs Service. For exports, ask for help at your local Department of Commerce office or the commerce department of the country you're interested in. Or ask your freight forwarder.

Most trade barriers take the form of tariffs, but they can be camouflaged as quotas on foreign goods or as maximum-frustration builders, like excessive marking and labeling requirements, excessive pollution control regulations, and unfair classification of imports for customs duties. These nontax barriers can be just as costly as the tariff kind—the cost of getting products qualified for all these special requirements still has to be passed along to the end user.

World economists are beginning to push the idea that in the long run, trade barriers only hurt our global economy. And governments are

Cruising the Caribbean

Under the Caribbean Basin Initiative (CBI), designated beneficiary countries in (surprise!) the Caribbean receive duty-free entry of certain merchandise into the United States, typically most goods produced in the Caribbean Basin region. Although the names on the list change from time to time, you can generally count on the following:

- Antigua and Barbuda
- Aruba
- The Bahamas
- Barbados
- Belize
- British Virgin Islands
- Costa Rica
- Dominica
- Dominican Republic
- El Salvador
- Grenada
- Guatemala
- Guyana
- Haiti
- Honduras
- Jamaica
- Montserrat
- Netherlands Antilles
- Nicaragua
- Panama
- Saint Kitts and Nevis
- Saint Lucia
- Saint Vincent and the Grenadines
- Trinidad and Tobago

You'll need to consult the newest edition of the Harmonized Tariff Schedule (see Chapter 5 for the complete skinny on this) to make sure the country you want to work with is a CBI beneficiary. Or better yet, ask your customs broker to do it for you.

beginning to listen, thus the recent trend toward free marketplaces, such as the European Union and NAFTA (see pages 31–33).

Can We Quota You?

An import quota is a limit on the quantity of a particular product that can be brought into the country over a specified period of time. The Land of Oz, for example, might put a limit on the number of ruby slippers that can be brought into the country each year—say, 10,000 pairs between January 1 and December 31. If a few really zealous slipper salesmen fill that quota by February 15, then it's tough luck for anybody else who might be importing ruby slippers for the rest of the year.

Andes Are Dandy

The Andean Trade Promotion and Drug Eradication Act, formerly known as the Andean Trade Preference Act, or ATPA, is another piece of legislation that allows for duty-free entry of approximately 5,600 products from U.S. markets to certain countries. In this case, the favored nations are those in the Andes mountain region of South America, specifically Bolivia, Colombia, Ecuador, and Peru. Enacted in 1991, the act was passed to deter drug production and trafficking in these countries and help them to establish legitimate businesses.

Most of these countries' products are duty-free, with certain exceptions, including textiles and clothing that are subject to textile agreements, some footwear, preserved tuna in airtight containers (sorry, Charlie!), petroleum products, watches, and watch parts subject to other duty rates, various sugar products, rum, and tafia (which is essentially the cheap version of rum).

Be sure to check the Harmonized Tariff System for the fine-print details on these products.

The United States divides its import quotas into two types: tariff-rate and absolute. Under the tariff rate banner, quota goods can be imported at a sort of "sale" price; you pay a reduced tariff or duty during a given period. There's no quantity limit, so you can bring in as much as you want, but when the special period ends, you pay a higher duty.

Absolute quotas are the quantitative ones. Once the limit's been bagged on the product, no more are let into the country until the next time period. Some absolute quotas apply to every country in the world, while others are aimed at certain nations.

Some absolute quotas become filled within moments of the period's official opening time, which is usually at noon on the designated effective date. To deal with this port rush, customs releases everybody's merchandise in prorated portions, based on a ratio between the quota limit and the total amount offered for entry. In this way, each importer gets an equitable chunk of the quota.

The Buddy System

Countries, like children, often play favorites. A country with "normal trade relations" with the United States is one that enjoys trade with Americans without additional barriers or duties. France, for example, is an American trading partner, or buddy, and therefore its imports get the standard rate on most products.

Kibbutzing Around

The United States-Israel Free Trade Area (FTA) agreement provides duty-free entry for certain Israeli products. Lest you think these goods are relegated to lemons and grapefruit off the kibbutz, think again. Kibbutzes (communal farms) export other items as well, including radiators for Mercedes and other upscale automobiles. According to the Jewish Virtual Library, a division of the American/Israeli Cooperative Enterprise, kibbutzes have a 36 percent export rate, and they provide over 8 percent of Israel's exports. Plastic and rubber products, metals, and food are all popular kibbutz products. And Israel is making a name for itself as a premier manufacturer of computers and computer peripherals.

Since some aspects of the FTA agreement differ slightly from the Caribbean and Andean schedules, make sure you check the rules before you buy to make sure you're with the program.

Some countries even get duty-free entry for most types of merchandise. Under a variety of programs, some developing nations receive the freebie treatment as a means of contributing to their economic growth.

To qualify for duty-free trade preferences, your merchandise must meet several conditions, including:

- Merchandise must be imported directly from the beneficiary country into U.S. Customs territory (no side trips or detours).
- Merchandise must have been produced in the beneficiary country, meaning that: a) it's entirely the growth, product, or manufacture of that country, or b) it's been substantially transformed into a new and different product in that country.
- At least 35 percent of the appraised value of the article must consist of the cost or value of materials produced in the beneficiary country and/or the direct costs of processing operations that were carried out in that country.

Smart Tip

Tip...

If your goods hit port after a quota has been filled, you're not stuck and out of luck. You can store them in a foreign trade zone (see pages 91–92 in Chapter 5) until the next quota period rolls around.

Since the rules may vary slightly from one trade initiative or pact to another, be sure to check with your customs broker or the director of the port of entry or district where your merchandise will make landfall in the United States.

The World Stage
Politics Plays a Role

We're beginning to realize that our planet belongs to all of us. The powers that be—and the importers and exporters out in the field—are moving toward a one-world economy. How are they accomplishing this? International traders contribute by working with (and, in many cases, making lifelong friends of) people all over the globe.

Free Association

The Compact of Free Association (FAS) grants duty-free entry to certain merchandise from the Marshall Islands and the Federated States of Micronesia. The compact renewed in 2003 for another 20-year coverage, which officially took effect in 2004. If you're trying to figure out why the acronym for an agreement beginning with the letter "C" starts with an "F," here's the answer: These island groups are considered freely associated states.

The following products don't qualify for duty-free status:

❍ Textiles and clothing that are subject to textile agreements

❍ Certain footwear, handbags, luggage, flat goods, work gloves, and leather apparel

❍ Certain watches, clocks, and timing apparatus in the Harmonized Tariff Schedule

❍ Certain buttons in the Harmonized Tariff Schedule

❍ Certain prepared or preserved tuna and skipjack

Governments contribute by writing policies that make importing and exporting easier and more profitable for everyone involved.

GATTing to Know You

The grandfather of modern trade policy is the General Agreement on Tariffs and Trade, or GATT, an international agreement designed to reduce trade barriers between countries. First instituted in 1947 when World War II was still a fresh wound in millions of minds, it's still the primary international trade instrument used around the globe.

GATT's prime directives are as follows:

• Trade should be conducted without discrimination.

• Domestic industry should be protected only through tariffs and not through restrictive rigmarole.

• All parties should reduce tariffs through negotiations.

• Members should work together to overcome trade problems.

GATT works in mysterious ways. Participants from 144 countries—members of the World Trade Organization (see next section)—meet in sessions called "rounds" to

Bright Idea

When emerging nations experience economic growth, so do the United States and other countries in the global market. So as an importer working with these countries, you're helping the world and its peoples grow healthier!

negotiate various issues. Unlike a square-dance round, a GATT round can last for years. One such conference, called the Uruguay Round because its first conference took place in (surprise!) Uruguay, began in 1986 and was finalized in Morocco in 1994. GATT negotiations have expanded from tangible products to include service industries, investments, government procurement policies, research subsidies, patents and other intellectual properties, and telecommunications.

Club WTO

Although it's administered by a Geneva-based secretariat, GATT is an agreement, not an actual group or society of nations. So the World Trade Organization (WTO) was formed in 1995 as the overseeing framework for the venerable GATT, a select society to which countries can belong. The WTO has over 150 members that account for over 97 percent of all world trade. At this time, 30 countries are negotiating membership.

In a move designed to either complicate or simplify administration (you be the judge), GATT's secretariat is also the WTO's secretariat, although the WTO also has a Ministerial General, a General Council that acts as a dispute settler, a Goods Council, a Services Council, and an Intellectual Property Council, as well as a host of committees.

The WTO's prime directive is to ease trade barriers around the world, help developing nations pull themselves up into the mainstream, and give smaller businesses in all nations more opportunities to join the world marketplace.

NAFTA

If you've been adult, conscious, and living in the United States within the last decade, you've heard at least something about NAFTA, the North American Free Trade Agreement. This

Beware!

"Intellectual property" means a product that somebody has patented, trademarked, or copyrighted and is protected by law. You can't import this merchandise without permission just because it's foreign to your country (and maybe no one would recognize it!) any more than you could sell the intellectual property of the fellow down the street.

No-Barrier North America

Thanks to NAFTA, all merchandise traded between the United States, Canada, and Mexico is fast becoming duty-free. This no-tariff status applies, save for a few exceptions, only to goods that originate in the NAFTA region. What exactly does that mean? Well, according to Article 401 of the agreement, the term "originate" is basically defined as:

○ merchandise entirely obtained or produced in the territory of one or more NAFTA parties

○ unassembled merchandise that hasn't been entirely obtained or produced in the NAFTA region but contains a 50 percent (if using the net cost method) to 60 percent (if using the transaction value method) regional value content

If you monkey around with your officially originating goods—if you transport them outside the NAFTA region and do anything more than unload or reload them for safer shipment—you lose the originating status.

Also, you can't try to beat the system by bringing a nonoriginating product into a NAFTA nation and then "trans-shipping" it on (see page 67 in Chapter 4). It won't qualify as a duty-free NAFTA product. To ease your mind and confirm all the down-and-dirty details of origination, learn more about NAFTA at www.export.gov or try the NAFTA Certificate of Origin Interactive Tool to assist you with forms at http://web.ita.doc.gov/ticwebsite/ticit.nsf.

15-year plan to phase out all barriers to trading goods and services among Canada, the United States, and Mexico took effect amid much ballyhoo on January 1, 1994. A similar agreement between Canada and the United States had already been in operation since 1989.

NAFTA's prime directives are to eliminate barriers to trade, promote fair competition, increase investment opportunities, and provide adequate protection for intellectual property rights. It specifically establishes trade rules for textiles and apparel, automotive goods, agricultural products, and energy and petrochemicals. It also defines standards for technical information and transportation among member nations.

Many Americans feared that since labor is so much cheaper in Mexico, NAFTA would have a super-Drano effect on domestic manufacturing jobs, sending them swirling down the proverbial drain. As yet, this hasn't happened, and it doesn't seem likely to. Instead, U.S. exports to Canada and Mexico have increased dramatically.

The European Union

The European Union is to Western Europe what NAFTA hopes to become to North America, a single marketplace for the goods and transactions of its 27 member nations. The membership roster:

1. Austria
2. Belgium
3. Bulgaria
4. Cypress
5. Czech Republic
6. Denmark
7. Estonia
8. Finland
9. France
10. Germany
11. Greece
12. Hungary
13. Ireland
14. Italy
15. Latvia
16. Lithuania
17. Luxembourg
18. Malta
19. Netherlands
20. Poland
21. Portugal
22. Romania
23. Slovakia
24. Slovenia
25. Spain
26. Sweden
27. United Kingdom

Candidate countries include Croatia, Former Yugoslav Republic of Macedonia, and Turkey.

These buddy countries, some working together since the late 1960s, have developed a common tariff for countries outside the union and have "harmonized" (or developed a single system for) most internal tariffs and other rules relating to the "four freedoms": free movement of goods, services, people, and capital. According to the Union's web site (www.europa.eu), Europe's mission in the 21st century is to:

- provide peace, prosperity, and stability for its peoples;
- overcome the divisions on the continent;
- ensure that its people can live in safety;
- promote balanced economic and social development;
- meet the challenges of globalization and preserve the diversity of the peoples of Europe;

Stat Fact

According to the U.S. Department of Agriculture, the European Union has lead imports of prepared or preserved vegetables to the United States since 2005.

▲

- uphold the values that Europeans share, such as sustainable development and a sound environment, respect for human rights and the social market economy.

War—What Is It Good For?

Absolutely nothing, so the song says. And it's not so great for trade, either. Wartime can challenge even the hardiest of traders, causing hiccups (sometimes lasting decades) to everyday trade functions and operations. And, keep in mind, it does not have to be your home country at war that will bring woe to your bottom line. If, for example, you trade with two countries who are at war, this puts you in the middle of a battle on the world stage. Try as you might to keep your two trading worlds separate, the import/export world is getting smaller every day, and your clients will find out about and question your loyalty to both them and their adversary.

War also can halt production of what you are importing. What if you have a trade partner in a country where all metal resources are now required to go to the production of munitions? So much for the metal windchimes you were buying by the gross. Your beautiful windchimes have been melted to make the belly of an airplane.

Sanctions

One of the biggest effects war can have on your business is trade sanctions. *Webster's Dictionary* defines a sanction as, "an economic or military coercive measure adopted usually by several nations in concert for forcing a nation violating international law to desist or yield to adjudication." That's a fancy way of saying that a country can bar import to and exporting from any country deemed to be breaking the international law. This can be a direct result of war, a conflict, or a country's actions toward its own people that are considered cruel and unnecessary. For example, the United States leveled sanctions on the Ivory Coast in 2006 due to "numerous violations of human rights and international humanitarian law," according to the President's executive order. U.S. sanctions are currently in effect for several countries, so be sure to check with the Treasury Department before you start shipping those baseball caps to North Korea.

Stat Fact
United States sanctions are currently in place for the following countries: Balkans, Belarus, Burma, Côte d'Ivoire (Ivory Coast), Cuba, Democratic Republic of the Congo, Iran, Iraq, Liberia, North Korea, Sudan, Syria, and Zimbabwe. Log on to www.treas.gov/offices/enforcement/ofac/programs/ for the most detailed and latest information.

The Trade Hit Parade

According to the International Trade Administration (ITA), the top ten countries importing into America (in order of largest import dollars to smallest) are:

1. Canada
2. China
3. Mexico
4. Japan
5. Germany
6. United Kingdom
7. Republic of Korea (South Korea)
8. Taiwan
9. Venezuela
10. France

The list of countries that spend top dollar on U.S. exports is quite similar, with a couple of differences. They are (in order of largest export dollars to smallest):

1. Canada
2. Mexico
3. Japan
4. China
5. United Kingdom
6. Germany
7. Republic of Korea (South Korea)
8. Netherlands
9. France
10. Taiwan

You needn't, of course, confine yourself to trade deals with importers and exporters in these countries—there are scads of other intriguing possibilities available, including the member countries of the Caribbean Basin and Andean pacts and the new kids on the Eastern Bloc, the former Soviet Union countries. But as a newbie on the international scene, you should familiarize yourself with our biggest trading partners and see what they have to offer. Then take your best shot, with them or with another country.

Stat Fact

Canada's greatest trading partner, in terms of both imports and exports, is the United States. The U.S. exports over $211 billion in goods to the northern neighbor, while accepting Canadian imports to the tune of $287 billion plus.

Canada

Canada and the United States have been economic buddies for most of our common history. We're also closer neighbors than you might imagine—more than 90 percent of all Canadians live within 160 kilometers of the U.S. border. Not surprisingly, a lot of trade crosses that border, and it's increased since the signing of the Canada-United States Free Trade Agreement in 1989 and NAFTA in 1994.

Canada has produced actors Jim Carrey and Michael J. Fox, hockey great Wayne Gretzky, and the beloved tale *Anne of Green Gables*. It's also one of the world's major producers of minerals. But did you know that one of its largest exports is automotive products (followed by nuclear products and wood)? And strangely, one of its largest imports is also automotive products, followed by nuclear products (like reactors, boilers, and parts) and electrical machinery.

The U.S. International Trade Administration (ITA) urges you to "Think 'CANADA FIRST!'" And with good reason. In a recent year, goods and services traveled across our Canadian trade borders to the tune of nearly $2 billion per day, every day. That's a lot of trade!

Except that it has a population about one-tenth the size of ours who pronounce "about" like "aboot," Canada is very much like the United States in terms of economy, environment, and marketplace. Pair this with the facts that Canada is a close-to-home travel destination and that most of its citizens are native English-speakers, and you have an ideal jumping-off point for the newbie exporter.

> **Smart Tip** Tip...
>
> Find out more about exporting to Canada—or any other country—on the U.S. government's export portal at www.export.gov. Check out the "Find Opportunities" section for market research, opportunities by industry, and country information.

> **Beware!**
>
> If you're exporting goods to Mexico, be sure your goods have packaging information in Spanish. If there's another language on the label, the Spanish text must be in the same font, size, and clarity as the other language. Or, you can slap on Spanish-imprinted stickers to cover up the English (or French, Swahili, or Urdu).

Mexico

When you think Mexico, think young. Thirty percent of its population is under 14. Think big. The United States and Mexico share more than 2,000 miles of common border, through which a recent annual $120 billion in American exports pass. Consider infrastructure. The old monopolized concessions have crumbled, and seaports, airports, satellite systems, railroads, and power systems are now being revitalized or reborn in the private sector. According

Smart Tip

Tip...

Interested in importing products from Mexico? Your most lucrative bets are in the areas of electrical parts and products, automotive vehicles and parts, mineral fuels and oils, and nuclear products.

to the International Trade Administration, the leading edges for U.S. exporters are in electrical machinery, sound and TV equipment, nuclear parts and machinery, and plastics.

Automotive parts and service equipment are also on this list, and anyone who's driven Baja Mexico's 1,000-mile route from Tijuana to Cabo San Lucas can attest to the abundant need for vehicle replacement parts.

One more thing to consider when you think Mexico: desirability. When Mexicans think of U.S. goods, they think quality and value. A close-to-home market with a steadily rising economy, predisposed to American products—what more could the newbie trader want?

Japan

Everybody knows Japan is a major exporter. Think Nissan, Toyota, Honda. Or Sony and Mitsubishi. But there is more to Japanese products than cars and television sets. The Japanese also export significant amounts of agriculture products a year, including fish, rice, fruits, and vegetables. In fact, Japanese fishing fleets account for 15 percent of all fish consumed in the world, according to the CIA *World Factbook*. They ship out lots of office machines and chemicals as well.

As you might suspect, much of these exports land in the garages, living rooms, kitchens, and offices of Americans. Japan conducts $138 billion in imports to the United States alone.

What does Japan import from us? Japan is an important source of tourist income for the United States, with a recent figure at almost $14 billion. That's a lot of Mickey Mouse ears. They also take in a large selection of consumer goods—more so than ever before, along with foodstuffs, raw materials, and manufactured products, including chemicals, semiconductors, business machines, optical and surgical instruments, and aircraft. U.S. exports to Japan are currently over $55 billion.

If you're looking at consumer products, keep in mind that the Japanese population is aging—only 14 percent of its population is under the age of 15.

Fun Fact

Japan developed a seclusionist policy in the early 17th century. The only point of international trade contact was the city of Nagasaki—and only with Chinese and Dutch traders. And although the Chinese were allowed quarters in town, the Dutch were based offshore on an island.

▲

Doing BISNIS

The new independent states of the former Soviet Union are a hot trade target these days. Just check in with the U.S. International Trade Administration's BISNIS (that's "BIS" for business information service and "NIS" for newly independent states) web site at www.bisnis.doc.gov.

Or talk to Peter P., who has traded frozen food. He says Russia is indeed a terrific market, although one with a philosophy all its own. "It's a very title-oriented environment," Peter says, "very bureaucratic, and in a lot of cases there's not a lot of flexibility. Everybody is very secretive. As a result, it's difficult to gain trust, and that's the nature of the people.

"You also have to be able to play by the rules of the business in Russia. There's very much an unwritten protocol," Peter says. "Those things are very evident from the minute you enter the building of a Russian company, especially a large one."

China

China presents a series of contrasts to the international trader. Although the days of Mao Tse Tung and the communist ideal are history, most of China's 1.3 billion people still live on a peasant level. But the country also boasts flourishing middle and upper classes that can afford the many luxuries we take in stride, from televisions, stereos, and cordless phones to designer clothes, family cars, and fine foods. The United States exports around $41.8 billion in goods to China, including those in the categories of electrical, nuclear, aircraft, and optics. What does China send our way in return? The United States accepts around $243 billion in imports from electrical items to toys, games, furniture, and bedding products.

China's infrastructure—airports and seaports, roads, bridges, telecommunications networks, and power plants—is critically underdeveloped, which means that, as a trader, you'll have to pay extra attention to the nitty-gritty of production, distribution, and marketing. But it also means that opportunities abound in infrastructure imports and also in consumer goods.

> **Tip...**
>
> ## Smart Tip
> "I lived and worked in China for three months," says Dan S., the cable trader in New Jersey. "I enjoyed it very much and [experienced] no language problems. If you're in Hong Kong, Beijing, Shanghai—the real metropolitan areas—English is spoken. But as soon as you go into the rural villages, English isn't the main language."

Germany

Another "car" country, Germany is famous for its exports of finely-engineered vehicles. The United States shells out over $84 billion for Germanic exports. But it pays to consider the country as a great importer as well, to the tune of $34 billion a year from the United States alone.

Smart Tip

Discover more about Germany on the Department of Commerce's Showcase Europe web site at www.buyusa.gov/europe.

Although unemployment is rampant, Germans still have a high standard of living and appreciate, especially at the end-user/consumer level, innovative, high-tech products with a modern flair. The newbie trader should consider multimedia merchandise, such as computers and software, electronic components, health-care and medical devices, synthetics, and automotive goodies. When you think Germany, keep in mind cutting-edge technology.

And, don't forget diversity. Germany's geographic regions are as culturally distinct as our own, with no more similarity between the Rhineland and Bavaria than between Alabama and New York. The common threads are technology, quality, and an emphasis on safety and environmental standards.

United Kingdom

Think David Beckham. Or (if you're a little older) the Beatles. How about Waterford crystal, Scotch whiskey, Sheffield steel? They are all U.K. exports. King Arthur's descendants across the Pond (England, Scotland, Wales, and Northern Ireland) have enjoyed economic growth since the early 1990s. Much of the United Kingdom's trade is with members of the European Union, but it's still a major American trading partner and one of our biggest European markets. (As a bonus, they speak English!) Minerals, vehicles, and pharmaceuticals top the import list, with a total of $51 billion spent in one year.

From their U.S. counterparts, U.K. denizens like to buy aircraft and aircraft parts, IT equipment, telecommunications equipment, medical equipment, and even nuclear parts and equipment. Exports to the U.K. total over $38 billion. And with a population of 60.6 million, it's also a fertile jumping-off point for the European Union, with more than 379 million consumers.

France

Champagne, cognac, Dijon mustard—these are just a few of France's substantial agricultural resources. But did you know that it also has a highly diversified industrial sector? Although unemployment is often high, a strong currency has lowered the cost of imports and kept inflation and wage increases low. As with other European countries, France is attempting to privatize many ventures previously owned and managed by the state.

Although we import all sorts of French gourmet foodstuffs into the United States, the French are a terrific market for our food exports. Fish and seafood as well as fresh, frozen, and processed fruits and vegetables are high on the take-out list, as are organic foods, candies, chocolates, and wild rice. Again, think desirability. French consumers like American food products, but they are a nation of savvy, sophisticated gourmets who aren't going to be wowed by inexpensive TV dinners. As a trader, your best bet in the foods sector will be with regional, trendy tastes, like Tex-Mex, Cajun, or nouvelle California cuisine. Products in the nuclear, pharmaceutical, and aircraft fields along with beverages, spirits, and, of all things, vinegar, amounts to over $33 billion in France to U.S. imports in just one year.

The French don't just sit around and eat, however. They rely on U.S.-produced nuclear products, aircraft, industrial chemicals, telecommunications equipment, and computers. The U.S. exports over $22 billion in goods to France each year.

Republic of Korea

Korea's gross domestic product is growing at a rapid clip, and the country's business environment is transforming, becoming more market-driven and less regulated. This is good news for the international trader.

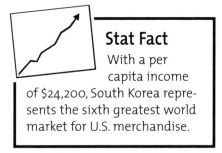

Stat Fact
With a per capita income of $24,200, South Korea represents the sixth greatest world market for U.S. merchandise.

Like France, when you consider South Korea, ponder food, especially beef, pork, seafood, wine, fruits, and pet food. Also think telecommunications—in Korea, there are more cell phones than land lines—and apparel. Don't forget infrastructure—goods that can be used in the construction of power plants, highways, and airports—as well as environmental technology, telecommunications, and energy products. South Korea maintains a friendly relationship with the United States (unlike its neighbor to the north), and spends about $27.6 billion a year on U.S. exported items. As for America, the feeling is mutual—and then some—with over $43 billion spent on South Korean imports each year.

Taiwan

With just 23 million people and few natural resources, Taiwan is a surprisingly significant U.S. trade partner. Because its resources are poor, it imports almost everything necessary for energy and industrial production as well as a tremendous amount of agricultural products. As for exports, Taiwan ranks as one of the world's largest suppliers of computer monitors, motherboards, image scanners, keyboards, and mice.

Taiwanese consumers, both individual and business, like foreign imports and don't mind spending money on them. Taiwan drops about $22 billion a year on U.S. exports, while the United States imports over $34 billion in products stamped "Made in Taiwan." As with Mexico, when you think Taiwan, think desirability. U.S. products and people have a favorable image in the Taiwanese lexicon, and this makes the country a terrific target for the international trader. As a bonus, while Mandarin Chinese is the official language of the country, English is the language of business.

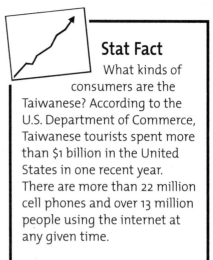

Stat Fact
What kinds of consumers are the Taiwanese? According to the U.S. Department of Commerce, Taiwanese tourists spent more than $1 billion in the United States in one recent year. There are more than 22 million cell phones and over 13 million people using the internet at any given time.

Singapore

A former British colony, Singapore has strong service and manufacturing sectors that offer many opportunities for the entrepreneur. From the United States, Singapore likes to import electrical machinery and equipment, computers and components, optical equipment, medical and surgical equipment, and aircraft and aircraft parts. The country spends around $20 billion on items exported by the U.S. In return, Singapore sends us disk drives, integrated circuits, computer parts, and pharmaceutical products, with total imports exceeding $15 billion annually.

The fact that it's the portal to Southeast Asia makes it a natural for the international trader—if you can't find a market in Singapore itself, you can almost certainly find one somewhere in the burgeoning Southeast Asian region. As you might guess, Singapore is heavily dependent on international trade. This is good because it puts up few trade barriers—more than 99 percent of imports enter Singapore duty-free. Something must be working, because the country has a per capita GDP equal to that of the four largest West European countries.

Tip...

Smart Tip
"In a lot of the countries I come in contact with, for example, Thailand, Singapore, and China, each culture treats business differently [than in the United States]," says Dan S. "In America, business is the first thing spoken as soon as you meet someone, whereas in Asian cultures, they want to get to know you on a personal level before they even sit down and talk business with you."

Venezuela

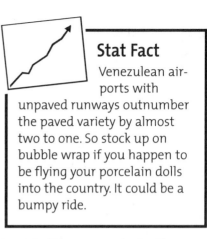

You might think of drug lords chasing down their enemies in the rainforest when you picture Venezuela, but let it go. Venezuela is a land of diverse landscape and many people. Bordering the Caribbean Sea and the North Atlantic Ocean, between Colombia and Guyana, Venezuela is home to 2800 kilometers of coastline, the Andes mountains, and the Guiana highlands. Its people are as diverse as the terrain, with 25.7 billion inhabitants with a

Stat Fact

Venezuelan airports with unpaved runways outnumber the paved variety by almost two to one. So stock up on bubble wrap if you happen to be flying your porcelain dolls into the country. It could be a bumpy ride.

median age of 26. You will hear the sounds of Spanish, Portugese, Arab, German, and African voices as you wander the open air marketplaces. Ninety percent of Venezuela's export earnings come from oil revenue, which also makes up a large portion (50 percent) of the country's federal budget revenues. The country is currently experiencing an automotive consumption rise. According to the CIA *World Factbook*, car consumption went up 70 percent in 2006. The United States is the country's main import and export partner, garnering about 50 percent of exports and just over 30 percent of imports. Exported products include petroleum, bauxite and aluminum, steel, chemicals, agricultural products, basic manufactures. Imports range from transport equipment (obviously!) to construction materials.

Netherlands

The Netherlands has always been on the cutting edge of economic and social development. During the 17th century, when the country was known as the Dutch United Provinces, it was a major economic and seafaring power. According to the CIA *World Factbook*, the country was a founding member of NATO and the European Union, and played a role in in the introduction of the euro at the turn of the century.

Stat Fact

The Netherlands has an almost-perfect literacy rate, with 99 percent of the population over 15 able to read and write. Time to reconsider your plan to export books?

Sitting like a puzzle piece between Belgium and Germany, the Netherlands opens its harbors to the North Sea to accept imports of $373.8 billion in the form of construction materials, foodstuffs, clothing, chemicals, and fuel. Top import partners include Germany, Belgium, and China.

Export-wise, the Netherlands depends heavily on the same type of materials to the tune of over $413 billion. Trade is most definitely the key to the Netherlands' success, garnering it stable industrial relations, low unemployment, and a budget surplus. Plus, its reputation as a strong trade and transportation hub for Europe is sealed by its past success and prime loction.

Trade Routes
Daily Operations

Now that you're versed in the ins and outs and whys and wherefores of import and export, let's take a look at operations. In this chapter, we explore what an international trader's daily work life is really like, what sorts of tasks you can expect to perform on a routine basis, and how they're completed.

▲

Trading Particulars

What you will be doing exactly during your peak hours and beyond will depend upon how you have structured your services. Some traders act only as sales representatives, finding buyers and taking commissions, and choose to steer clear of the shipping, documentation, and financing aspects of the deal. Others are happier offering a full line of services, buying directly from the manufacturer and taking on all the responsibilities of the transaction from shipping to marketing. These traders often specialize in either import or export and stick to the merchandise industry they know best.

The Exporter at Work

No matter how exotic you want to get, your most basic tasks will be obtaining merchandise, selling it, transporting it, and getting paid for it. Since exporting is usually considered to be easier than importing (less red tape), we'll start with an exporter's project. But even if you have your heart set on importing, pay close attention. Exporting and importing are two sides of the same coin, so what you learn here will stand you in good stead whether you're shipping into or out of the country.

Let's say you've noticed on your trips through Italy that, while the Italians are the original experts on cappuccino, espresso, and all those other gourmet coffee drinks, nobody really takes their "go juice" along with them in the car. You've decided that "go cups," those insulated plastic coffee mugs we take for granted from every fast-food and gas station/convenience emporium, would go over well in Italy. You've contacted a Miami manufacturer and gotten his OK to represent his product (which we'll now call "yours"). Then you've contacted an Italian company and sent them your brochure and price list and, when they've asked for it, a sample. They love it! And they e-mail you with a request for a *pro forma invoice*.

The pro forma invoice is a quotation—an invoice that the buyer gets to approve before it becomes fact. Keep in mind, however, that once your buyer accepts it, you're stuck with it, too, so think it through carefully. It contains a lot of information, including:

- Price
- Shipping date and terms
- Letter of credit information, including bank to be used and expiration date
- Necessary documents
- Packing or labeling requirements

The Pro's Pro Forma

Check out the sample pro forma invoice on page 49. The From, To, and Date sections should be self-explanatory. (If they're not, we've got some real problems.) Below the date is your quote for the number of cups you understand the importer wants and the amount you're charging per cup. USD is international shorthand for U.S. dollars. Since the Canadian dollar and the Mexican peso can also be quoted with the $ sign, you're making it clear by using USD that you're talking American money.

The term EXW on the next line means Ex Works, or at your works—your (or your customer's, the manufacturer's) shop, warehouse, or factory. This is telling the Cappuccino Imports people the price for 5,000 go-cups if they arrange to pick up the shipment at your place. The term CIF on the next line is import/export shorthand for cost, insurance, and freight. This is your price—after adding in freight costs—if you pay for shipping the 5,000 go-cups, insured, to Rome, which, of course, will make it much easier for the Cappuccino Imports people to pick them up.

Beware!

You can see the importance of getting quotes from your freight forwarder before you send out your pro forma invoice. If you guesstimate, without bothering to check prices, that it will cost you $200 to ship the cups to Rome, and in reality the cost is $2,000, you're not only going to lose some of your profit, but you're going to give yourself a headache from self-administered slaps to the forehead.

The Export Path

OK, exporter—you've found a buyer for your merchandise. You're a player. You're ready to roll. So now what do you do? Follow the export path:

1. Generate the pro forma invoice—give the importer a quote on your merchandise; negotiate if necessary.
2. Receive the letter of credit (L/C) from your bank.
3. Fulfill terms of the L/C.
   a. Have the merchandise manufactured if necessary.
   b. Make shipping and insurance arrangements.
   c. Pack the merchandise.
   d. Have the merchandise transported.
   e. Collect shipping documents.
4. Present shipping documents to your bank.
5. Pass Go. Collect your payment and give yourself a pat on the back!

▲

Pro Forma Invoice Particulars

Here's a rapid-fire review of a pro forma invoice's main ingredients. For your first few efforts, you might make copies of this list and check off the items as you go.

❑ Product description

❑ Price

❑ Terms of sale (How is your merchandise going to be picked up or shipped? When will ownership—or title—change hands?)

❑ Terms of payment (How are you going to be paid? L/C, prepayment, 90-day time?)

❑ Length of time prices are valid

❑ Length of time necessary for shipping

Remember to check shipping dates and prices and special documentation questions with your freight forwarder *before* you issue the pro forma invoice.

You won't see the little numerals in the Terms & Conditions section on most pro forma invoices—we've put them in to make it easier to explain each point. So are you ready? Follow along on the sample on the next page:

1. A *sight letter of credit* means a letter of credit, a sort of bank draft, paid as soon as you've fulfilled the conditions spelled out in it. This is in contrast to a time or term letter of credit, which gets paid after a period of time.

2. The 2 percent discount is an incentive for the Cappuccino Imports people to prepay, but it's not something they have to do. And, of course, you can make the discount, assuming you want to offer it, any amount you like.

3. This item is a hint: Italians, it would be nice if you opened the letter of credit at The Bank of Berry. As the exporter, you can specify that it must be opened at your own bank, but here we're giving them an option.

4. This is another little courtesy. It will save the Cappuccino Imports people some money and, in this case, won't cost you a whole lot more. Again, though, make sure you've figured your packing costs properly before offering the quote. When you're shipping items like fine china or crystal, packaging and packing is going to be a much bigger issue than it would be for plastic cups. And when you're shipping steak or seafood, it's also going to be a big issue, so get in the habit of checking this stuff out before you open your pro forma mouth and insert foot.

5. This protects you from the buyers hemming and hawing until sometime next year or the year after when it might cost you more to obtain the go-cups.

Sample Pro Forma Invoice

From: Coffee Holic Exports
        123 Cafe Street
        Berry, FL 30000, USA

To: Cappuccino Imports
        456 Via Espresso
        Ostia Antica, Italy

Date: June 4, 200x

For: 5,000 (five thousand) Coffee Go-Cups, Style A
        @ USD 3.00

Shipping Terms: EXW Miami, Florida, USA   USD 15,000.00
                        CIF Rome   USD 16,000.00

Other Terms and Conditions:

1. Sight letter of credit in U.S. dollars on a U.S. bank
2. 2% additional discount from EXW cost ($300.00) for advance payment
    in U.S. dollars (check payable at a U.S. bank)
3. Our bankers: The Bank of Berry, Berry, Florida, USA
4. Export packing included
5. Prices good for 90 days
6. Shipment: within 60 days after receipt of check or letter of credit;
    please open letter of credit for 90 days total

Thank You!

Pro Forma Invoice

From: _____

_____

_____

To: _____

_____

_____

Date: _____

For: _____

_____

Shipping Terms: _____

_____

Other Terms and Conditions: _____

_____

_____

_____

_____

_____

_____

_____

_____

_____

_____

_____

Thank You!

6. This item gives you time to have the cups manufactured, packed, and shipped before the letter of credit runs out. You don't, of course, have to stipulate this amount of time; it can be more or less, depending on what's comfortable for you and your supplier. Keep in mind that you may need to have the cups specially labeled or include some kind of user information, such as whether they are

> ### Bright Idea
> Last but not least on the pro forma invoice, don't forget the Thank You! People the world over appreciate courtesy. It will often take you further than you'd imagine.

dishwasher safe or contain hot beverages that may burn, and that this will have to be translated into Italian. All this can take extra time. Also be sure to allow for plenty of shipping time. There's nothing worse than finding out that the ship your cups are booked on sails one week before they're ready to go, and there are no others available.

Documentation

There's one other item to think about on a pro forma invoice: special documents. Some countries require certification for certain items—for example, food and pharmaceutical goods. Other countries, particularly those in Latin America and the Middle East and some Sub-Saharan countries, tend to require legalization or consularization of documents, which is another way of saying they like to have a special fee paid for the privilege of stamping the document "legal." Many countries have abolished this requirement, as the process makes it extremely difficult (if not impossible) to document via electronic methods.

Frequently, your customer will inform you of this requirement when she asks for your pro forma invoice. But don't assume. Do your homework. Check with your freight forwarder. If he thinks special documentation will be required and your customer hasn't asked for it, make sure your invoice says "Price does not include legalization" or whatever the documentation may be. Bring the issue up again in the cover letter you send with the pro forma invoice. Make sure you've covered all the angles.

Take a Letter

Now, about that cover letter. This is another nicety, a sort of "courtesy stamp" that can set you apart from the crowd as the kind of company with whom potential importers will want to work (see page 52). The first paragraph speaks for itself: It thanks your customer for his order, reiterates what he's purchasing, and indicates that you plan to work with him over the long haul—you're not just a fly-by-night operator. He's now got a friend in the business: you!

Sample Pro Forma Invoice Cover Letter

COFFEE HOLIC EXPORTS

123 Cafe Street • Berry, FL 30000 • USA

(305) 000-0000 • (305) 000-0000

e-mail: CoffeeHol@Holiday.com

June 4, 200x

Sr. Antonio Franco

Cappuccino Imports

456 Via Espresso

Ostia Antica, Italy

Dear Signore Franco:

Thank you for your order of our Coffee Go-Cups! Please find herewith our proforma invoice. We believe your customers will love the cups, and we look forward to a long and mutually prosperous relationship with you and your firm.

Please advise either when payment is to be sent or the name of the opening bank and letter of credit number.

Again, we thank you for your order and look forward to hearing from you soon.

Very best,

Charlie Holic

Charlie Holic

Coffee Holic Exports

CH/ta

Paragraph two offers two important points. It's asking whether the order will be prepaid by check or whether the customer plans to pay by letter of credit, otherwise known as an L/C. The opening bank is the customer's bank. This bank cannot issue a letter of credit number until the letter of credit itself has been issued. So what you're saying here is "Tell me the L/C is on its way."

The last paragraph is a typewritten, faxable smile and handshake, the same treatment you'd give your Italian customer if you were dealing with him in person. Don't hesitate to use it!

Now, how are you going to get this terrific cover letter and the pro forma invoice to your customer? Not necessarily by mail. Anyone who's had the experience of sending a "wish you were here" postcard from a foreign clime to the folks back home knows that you usually arrive home from vacation long before the postcard does. And vice versa. Mailing documents to other lands is not a speedy process. And in Third World countries with shaky infrastructures, it can be downright miraculous if your mail arrives at all.

Many international traders continue to rely on the good old fax machine. It's quick, it's reliable, and it's relatively inexpensive. You'll probably do a lot of your preliminary negotiations by e-mail, which is even faster and less expensive, but a faxed pro forma invoice, a sheet of paper your customer can hold in his hand, lends a more formal note. Even better, consider e-mailing your documents with a request for receipt as well as faxing them so you have all bases covered and have proof that contact has been made with your client.

Let's Talk Shipping

Now that you've gotten a feel for the pro forma invoice, let's talk shipping terms. Remember that your price quote will vary depending on how you or your customer decide to send the merchandise. In the coffee go-cup order, for example, there's a $1,000 difference between the price if the customer arranges for the order to be picked up or if you send it off to Rome for him. Your freight forwarder can make all these actual arrangements for you and carry them out, but you need to understand them to quote your prices profitably.

Shipping Terms on Parade

Terms of Sale	Exporter's Job and Responsibilities	Buyer Takes Title At
EXW—Ex Works	Pack and label merchandise; have it ready for loading	Exporter's facility
FCA—Free Carrier	Pack and label merchandise; have it ready for loading; load truck	Exporter's facility
FAS—Free Alongside Ship	Ship to port or airport; pay truck freight	Ship or plane, departure city
FOB—Free on Board	Ship to port or airport; have loaded; pay freight forwarder	Ship or plane, departure city
CFR—Cost and Freight	Ship to destination port or airport	Destination port or airport
CIF—Cost, Insurance Freight	Ship, insured, to destination port or airport	Destination and port or airport
CIP—Cost, Insurance Paid To	Ship, insured, to destination port or airport; then have delivered by ground transport	Importer's facility
DDU—Delivered Duty Unpaid	Ship, insured, to destination port or airport; then have delivered by ground transport; pay customs duties	Importer's facility
DAF—Delivered at Frontier	Ship to border; pay truck freight	Specified border point

- *Ex Works (EXW)*. This one you already know! This is where the merchandise is picked up at your "works"—your shop or warehouse, or your supplier's warehouse or factory. The unstated agreement here is that you'll have the product ready to go, properly packaged for shipping, stacked on a shipping pallet if necessary, and properly banded and labeled. You'll also, of course, have the merchandise ready and waiting at the time the customer has specified for pickup.

In an EXW transaction, your responsibility for the merchandise ends when the customer or his representative picks up the goods. He's taken legal possession or title. If the go-cups are lost at sea in a freak storm or are blasted out of the sky by the aliens, you're off the hook and you still get paid under the terms of the letter of credit.

- *Free Carrier (FCA)*. This is the same thing as EXW, except that it means you'll load the truck or minivan or whatever carrier the customer sends to pick up the goods. Since this is basically a courtesy, you should plan on charging the same price for FCA as you would for EXW. You won't see this term used for ground transportation—when you're shipping by truck or rail—because in this case it's basically the same thing as FOB, which is described later.

- *Free Alongside Ship (FAS)*. This means that you as the exporter will have the merchandise delivered, just as it sounds, right alongside the ship (or air carrier). In other words, instead of just having the goods ready for pickup, you'll deliver them to the ship or plane to be loaded. "Ship" can also mean a warehouse in the

What a Tramp!

While you might book yourself on any one of a plethora of ritzy cruise lines with six pools, three movie theaters, and ten restaurants, there are only three types of ocean carriers on which to place your merchandise:

○ *Conference lines*. This is neither the parent-teacher type of conference nor the football team type but an association of carriers that join together in Ocean Freight Conferences to establish common shipping rates and conditions. They offer two fee schedules—the regular one and the lower one they'll give you if you sign a contract to use only their ships during the contract period.

○ *Independent lines*. These lines operate on their own and usually offer rates about 10 percent lower than their conference competition. So why wouldn't you just go with them and forget the conferences? Because the independents' space is based on availability, and there isn't always room for your goods.

○ *Tramp vessels*. This is the kind of ship Indiana Jones sailed back to the States with the Lost Ark on board. They can be conference or independent, but they're called tramps because instead of operating on a fixed schedule, they tramp around the world, seeking out whatever bulk cargoes might be available at the last minute.

port area where the steamship line will later pick up the go-cups and whatever other goodies are waiting for pickup and take them to the ship. The point is that you pay for transportation to the ship or ship's warehouse, whichever your customer has specified, and you have responsibility for the cups until the shipping line representative signs for them and takes over the title. If the coffee cups meet with a nasty accident on the freeway in this instance, they're your responsibility and your problem. You'll have to replace them if you want to get paid.

How much do you charge for FAS delivery? That's up to you. If you live near the point of delivery and the load is light, say, 50 Styrofoam statuettes, you'll probably hop into your station wagon and deliver them yourself. Or you might call UPS or Joe's Cheap Delivery Service.

But chances are you'll rely on a common carrier, one of those fleets of semis you see rumbling down every interstate in the land—especially if you live someplace like Pocatello, Idaho, which is not exactly next door to a major seaport.

The Merchandise Love Boat

- *Free on Board Vessel (FOB).* This term means that you not only have the merchandise delivered to the port, but you also see that it's loaded on board the ship, or vessel. Here you're taking on several additional charges. For starters, there's the transportation fee to the port. Then there are the terminal receiving charges (TRC), or wharfage, which the shipping line charges to load your go-cups onto the ship. And then there's the freight forwarder's fee.

In this instance, your responsibility does not end until the merchandise is safely loaded onto the ship and signed for by the captain or his representative. So, again, you can charge what you like for the added anxiety.

Be sure you check with your freight forwarder before committing yourself to an FOB price quote. Steamship line prices can vary among ports. And trucking or common carrier prices will vary among cities. You'll also want to double-check the matter of legalization or consularization fees, because if they're necessary, you'll have to supply your

Beware!
Make sure you know exactly which port or airport your merchandise is to be shipped from. If the letter of credit specifies Los Angeles International Airport, for example, and you send your coffee cups out from Burbank, only a few miles away, you could end up not getting paid because you didn't follow directions. You might want to avoid this by simply stating California Airport or West Coast Airport instead of naming a specific one.

importer with a certificate of origin, packing slip, and invoice stamped by somebody in the importing country's local American embassy. What's a certificate of origin? A form signed by your local chamber of commerce verifying that the product was manufactured in the United States.

Fun Fact
Even though nobody travels by steam anymore, shipping lines are still referred to as steamship lines.

FOB prices are usually requested and quoted with the port of departure listed, as in FOB airport, Seattle, or FOB vessel, Panama City, Florida, or just FOB Panama City, Florida, without the words "vessel" or "airport."

- *Cost and Freight (CFR).* Here you're taking on even more responsibility. This means you'll not only transport the packaged go-cups to the port or airport and have them loaded onto the ship, but you'll also pay the shipping charges. You might see CFR written as C+F or C&F, but these are elderly forms and have basically been retired from service.

- *Cost, Insurance, and Freight (CIF).* You might recognize this one from the pro forma invoice. It means that you're paying to ship the coffee cups to Rome and you're also paying the insurance to cover their safe arrival. Marine insurance usually includes transportation to the port as well as on board the ship, so if something hideous happens anywhere en route, you're responsible, but you're also insured. Again, as in every example above, you can tack on whatever fee you like. CIF prices and quotes are written with the destination listed, as in CIF Rome.

- *Cost, Insurance, and Freight Paid To (CIP).* This one tacks on one more stipulation. You'll arrange and pay for having the coffee cups insured, trucked to the port or airport, shipped or flown to Rome, and then delivered directly to your customer's door (or other specified location) by local ground transportation. Of all the shipping terms we've just reviewed, this is the only one you won't see applied to air freight as well as ocean. Why? Because CIF and CFR will cover your shipment. You also won't see this term used for ground transportation.

- *Delivered Duty Paid (DDP).* Not to be confused with DDT, DDP is like CIF, except that besides having the coffee cups insured and shipped to Rome, then delivered to your customer's door, you also pay all customs duties. This is not so hot for you as the exporter (although you'll

Beware!
The insurance granted by an airline's waybill is not the same as the insurance certificate that may be required on your letter of credit. Make sure you've got the real thing or you may not be in compliance with the L/C, which means you may not get paid.

Thanks, But No

Listen up, importer! It's not always in your best interest to let the exporter ship her merchandise CIF (cost, insurance and freight). Having her pay the freight and insurance and handle all the paperwork may sound wonderfully simple (and it is), but the money's going to come out of your pocket anyway. Possibly more than is necessary. Why? There could be a couple of reasons: She might be tacking on a tidy little sum for her trouble. Or she might not have done her homework and shopped around for the best prices. Either way, you won't know unless you do your homework.

Ask for the weight and dimensions of the shipping containers and how many containers there will be. Then get on the horn with your customs broker and get your own price quotes. If you discover that you can do better than what the exporter has quoted, re-negotiate. Say you want your goods shipped EXW (ex works), FCA (free carrier) or FOB (free on board). Then make sure the letter of credit specifies your preferred carrier.

On the other hand, if you're a newbie importer and you decide that the difference in price between the exporter's quote and the ones you've received is minimal, it might just be worth it to let her carry the ball—at least for your first few forays until you learn the shipping ropes.

do your homework before you agree so you know how much money to tack onto your invoice, right?). But if you're the importer, especially a newbie, it's a nice way to have someone who knows the ropes take over the tough stuff. You should be aware, though, that DDP is not the most common way for the exporter to ship, so don't expect to have it handed to you without some negotiation.

- *Delivered at Frontier (DAF)*. This term applies to ground transportation only and means the merchandise gets dropped off at the border, or frontier. You pay the freight costs to the drop-off point and take responsibility for getting the shipment to that location.

The Import/Export Referee

Now that you know how to get your merchandise shipped, let's talk about getting you paid. Over the centuries, international traders

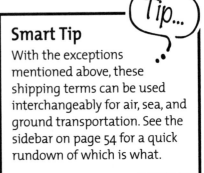

Smart Tip

With the exceptions mentioned above, these shipping terms can be used interchangeably for air, sea, and ground transportation. See the sidebar on page 54 for a quick rundown of which is what.

have devised the letter of credit as an honorable, safe method of insuring that the importer gets the goods he's paid for in the manner he wants them shipped from an exporter who could be halfway around the world. At the same time, the letter of credit assures the exporter that he will get paid for his merchandise once he's sent it across international borders to someone he may never even have seen up close and personal.

The letter of credit does this by acting (with the help of the people at the bank) as a sort of import/export referee, making sure that the exporter has carried out the importer's instructions down to the last dotted "i" and crossed "t" before it hands over payment to him. For the exporter's peace of mind, the letter of

Smart Tip

Tip...

International shipping terms are sometimes referred to as "Incoterms," from the International Chamber of Commerce. Incoterms are a worldwide standardization of what once was a Tower of Babel of different definitions. Another set of standard definitions, The American Standard Foreign Trade Definitions, is rarely used.

Exporter's Letter of Credit Checklist

As the exporter, there are a number of items you'll need to know or negotiate before the importer sends you the letter of credit. Here's a handy checklist to help you make sure you've covered all your bases. You might want to make copies of this list and check things off as you go.

❑ What will be the advising (your) bank? _____

❑ How much time will you have to ship your merchandise after you receive the L/C? _____

❑ How much time will you have to get your documents to your bank? ____

_____

❑ Will the letter of credit be irrevocable? The answer should be yes. _____

❑ Is the L/C payable at sight (when you present the done-deed documents, not after another 30, 60, or 90 days)? The answer should be yes. _____

❑ Will you pay your bank charges, and will the importer pay his? _____

❑ What will your bank charges be? _____

❑ Are there any special requirements? If so, what are they? _____

_____

❑ Remember: When the L/C is opened, get the name of the opening bank and the L/C number.

credit guarantees that his payment is already in the bank and that once he's carried out the instructions embedded in the L/C, he'll receive the money.

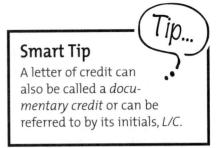

Smart Tip

A letter of credit can also be called a *documentary credit* or can be referred to by its initials, *L/C*.

Let's run through a letter of credit transaction and show you exactly how the whole thing works. Letters of credit can take on various "looks," from the flowery formal business letter to the snappy let's-get-to-the-point list to the unimaginative-but-works fill-in-the-blanks form, depending on the issuing bank's modus operandi. But whatever the style, each L/C will contain the same information and will be used the same way. Check out the samples on pages 62 and 63 to get an idea of what typical L/Cs can look like.

Signore Franco of Cappuccino Imports zips down to his bank, the Banco della Roma, and applies for a letter of credit in the amount of USD 16,000, the amount he needs to have the exporter, Coffee Holic, send him the 5,000 coffee go-cups CIF Rome. (CIF, remember, is cost, insurance, and freight paid to Rome.) The bank

Importer's Letter of Credit Checklist

When you're the importer, you'll need to ascertain a number of points before issuing your letter of credit. Here's a handy checklist to help you make sure you have everything present and accounted for. Why not make copies so you have it on hand for each transaction?

❑ Will the letter of credit be confirmed? _____

❑ What will your bank charges be? _____

❑ Is the L/C payable in the exporter's desired currency? What is that currency (U.S. dollars, Mexican pesos, etc.)? _____

❑ How much time do you want to allow for shipment? _____

❑ How much time do you want to give the exporter to get his documents to the bank? _____

❑ What documents will you need? _____

❑ Is everything in the letter of credit on the pro forma invoice? _____

❑ What are your shipping requirements? _____

❑ What about insurance? _____

❑ Remember: Notify the exporter of your bank and letter of credit number.

checks Sr. Franco's account to make sure he has USD 16,000 available. It may freeze this sum until the letter of credit becomes payable. But then again, the bank may not.

You should note that the Banco della Roma is an international bank and is used to dealing with L/Cs. If Sr. Franco had gone to a dinky bank without an international department, then either he'd have been bundled out the door to find another bank to work with, or his bank would have found an international affiliate to help it through the ropes. But in this instance, it's not a problem.

> **Smart Tip**
>
> The importer is some-times referred to as the *applicant* or *opener* since he's the person applying for or opening the L/C, while the exporter is called the *beneficiary* because he ultimately benefits by deposit into his account.

Sr. Franco tells his bank exactly which documents he'll want from the Coffee Holic people. In this case (see page 63), he's asked for:

- Full set of clean, on board air bills of lading, issued "to order"
- Commercial invoice, original and five copies
- Packing slip, original and five copies
- Insurance certificates

Sr. Franco's bank neatly condenses all this into L/C format and sends the letter of credit to the Coffee Holic people's bank in Berry. When The Bank of Berry receives the L/C, it sends it on to Charlie Holic, the exporter. Again, if Charlie's bank is the dinky-town type and doesn't know how to deal with L/Cs, it will either send him packing or find an international bank to help with the transaction. But, as in Rome, this bank is used to dealing with letters of credit.

So now the ball is in Charlie's court. It's up to him to carry out every detail of the letter of credit exactly as it's spelled out. This includes using a particular ocean carrier or sending the go-cups from a particular port, if that's what's specified. Here, Charlie has it pretty easy. He can ship from any East Coast port on any carrier, so long as the cups end up in one piece in Rome on or before September 1, 200X.

> **Smart Tip**
>
> The importer's bank is called the *opening, originating,* or *issuing* bank, while the exporter's bank is known as the *advising* bank because it advises the exporter of the L/C.

Once the coffee cups have made it to Rome, Charlie takes a trip to the bank with all the documents—including the bills of lading, the commercial invoice with all its copies, the packing slip with all its copies, and insurance certificates—proving that he's done his job as set out in the letter of credit. The bank people, in their capacity as "import/export referee," check over all these documents and assure themselves that everything is copacetic. Then they have Charlie's

Sample Letter of Credit #1

The Bank of Berry

Specialists in Small-Town & International Banking
Berry, Florida 30000, USA

July 2, 200x

Coffee Holic Exports
123 Cafe Street
Berry, FL 30000, USA

Dear Sirs:

Our correspondents, Banco della Roma, request us to inform you that they have opened with us their irrevocable letter of credit in your favor in the amount of Maximum Sixteen Thousand and 00/100 ($16,000.00) Dollars by order of Cappuccino Imports, 456 Via Espresso, Ostia Antica, Italy.

We are authorized to accept your 90 days sight draft, drawn on us when accompanied by the following documents, which must represent and cover full invoice value of the merchandise described below:

1. Signed commercial invoice in original and 5 copies
2. Full set of clean ocean bills of lading, dated on board, plus one (1) non-negotiable copy, if available, issued to the order of Banco della Roma, notify: Cappuccino Imports, 456 Via Espresso, Ostia Antica, Italy, indicating Credit No. 0123
3. Insurance certificates in duplicate, in negotiable form, covering all risks, including war risks, strikes, and mines, for the value of the merchandise plus 10%

      Covering: Coffee Go-Cups, Style A
                     As per pro forma invoice dated June 4, 200x
                     CIF Rome
      Merchandise to be forwarded from Miami to Rome
      Partial shipments prohibited
      Transshipments prohibited

The above-mentioned correspondent engages with you that all drafts drawn under and in compliance with the terms of this credit will be duly honored on delivery of documents as specified, if presented at this office on or before October 1, 200x. We confirm the credit and thereby undertake that all drafts drawn and presented above will be duly honored.

Jennifer Schneider Jordan

for The Bank of Berry

Sample Letter of Credit #2

The Bank of Berry
Berry, Florida, USA

Opening Bank L/C No.: 0123   Our Reference No.: 0456D

July 2, 200x

1. By order of Cappuccino Imports, Ostia Antica, Italy, we advise this irrevocable Documentary Credit No. 0123 in favor of Coffee Holic Exports, Berry, Florida, USA, in the amount of USD 16,000.00 (Sixteen Thousand and 00/100 United States Dollars) available at sight, against your drafts, accompanied by the following documents:

2. Full set of clean on board bills of lading issued to order of shipper, marked notify applicant, freight prepaid

3. Beneficiary's signed commercial invoices in original and five copies

4. Packing slip in original and five copies

5. Insurance policy in negotiable form issued to our order and showing claims payable at destination for the full invoice amount plus 10% covering all risks, SRCC, and war clause

6. For: 5,000 Coffee Go-Cups per pro forma invoice dated June 4, 200x

7. Shipment from: East Coast port

8. Shipment to: Rome, Italy

9. Shipment not later than: September 1, 200x

10. Date of Expiry: October 1, 200x

11. Part Shipments: Prohibited

12. Transshipments: Prohibited

13. Documents must be presented within ten days after shipment

14. Banking charges in the United States for the account of beneficiary

15. Applicant's bank: Banco della Roma

16. We hereby confirm this letter of credit.

Jennifer Schneider Jordan

for The Bank of Berry

payment, which has been waiting patiently all this time in Sr. Franco's account at the Banco della Roma, transferred to Charlie's account.

Meanwhile, back at the FedEx counter, all the documents Charlie (or his freight forwarder) assembled in the course of shipping the coffee cups are sent to the bank in Rome to be handed over to Sr. Franco.

End of transaction. Which is pretty simple, really!

The L/C Revue

Now that you understand why and how a letter of credit works, let's go over each item in the L/C in a sort of choreography, one step at a time. Follow along on the Sample Letter of Credit #2 on page 63 as we review (or is that revue?).

> ### ! Beware!
>
> Unless otherwise stated, a letter of credit is *irrevocable*. This means that once it's been opened, neither the importer nor the exporter can change his mind about anything in it without a tremendous amount of hassle. So whether you're acting as importer or exporter, make sure you know, understand, and can carry out what you're committing to.

1. This gives the basic information—who the L/C is from, who it's written to, how much money it's for and in which currency, and—important!—states that this is an *irrevocable* letter of credit. This is standard operating procedure, but worth repeating. You don't ever want to accept a revocable letter of credit because that would mean that the importer could back out of the deal any time he felt like it. This section also gives the information that this L/C is *available*

Something Smelly in Denmark

All letters of credit are generated through banks. Usually, the importer will arrange for your bank to be the advising bank, but occasionally he'll use another American bank. If this is OK with you, go for it. If not, you can ask that your bank be included in the loop. You'll have to pay their fees on top of whatever other bank charges you're committed to, but you'll have the security of knowing that the folks you're familiar with are on the job.

If you ever receive an L/C directly from an importer, be on guard! Letters of credit can only come from banks, so an L/C generated by any other entity is a dead giveaway that something is smelly. Turn the letter of credit over to your international banker and let him or her take it from there.

at sight, which, as you already know, means that the money will be paid as soon as the terms of the L/C are met; it's not a time draft to be paid out over a designated period.

2. This section spells out that the merchandise is to be sent CIF (cost, insurance, and freight) by sea. How do you know this? Because it calls for a *full set of clean on board bills of lading*, for starters. Bills of lading are forms issued by the sea, land, or air carrier to verify the merchandise they're transporting. The term on board is used by steamship lines to indicate that, yes, the merchandise is on board the ship as opposed to sitting on the dock. This way, the exporter knows his product is actually underway and not baking in the sun waiting for the next available ship to come along. *Full set* is another term used exclusively by steamship lines and refers to the three original bills of lading traditionally issued and signed by the captain or one of his subordinates, so that's how you know the order is to be sent by sea. The steamship line people, being nice guys and gals (and anxious for your repeat business), will provide you with as many copies marked *non-negotiable* as you need. *To order of shipper* means that the merchandise is consigned to the steamship line and not to the importer, although the shipper will turn the goods over to the importer when they reach their destination. (More on this weird-but-true point later.) The *applicant*, to be notified when the merchandise reaches its destination, is the buyer (in this case Cappuccino Imports). Last but not least, the section clearly says *freight prepaid*—and that's

---

The Negotiator

A negotiable bill of lading is like a signed check with nobody's name on the "pay to the order of" line. The shipper can give it—and thus the merchandise it describes—to anyone you choose. So if something goes wrong with the letter of credit after your shipment has already arrived on foreign shores and your customer won't accept the merchandise, you can hustle and find someone else to buy it.

A non-negotiable bill of lading, on the other hand, is like a check made out to a specific person. Only that person (or company) can take receipt of the merchandise; if something goes wrong after it arrives on foreign shores and you want to sell the goods to someone else, you'll have to start the whole shipping document process over again.

Which should you use? It all depends on your preferences and the specifics of each transaction. As a newbie, ask for advice from your customs broker.

how you know that the coffee cups are being sent CIF. Got it? Good!

3. This sentence says that the *beneficiary* (the exporter, remember?) must provide not a pro forma invoice, but the familiar, ordinary one he uses for routine transactions, signed in his own hand, along with five copies.

Beware!
Exporting and procrastination don't mix. Start arranging your shipment as soon as you receive the letter of credit.

4. The packing slip called for here is, like its compatriot, the invoice, not some exotic hybrid but the ordinary, everyday packing slip with copies that Charlie Holic uses all the time.

5. An insurance policy for your merchandise is a must—and not difficult to obtain. Your freight forwarder can make all the arrangements. The acronym SRCC means *strikes, riots,* and *civil commotion.* The importer wants the coffee cups covered for risks, such as storms at sea, running up on reefs, or run-ins with icebergs (yes, he's seen *Titanic*). And he also wants the shipment covered for possible torpedo or other war damage and any other violent act of man that can be thought up.

I, Applicant

As the importer, you get to apply for the letter of credit. Your bank will provide you with a form on which to submit all the necessary information. You can check out the sample on page 68 to see what the finished product will resemble.

Now, about those bank charges. If you don't already have an account with an international bank, you will be required to place all the funds guaranteed by the L/C into the institution's coffers. If you're already a customer with a gold star next to your name, the bank will set you up with a line of credit against your account. Either way, the bank sets the L/C funds into a sort of escrow account and holds them for you until the close of the transaction.

Aside from the money you need to pay the exporter, of course, there are various bank fees for letter of credit transactions. These include advising, assignment, payment, and transfer fees. The exact charges will depend on the bank, but you can expect to pay between $1,000 and $1,500 for a $50,000 transaction. Talk to your banker before you embark on a project. (See Chapter 13 for the details on developing a banking relationship.)

6. This one's simple: These are the 5,000 go-cups precisely as spelled out in the pro forma invoice. Type in this same phrase describing your merchandise per *pro forma invoice dated (whatever)* on every document you ultimately hand over to the bank.

7. This one's simple, too! For review, remember that "East Coast port" gives Charlie Holic the freedom to choose any East Coast port he wants to ship from.

> ⚠️ **Beware!**
> Be sure your insurance covers your merchandise from your driveway to the importer's door. Don't leave gaps in the coverage area—strange things can happen on piers or in air cargo bays.

8. Another obvious one—the destination port.

9. This is the absolute latest date for the carrier to leave port with the merchandise on board—the last possible date Charlie Holic can send his coffee cups off to Rome. One day later and he runs a serious risk of not getting paid because he's violated the stipulations in the letter of credit.

10. The *date of expiry* is the date the letter of credit expires. Like time and tide, the L/C waits for no one. If you aren't at the bank by the date of expiry with all your documentation in hand and correct, you don't get paid.

11. *Part or partial shipments* are those sent in batches rather than as a complete set. Cappuccino Imports might want Coffee Holic to send a part shipment if it planned to sell only, say, 1,000 go-cups at a time and didn't want to warehouse the entire 5,000-cup order. In this case, though, the importer is eager to get all the merchandise at once. And he doesn't want to pay the extra expense of multiple shipments.

12. *Transshipment* is the cargo opposite of nonstop. In other words, it means that the merchandise is off-loaded somewhere en route to the final destination, new bills of lading are issued, and the whole process starts over again. Not nonstop and not fun to keep track of.

13. This section spells out how long the exporter has to get the shipping documents (bills of lading, invoices, and packing slips) to the importer so that he has them ready to show his home-turf customs people when the merchandise arrives. It's not cool to make him wait for the documents because, if the goods arrive before the documentation, he'll have to leave all those eagerly awaited coffee cups sitting in a warehouse and pay storage fees. Sending documents ASAP will ensure you have a customer for life. And ensure that you get paid ASAP!

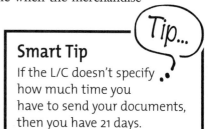

> **Smart Tip**
> If the L/C doesn't specify how much time you have to send your documents, then you have 21 days.

Sample Request to Open L/C

Request to Open Documentary Credit
(Commercial Letter of Credit and Security Agreement)

To: Banco della Roma

From: Cappuccino Imports

Please open for our account a letter of credit in accordance with the undermentioned particulars. We agree that, except so far as otherwise expressly stated, this credit will be subject to the Uniform Customs and Practice for Documentary Credits, ICC Publication #500. We undertake to execute the bank's usual form of indemnity.

Type of Credit:	Irrevocable
Method of Advice:	Fax, full details
Beneficiary's Bank:	The Bank of Berry
In Favor of Beneficiary:	Coffee Holic Exports
	123 Cafe Street
	Berry, Florida 30000, USA
Amount or Sum of:	USD 16,000.00
Availability:	Valid until October 1, 200x

This credit is available by drafts drawn at sight, accompanied by the required documents.
Required Documents:

1. Invoice in original and five copies
2. Full set of clean, on board bills of lading to order of shipper, marked notify applicant, freight prepaid
3. Packing slip in original and five copies
4. Insurance policy in negotiable form showing claims payable at destination for full amount plus 10% covering all risks, SRCC, and war clause

Quantity & Description of Goods:	5,000 Coffee Go-Cups, Style A, per pro forma invoice dated June 4, 200x
Price Per Unit:	USD 3.00
Terms & Port:	CIF Rome
Ship From:	East Coast port
Special Instructions:	Part shipments prohibited
	Transshipments prohibited
	Documents must be presented within 10 days after shipment
	Banking charges in the U.S. for the account of beneficiary

14. This means that the beneficiary, or exporter, will pay his own bank's L/C charges and the importer will pay the fees charged by his bank. Occasionally, either exporter or importer will pay all fees. When do you pay? Not to worry— your bank usually deducts the charges from your L/C payment before it turns the funds over to you.

15. This, remember, is the importer's bank.

16. When your bank *confirms* the letter of credit, it is saying that, so long as you conform to the terms of the L/C, it will pay you, come hell or high water.

A Day in the Life

What does a trader's day really look like? What does he do in between preparing pro forma invoices, requests for letters of credit, and shipping documents? Here's a behind-the-scenes peek, courtesy of Michael R., the international trade consultant in Germany:

○ First hour. Read statistics printed overnight by the computer to see if each representative/agent has fulfilled his plans and initiate changes if necessary.

○ Work on the internet for one or two hours to see what inquiries have come in, then answer them personally or forward them to past or present clients who may be interested.

○ Have short meeting with colleagues to see if assistance is needed, then support them or troubleshoot.

○ Look at the day's newspapers to see whether there's any movement within my industry where I should act fast.

○ Take a coffee break.

○ Look at the mail and handle or forward items.

○ After lunch, take time to reflect on what has and what should have happened.

○ Discuss problems and/or chances for the future with prospects and/or business partners.

○ Look again at e-mail and the internet for any news or try to find new situations.

○ At the end of the day, there should be about an hour to discuss again with colleagues how the day went and/or problems that came up.

○ One or two evenings a week, attend business events or meetings with partners for discussion.

Oops!

This is all dandy, you say, but what happens if somebody goofs? Surely, life being full of surprises as it is, someday something is going to go wrong with the letter of credit transaction. Well, you are right. So what do you do? Panic! No, no—just kidding!

Keep your wits and call your bank. Your bank then contacts the importer and explains the problem, euphemistically called a *discrepancy*, such as, "The air carrier screwed up and delivered the merchandise 30 miles from where it should have landed." Or "Because of calving icebergs, the ship is still in the North Atlantic, 500 miles and two days from where it's supposed to be." The importer can then forgive these little transgressions and agree to pay you anyway. Or (ominous drum roll) she can decide not to accept the whole shebang, and the letter of credit is immediately rendered null and void. Then all your (hopefully) carefully garnered documents get returned to you.

So what happens to your merchandise, the stuff that's sitting in the North Atlantic or on an airstrip in East Nowhere? If you can't come to an agreement and save the deal, you can have the merchandise put into a warehouse while you find a new buyer. You'll have to start all over again with a new letter of credit and new shipping documents, but you can still sell those goods to somebody else.

> ### Smart Tip
> Some exporters who deal with importers in volatile areas, like parts of Africa or the Middle East, arrange for a bank in a stable country to confirm the L/C so that they're guaranteed payment.

Is That All There Is?

So you're probably thinking, Is that it? One mistake and kaboom! All my work goes down the tube? Well, not necessarily. You can always ask the importer for an *amendment* to the letter of credit. After your bank contacts her bank, which then contacts her, she may agree to extend your deadline, which is great! Or she may agree to extend the deadline but penalize you by lowering the price, which is not so great. So keep in mind that you don't have to accept the amended L/C that comes down the pike to you.

Here's what you do if you don't like the amended letter of credit: Pop on down to your bank, hand over the darn L/C along with a letter stating that you are rejecting the thing, and

> ### Smart Tip
> Ask your international banker for a copy of Publication 500, otherwise known as *ICC Uniform Customs and Practice for Documentary Credits*. Or order it from www.iccbooks.com. This must-read, published by the International Chamber of Commerce, sets forth the guidelines for all letter of credit transactions.

have them give you a receipt. Then, send a letter to the importer telling her why you've rejected her amended L/C. Hopefully, she'll generate another amendment and you can get your deal back on track.

Cash Is King

Although the letter of credit is the safest way to ensure payment (especially for newbies) and is a common method of payment, there are other ways to negotiate an international trade transaction. Here's a rapid-fire list of other ways and means:

- Cash in advance
- Open account
- On consignment
- Collection draft

Cash is always good, so you might think (and rightly so) that the first of this lot is the best. But the other methods have their good points, too. Let's go over each transaction in more detail.

- *Cash in Advance.* The importer pays for the merchandise before it's even shipped. With this method, the buyer must implicitly trust the exporter to follow through on the deal. You might see it used in a strong seller's market when demand for a product is sky-high, or for small deals where both parties agree that the cost in time and money isn't worth investing in a method such as a letter of credit.

  As a variation on a theme, sometimes when a manufacturer needs a lot of upfront money, he may demand partial cash in advance, such as 25 percent, to offset his costs.

- *Open Account.* The buyer has an account with the exporter. When she receives the merchandise, she sends payment to the seller. In essence, the exporter is offering credit to the buyer, and this can be risky. As with the cash in advance transaction, this type of account is used when the exporter feels comfortable with his buyer. However, where cash in advance puts all the risk on the importer, open account puts all the risk on the exporter's shoulders.

  Another tack that's gaining popularity is to use an open account and buy credit insurance in case the deal sours. This payment method is cheaper than an L/C: $250 or so vs. the $1,000 to $1,500 for a letter of credit. To find out more about credit insurers, check out the web site for the International Union of Credit

▲

On the Road

A trader isn't always at home behind his desk. What does he do when he's out on the road? Here's another behind-the-scenes peek, courtesy of Jan H., the Belgian tire trader:

Note that Jan's day, in typical European fashion, evolves through a 24-hour clock, or what we think of as military time. In this system, the hours of 1 in the morning to noon are expressed as 1:00 to 12:00. For every hour after noon, you add onto 12, so that 13:00 is 1 o'clock (12 + 1) and midnight is 24:00 (12 + 12).

Day in Belgium

07:00–09:00: Office work, e-mail, fax offers, mail, etc.

09:00–12:00: Drive to airport, meet customer from Finland; back to warehouse, customer chooses products

12:00–13:00: Lunch with customer, general discussions

13:00–18:00: Visit with a customer from Nigeria; long discussion, haggling over prices, payment terms, etc.; supervise loading of containers bound for the United States; phone calls, fax, e-mail; arrival of a customer from France, discussions

18:00: Quick trip home to change and shower

19:00–??: Pick up French customer at hotel, have cocktails, dinner, and more negotiations

Day on the Road in Germany

05:00: Leave home for 400-km drive

08:00: Arrive at first supplier; discussions and purchase of goods

10:00: Leave for next supplier

11:00: Next supplier; discussions without any result

12:00: Visit customer, make a sale

13:30: Visit another supplier; more discussions

15:00: Leave for another 300-odd km drive

18:00: Arrive at hotel; check e-mail on laptop, phone calls

19:30: Sauna and swim at hotel pool

20:30: Dinner with supplier, then to bed!

Day in Miami

07:00: Swim in hotel pool; breakfast, phone calls, and faxes

08:30: A good friend, customer, and supplier, picks me up; go to his office, business discussions

13:00: Free afternoon; go to shopping mall and hotel pool; check e-mail, make a few phone calls

19:00: Dinner and a show with friend

23:00: Bed

and Investment Insurers at www.berne union.org.uk. It is the leading international organization and community for the export credit and investment insurance industry with over 70 member companies spanning the globe.

- *On Consignment.* The seller ships his merchandise without any sort of payment and doesn't get paid until the importer sells the goods in her own country. This system is by far the riskiest and is not advisable for any deal, because if the buyer can't liquidate the product, she'll return it without payment, thus sticking the exporter with both an Excedrin headache and unnecessary shipping costs.

- *Collection Draft.* This method is similar to the letter of credit in that the bank acts as the go-between for buyer and seller. In a collection draft transaction, the exporter ships the merchandise. His bank then sends the bill of lading and other specified shipping documents (which are necessary to collect the goods down at the dock) to the importer's bank, which keeps a tight grip on the documents until the importer coughs up the exporter's payment. Once this has been extracted, the bank releases the documents to the importer, sends the funds to the exporter, and everybody's happy. Bank charges for collection drafts run between $250 and $500.

> **Smart Tip** *Tip...*
>
> *Air waybills* (bills of lading from air carriers) are never negotiable. (Think FedEx. Would it accept a package with nobody's name and no street address on it? Heck no.)

A Date with a Draft

Now, lest you thought you were done with all this, there's more: To complete the collection draft, the exporter has to draw up the draft part of the deal, which is basically the buyer's order to pay. There are three types of drafts:

- *Sight draft.* This requires payment before the importer can get her hands on the goods. The exporter retains title until they've reached their destination and are paid for. It's called a sight draft because as soon as the merchandise has arrived and is theoretically "in sight" of the dock, the draft is payable. The risk here is that the buyer may change her mind while the merchandise is somewhere out at sea and decide to forget the whole deal. Then it's the exporter's responsibility to pay return passage for his stuff.

- *Time draft.* The exporter extends credit to the importer. She has a certain amount of time, say, 30, 60, or 90 days from the moment she picks up the merchandise and accepts the draft, to make payment.

> **Smart Tip** *Tip...*
>
> A collection draft transaction can also be called a *cash against documents* transaction.

▲

Hometown Money Makes Good

If you receive a check from your importer's bank, the Banque de Paris in France, for example, but it's drawn on the Bank of Omaha, Nebraska, can this be right? Sure it can! Lots of international banks have accounts at American banks and will write drafts on those gringo accounts just so you can be paid in homegrown money.

You can also be paid in U.S. dollars by wire transfer, in which funds from the importer's bank are wired directly to your account at your home bank.

All this works in reverse, too. When you're the importer, you can have the exporter paid in his native currency, whether it's Mexican pesos or Thai baht, you can have your money wired to his account.

With some time drafts, payment is due within a specified number of days after "sight," or arrival of the goods. In this case, the draft is called a date draft.

- *Clean draft.* The shipping documents are sent to the importer at the same time as the merchandise. This is basically the same as sending the goods on open account and is extremely rare. Again, it's used only when the exporter has extreme confidence in his customer.

Rituals and
Red Tape

e've figured out how to ship your mer-

chandise and how to get you paid once the goods arrive. Sort of.

But what about all those documents we've been discussing?

The ones you need to get signed off on the letter of credit or col-

lection draft? Yeah, those!

Most shipping records are known as collection documents and in some ways are exactly the same as cash. Why? Because once you present the documents to the bank, demonstrating that you've fulfilled the conditions of the L/C, the bank issues payment. Now, you can have your freight forwarder handle all the paperwork so that all you have to do is trot down to the bank with the completed documents in hand when he's finished, but as the exporter, you need to know how each link in the chain functions. You need to understand these documents when you're the importer, too, because either you or your customs broker will use them to claim your cargo once it arrives at the harbor, loading dock, or airport.

So here they are for your review, like big-name stars in a Hollywood movie, listed in alphabetical order:

- *Bill of Lading.* "Lading" means freight or cargo, so a bill of lading is basically a receipt from the cargo handler—the steamship, air, or truck line—showing that it's got your goods. To make things official, the document is signed by the captain (on a ship) or other agent of the transporter as binding evidence that the merchandise has been shipped. There are various permutations of the bill of lading, including:

  - *Clean or Clean on Board.* This does not mean clean as in sprayed-with-Lysol, but clean as in the transport company hasn't noted any irregularities in the packing or the condition of the goods. This is the standard bill of lading.

  - *Foul.* Not to be confused with the baseball term, a foul bill of lading is the opposite of the clean one—it indicates that the transport company has discovered, for example, something sticky leaking from those boxes marked "blood byproducts." If your bill of lading gets marked "foul," you'll want to exchange the bum container for a "clean" one and have the shipment relabeled before it's presented to the importer.

  - *Straight.* This one is non-negotiable—like a check with the name of the payee filled in—it spells out whom the merchandise is consigned to. Because it prohibits release of the goods to anyone but the person specified on the documents and thus offers the most protection, the straight bill of lading is usually preferred by newbie importers.

  - *On Board.* This one confirms only that the cargo has been placed on board the vessel and carries no other guidelines or stipulations. It's an elderly shipping term and isn't used much these days.

  - *On Deck.* This is relevant only if the goods, such as livestock, must be transported on the deck of the ship.

 Beware!
Some countries require more information on shipping documents than others. Be sure to check with your customs broker to make sure the form you're using covers everything.

- *Order.* A negotiable bill of lading that must be endorsed by the shipper before it's handed over to the bank for collection. An order bill of lading is usually made out to the bank or customs broker, or it can be left blank—again, like a blank check.

- *Order Notify.* This is like the order bill, except that the consignee (the buyer) and sometimes the customs broker must be notified when the ship reaches port. This is particularly keen if you're the importer because the shipper will notify you in advance when the vessel will arrive.

- *Through Bill of Lading.* This is the "pass it on down" bill used when several carriers are involved if, for example, the merchandise needs to go by rail or truck to the port and then by ocean, or vice versa.

- *Certificate of Manufacture.* Used when the buyer pays for the goods before shipment, this document verifies that the merchandise has really been manufactured and really does fulfill the general product requirements (see page 78). In other words, it's proof that the goods are on hand and ready for shipment.

- *Certificate of Origin.* Some countries require a separate certificate of origin (see pages 80–81), even though this information is provided on the commercial invoice. The certificate is especially important when you're importing goods that require regulatory approval, such as medical equipment or food. Our own Food and Drug Administration, for example, requires a certificate of origin for every imported product. Some countries will count a piece of paper with your signature below the statement "I certify that these goods were manufactured in the United States of America" as acceptable. Others want the statement

Build a Better Bomb

Although you don't need a license to export most merchandise, you'll need a validated export license to ship goods that the U.S. government wants to control, such as articles of war, advanced technology, and products in short supply. Obtaining a validated license can be time-consuming, costly, and, in some cases, impossible. (It's not a good idea, for example, to try shipping SCUD missiles to the Middle East.) If you're an export novice, you should probably leave exporting sensitive materials to somebody else, but if you simply must send sensitive materials, be sure to contact the Department of Commerce first. They can tell you if your potential export is on the *Commerce Control List* (CCL), which means it needs a validated license.

Sample Certificate of Manufacture

From: Coffee Holic Exports
              123 Cafe Street
              Berry, FL 30000, USA

To: Cappuccino Imports
              456 Via Espresso
              Ostia Antica, Italy

Date: July 15, 200x

Opening Bank: Banco della Roma

L/C or Other Reference No.: 0123

Merchandise: 5,000 Coffee Go-Cups, Style A

We hereby certify that the above-described merchandise has been manufactured as of <u>July 30, 200x,</u> and is available for shipment as of <u>August 1, 200x.</u>

By: *Charlie Holic, Owner*
          (signature and title)

Certificate of Manufacture

From: _____

          _____

          _____

To: _____

          _____

          _____

Date: _____

Opening Bank: _____

L/C or Other Reference No.: _____

Merchandise: _____

We hereby certify that the above-described merchandise has been manufactured as of _____, and is available for shipment as of _____.

By: _____
        (signature and title)

notarized, on a form from your local chamber of commerce, or on a special form for that particular nation.

Smart Tip *Tip...*

You can purchase a number of these forms through Unz & Co. at www.unzco.com.

- *Commercial Invoice.* The commercial invoice is the same as any invoice used by a domestic company and is essentially a finished version of the pro forma invoice.

You can make up your own commercial invoice on your trusty desktop computer or buy preprinted blank forms with carbon copies at an office supply store. When you fill in those blanks, you'll want to be sure you've added the same particulars you have on your pro forma invoice and the L/C number, if you're using an L/C. Plus, you'll need to add the terms of the sale (i.e., FOB or DDP) and—important!—a statement certifying the goods were manufactured in the United States, followed by your signature. This will help skate the merchandise through customs. Check out the sample commercial invoice on page 82 to get an idea of what yours should look like.

- *Consular Invoice.* Not every country will demand one of these—the ranks are mostly filled by emerging nation types. Basically, a consular invoice is one for which you fill out a form available from the local consulate office here in the States, pay a nominal sum and go on your merry way. The presumed idea behind the invoice is to ensure that overpriced or underpriced goods don't enter the country, but in actuality it's a sort of collection plate for the national economy.

- *Dock Receipts.* This receipt is used if the importer is responsible for shipment from the U.S. port—it verifies that the merchandise has indeed made it as far as the dock.

- *Inspection Certificate.* The importer may request one of these to certify the quantity, quality, and/or conformity of the product. Say, for example, that you are bringing in cookie-making equipment from whatever country the Keebler elves live in. You may want to have an inspector check the machines to make sure they're in good working order before you take title. You can elect a standard export inspection, which is done by a (surprise!) standard inspector nominated by the exporter or shipping line, or you can hire a specialized private company to do the job.

Dollar Stretcher

Instead of paying a printer, you can generate a number of these documents yourself—personalized for your company—with a simple and inexpensive desktop publishing program. Or use the blank forms we've provided throughout this chapter. And remember to check their suitability with your customs broker!

Sample Certificate of Origin

I, __Charlie Holic__ , __Owner__ of __Coffee Holic Exports__ , declare that the

   (name of person)   (title)   (name of company)

goods described herein are the product of the United States of America.

Marks & Numbers	No. Containers	Gross Weight or Quantity	Description
As Addressed 1 thru 50	50	5,000 pieces	Coffee Go-Cups

Certified by: __*Charlie Holic*__   Date: __July 10, 200X__

           (signature of person named above)

This space for notary, if required:

The __Berry__ Chamber of Commerce, a recognized chamber of commerce under the laws of the state of __Florida__ , has examined the manufacturer's invoice or shipper's affidavit on the above-described goods and, to its best belief, certifies that the merchandise originated in the United States of America.

By: __*Shelby Anne Bean, President*__

      (signature and title)

Certificate of Origin

I, _____ , _____ of _____ , declare that the
   (name of person)   (title)   (name of company)
goods described herein are the product of the United States of America.

Marks & Numbers	No. Containers	Gross Weight or Quantity	Description

Certified by: _____   Date: _____
               (signature of person named above)

This space for notary, if required:

The _____ Chamber of Commerce, a recognized chamber of commerce
under the laws of the state of _____ , has examined the manufacturer's
invoice or shipper's affidavit on the above-described goods and, to its best
belief, certifies that the merchandise originated in the United States of
America.

By: _____
            (signature and title)

Sample Completed Commercial Invoice

Date: July 15, 200x

From: Coffee Holic Exports
               123 Cafe Street
               Berry, FL 30000, USA

To: Cappuccino Imports
               456 Via Espresso
               Ostia Antica, Italy

Merchandise Ordered: 5,000 Coffee Go-Cups, Style A

On Order or L/C No.: L/C 0123

Shipping Terms: CIF Rome

Price: USD 16,000

We hereby certify that these goods were manufactured in the United States of America and that this is a valid, true and correct invoice.

By: *Charlie Holic*   Owner
          (signature)   (title)

Commercial Invoice

Date: _____

From: _____
_____
_____

To: _____
_____
_____

Merchandise Ordered: _____

On Order or L/C No.: _____

Shipping Terms: _____

Price: _____

We hereby certify that these goods were manufactured in the United States of America and that this is a valid, true and correct invoice.

By: _____
(signature)   (title)

Sample Packing List

From: Coffee Holic Exports
            123 Cafe Street
            Berry, FL 30000, USA

To: Cappuccino Imports
            456 Via Espresso
            Ostia Antica, Italy

Date: July 15, 200x

Per your order No. _____L/C 0123_____ , the following merchandise has been shipped to __Rome__ , departing _August 3, 200x_ , by _ship_ .

Item No.	Quantity Ordered	Quantity Shipped	Description
Style A	5,000	5,000	Insulated Plastic Coffee Go-Cups

No. containers & type: _____50 cardboard boxes_____

Weight per container: _____4 kilos_____

Dimensions of each container: _3.5 x 3.5 x 3.5 meters_

Containers numbered: __1/50_____

Marks: __Cappuccino Imports_____
        __Ostia Antica, Italy_____
        __Boxes 1/50_____

Packing List

From: _____

_____

_____

To: _____

_____

_____

Date: _____

Per your order No. _____ , the following merchandise has been shipped to _____ , departing _____ , by _____.

Item No.	Quantity Ordered	Quantity Shipped	Description

No. containers & type: _____

Weight per container: _____

Dimensions of each container: _____

Containers numbered: _____

Marks: _____

_____

_____

▲

- *Insurance Certificate.* This confirms that marine insurance has been provided for the cargo and indicates the type and coverage. We'll cover insurance in greater detail in Chapter 10.

- *Packing List.* The packing list or packing slip is a sort of shopping list of the merchandise in the shipment, along with information on how it was packed, how the various items are numbered, and the serial numbers, if applicable, and weight and dimensions of each item. The packing list is an important ingredient in the letter of credit because it (again) verifies the shipped goods and shows to whom they're consigned.

Beware!
Do you need to fill out an SED, or *shipper's export declaration,* for shipments to and from U.S. territories and possessions? The answer depends on where you're shipping to and from. Check with your freight forwarder or customs broker, or call the Foreign Trade Division Regulations people at the Census Bureau at (301) 457-2238.

- *Shipper's Export Declaration.* This one is required by the U.S. government on all exports in excess of $2,500 or ones that require an export license. The reason behind it is to give the folks down at the Census Bureau fodder for their statistics (which you, for one, will probably want to take advantage of during your market research phase), and it gives all the usual information, including product descriptions, value, net and gross weight, and license information.

The Importer at Work

Once the letter of credit has been issued, the exporter's job is to get the merchandise from one country to the other. When the goods arrive, however, the importer takes over. Like a nanny for merchandise, her job is to shepherd the new arrivals through customs so that she can get on with the important—and more exciting—work of sales.

So how is this done? Well, let's face it. The customs broker does most of the nanny work. In fact, unless you have an import license, for which you have to take a government-administered test, in most cases, you can't shepherd your own merchandise through customs.

Still, it's important for you to know how your merchandise gets imported. The more you know, the better you'll be able to help your customs broker—and yourself. There are four basic steps to taking your goods through customs:

1. *Entry.* Deciding where and how you'll enter your merchandise
2. *Examination and valuation.* Determining the legality and tariff or duty value of your goods

The Import Path

OK, importer. You've found the merchandise you want to buy and then resell. You're a player. You're ready to roll. So now what do you do? Follow the import path:

○ Receive pro forma invoice, the exporter's quote on the merchandise; negotiate if necessary.

○ Open a letter of credit at your bank.

○ Verify that the merchandise has been shipped.

○ Receive documents from the exporter.

○ See merchandise through customs.

○ Pass Go. Collect your merchandise and give yourself a pat on the back!

3. *Classification.* Determining the percentage of tax that will be charged on the value of your merchandise

4. *Payment and liquidation.* Coughing up the cash to pay the tariff or duties

But let's take this one item at a time.

Entry

There are two main types of import entry into the United States: informal and formal. Neither has anything to do with tuxedos or evening gowns but rather indicate how much money the merchandise is worth and what it contains. Generally, an informal entry is one valued at $2,000 or less, while a formal entry covers imports of $2,000 or more. Certain goods must always make a formal entry. OK so far? Good.

Now, if the goods you're importing are informal and you're importing them for your own use or to sell at your own shop, then customs will allow you to process the entry yourself. If, however, you're an international trader and you're importing for the purpose of resale or distribution, then you need a customs broker to handle the entry for you. Since this book is all about the business of being an international trader, we're going to go with the formal entry version of the customs game.

Smart Tip

Tip...

One more time: A *negotiable* bill of lading or document is one that can be used to claim title to the merchandise; a *non-negotiable* one cannot.

The Tuxedo Entry

	Informal Entry	Formal Entry
Merchandise worth	Less than $2,000	More than $2,000
Being imported by individual for personal use or to sell in own shop	You can process through customs yourself.	You must employ a customs broker.
Being imported by trader for resale or distribution	You must employ a customs broker.	You must employ a customs broker.

The Merchandise Passport

What do you do if you want to travel abroad with your sales samples so you can show them to prospective buyers? Well, you could go through the whole complicated import process in each country. Or you can take your samples on the Grand Tour duty-free with an ATA carnet. ATA is an acronym for the combined French and English words "Admission Temporaire/Temporary Admission" and means exactly what it says, in whichever language you choose. The carnet, a sort of passport for merchandise, is an international customs document that gets the goods into certain countries without any duties paid until they're returned to home port.

A carnet is:

○ valid for one year

○ good for as many international stops as you care to make with it during that year

○ used not only for commercial samples but advertising materials and professional equipment as well

Currently over 69 countries and territories recognize the ATA carnet, including most European countries, Canada, India, China, Korea, Taiwan, Singapore, and South Africa. Visit www.atacarnet.com for a complete list.

Customs Limbo

According to U.S. Customs, goods brought into the country are in a sort of import limbo—not considered legally entered—until after the following actions have been taken:

- Shipment has arrived within the port of entry.
- Delivery of merchandise has been authorized.
- Customs duty has been paid.

When your merchandise arrives at the U.S. port of entry (the dock, airport, or border), the carrier submits the bill of lading or air waybill to the on-site customs office. This document is now known as evidence of right to make entry.

The shipper notifies your customs broker—and the clock starts ticking. Your broker has 15 days to provide the necessary documents to get your goods out of hock. You and your broker will probably already have a fair idea of when your merchandise is due to arrive because the exporter will have notified you of its ETA and the vessel it's coming in on.

Bringing Home the Bacon

Let's say you've been in contact with a ceramics studio in Ireland and you're planning on contracting with the company as the exclusive representative for its series of ceramic pigs. The company ships you a box of the little fellows to use as samples so that you can presell the line.

Now, you can bring home your ceramic bacon duty-free with a Temporary Importation Under Bond (TIB). With a TIB, you post a bond for double the estimated duty amount, thus assuring the customs people that you'll cover the import fees should you fail to return the samples to Ireland within one year. This period may, with the grace of the district or port director, be extended for up to three years.

TIB fun facts:

- ○ Cars, bikes, boats, balloons, and planes brought into the States for the purpose of engaging in a race or contest can travel on a TIB.
- ○ So can railroad equipment brought in for firefighting or other emergencies.
- ○ So can animals and poultry brought in for exhibition, competition, or breeding.
- ○ And so can fine art or theatrical materials brought in for show.

Released from Custody

Next up is *entering your merchandise*. The most common type of entry is called *entry for consumption*. This, of course, is consumption as in "to be consumed" (i.e., used or sold), and the customs people have handily broken down this stage of the process into two parts:

1. Filing the documents necessary to determine whether merchandise may be released from customs custody; and

2. Filing the documents that contain information for assessing duty and for statistical purposes.

Here's a list of the entry documents your customs broker will need:

Beware!

If you don't file for entry of your merchandise within 15 days, Customs considers it abandoned and puts it into a bonded warehouse of its own under *general order*, otherwise known as G.O. After a one-year holding period, G.O. goods are sold at public auction unless they're perishable or explosive, in which case they get dealt with a lot sooner.

- Entry manifest (also known as Customs Form 7533) or Application and Special Permit for Immediate Delivery (aka Customs Form 3461)

- Bill of lading or air waybill (also known as the *evidence of right to make entry*)

- Commercial invoice or pro forma invoice if the commercial one can't be produced

- Packing lists

- Certificate of origin, if necessary

- Customs bond (which is posted by your broker and assures customs that they'll get the duties, taxes, and any penalties out of you one way or another)

You can see why it's so important to do your homework and make sure the exporter sends you copies of all documents ASAP.

Out on Bail

After customs has gone through all these documents, accepted the bond, and decided that everything's legal and up to snuff, the merchandise is released. Sort of. You could say it's out on bail, pending the last two phases of the customs game.

The first of these is the entry summary documentation. Now your broker has ten days to deposit the estimated duties and file the necessary documentation, namely:

- Entry summary (also known as Customs Form 7501)

- Any other invoices and documents necessary for the assessment of duties, collection of statistics, or other determination that you've met import requirements

Hold on to Your Hats

Now, let's back up a little. Just because your merchandise has arrived at the port of entry, you don't have to rush home with it right away. In fact, you don't even have to enter it immediately. You can choose instead to stash it in a bonded warehouse or transport it to a foreign trade zone.

A *bonded warehouse* is a yard, shed, (surprise!) warehouse, or other storage area within customs territory where you can store your imported merchandise for up to five years without paying duty. While your goodies are in the bonded warehouse, you can clean, sort, and repack them, but that's it. You can't assemble them or attach them to something else and create a new product in the process. It's called a bonded facility because the owner has to post a bond with customs.

> ## Smart Tip
>
> In special cases, such as with perishable items, Customs will issue a permit for immediate release of goods. (Customs isn't stupid; they don't particularly want 500 kilos of fish sitting on their dock for five days or more. Especially not in summer weather.) You can't make up your mind at the last minute, however; you must apply for the permit before your merchandise has arrived.

A *foreign trade zone*, or FTZ, is a sort of customs limbo, in which you can store and also process your imported goods without having to pay duties or jump through the usual customs hoops. Although it sounds like it might be a chunk of foreign land floating somewhere above the surface of American soil, an FTZ is much more prosaic. It's usually a large warehouse located near a port of entry, say in an industrial park or on the docks, with rental spaces available for importers. And unlike the bonded warehouse, the FTZ allows you the freedom to assemble or manufacture your goodies into any other product you choose. So what's the catch? Believe it or not, there isn't one. Local governments set up FTZs to promote international trade, which, in turn, stimulates economic growth.

What the FTZ means to you is savings. If you plan to export the merchandise immediately and you're only holding it in the United States for a short time, you get away with not having to pay customs duties. If you're going to enter the products into the country, you can alter or modify them to lower the import costs. For example, you might bring in fancy sequined fabric squares from Thailand and sew them onto American-made cushions to create decorator throw pillows. When you're ready to bring them out of the foreign trade zone, you pay duties on the throw pillows. If duties on throw pillows are cheaper than those on the sequined fabric squares, the FTZ saves you money.

Another FTZ bonus is that you can duck around the import quota issue. If U.S. Customs allows only so many straw hats, for example, per year and that quota has already been filled, you might hold onto your hats in your FTZ space until the next quota period rolls around.

You would probably use the bonded warehouse when planning a quick in-and-out entry for your merchandise, while you'd use the FTZ when you need to manipulate your products as we've explored. As always, the best way to choose which to use is to consult your customs broker or freight forwarder. There are several different types of entry covering everything from personal baggage to large commercial shipments. The three types you will probably deal with are:

> **Smart Tip** — Tip...
>
> We are not the only country with foreign trade zones. Every country uses a different term, but the idea is the same. As an exporter, you can use these zones to receive goods that will be reshipped in smaller lots to customers in the region.

1. *Consumption entry.* You already know this one, used when the merchandise is intended for immediate resale. This type is the most common.

2. *Immediate transport entry.* This is used when you want the goods whisked to another location within the United States for customs clearance, for instance, if you've arranged to have them brought in by ship to New York, but you want to store—and assemble—them in an FTZ in Ohio.

3. *Warehouse entry.* This is sort of a layaway plan. You leave your imported goods in a customs-bonded warehouse and withdraw them in portions. Each time you make a withdrawal, you pay duty on that part.

Examination and Valuation

After you've decided to enter your merchandise, customs will inspect your shipment to make sure it can legally enter the country and to determine its tariff or duty value. Why do they want to dip into your goods? They're checking to see:

- if your merchandise is marked with the country of origin or requires special markings or labeling and, if so, that it displays it
- if the shipment contains prohibited articles
- if the merchandise is correctly invoiced
- if the merchandise is either in excess or shortfall of the invoiced quantity
- if the shipment contains illegal drugs

They're also checking the dutiable status and value of your goods. The value is the price you've actually paid for the merchandise, plus amounts for the following items if not included in the price. (You can see why it's important to make sure everything is listed on the commercial invoice.)

Go, Dog!

Contrary to the flashier techniques you may have seen on Miami Vice, the drug smuggler's method of choice often involves the (relatively) simple act of tucking narcotics into legitimate cargo shipments. But bad guys, beware! The U.S. Customs Service's Canine Enforcement Program is on red alert at ports of entry around the country and our territories.

You can check out the canine of the month as well as other sniff-detective pooches on Customs' web site at www.cpb.gov/xp/cgov/border_security/canines/canine.xml. The dogs also have their own set of collectible cards, each listing port of entry worked, age, breed, weight, year started in customs, and largest or most notable seizure.

- Packing costs incurred by the importer
- The value of any assists (An assist can be a tool, die, mold, engineering drawing or artwork, something that assists in the assembly and sale of the product.)
- Any selling commission incurred by the importer
- A royalty or license fee required from the importer as part of the sale
- The proceeds accruing to the exporter of any subsequent resale, disposal, or use of the imported goods

Classification

The Customs Service classifies goods according to tariff schedules. Different types of goods are assigned different percentages on which they're taxed. The amount of duty varies dramatically depending on exactly what the products are and what specifically they're made of. Cotton knit shirts, for example, may be taxed at 17 percent, while nonknit cotton shirts might be taxed at only 8 percent. During the classification step, the customs people will decide exactly which category your merchandise falls into.

Their decision is based on an extremely complicated set of rules called the Harmonized Tariff Schedule of the United States. The word "harmonized" refers to the fact that it harmonizes with, or matches, the tariff schedules of the rest of the industrialized world. The harmonized schedule comes in a book big enough to serve as a booster chair for a hefty three-year-old and is jam-packed with enough

Last Person in America

U.S. Customs insists that each item imported into the country be marked or labeled with the country of origin. This marking must be done so that it's readily visible to the ultimate end user, "the last person in the United States," as the customs people word it, "who will receive the article in the form in which it was imported."

In other words, if you're importing ceramic pigs from the Emerald Isle, each little porker must be stamped or labeled "Made in Ireland" on its underside, so that the last person in the United States can tip over the little chap and read where he came from. You can't settle for a "Made in Ireland" marking on the box in which a dozen pigs are shipped, because the ultimate consumer will probably only be buying one piglet at a time.

There are, of course, exceptions to this rule, and they're rather eclectic, ranging from playing cards to rags to wood shingles (except red cedar ones) to hairnets to certain types of fish hooks to cut flowers to Christmas trees. Since you can't know and probably could never guess the extent of all these exceptions, it's best to check with your customs broker while you're still in the final negotiations stage with the exporter. You don't want someone shipping you 1,000 bales of barbed wire you can't use because it's unmarked; nor do you want to pay extra for the marking of 5,000 ceramic bricks from Mexico when it's unnecessary.

---

classifications, sub-classifications, and sub-sub-classifications to satisfy even the most nit-picking person on earth.

Cotton fabric, for example, is classified by whether it's bleached or unbleached, printed, composed of yarns of different color or dyed, whether it's pure cotton or a mix of fibers, the number of single threads per square centimeter, yarn sizes in the warp, whether the fabric is or is not napped, etc. Even fish livers must be classified by how much oil, fat, or grease they contain. Now you see why you need a customs broker!

The broker, while versed in the harmonized system and armed with the basic HS number for your merchandise, is not the one who hands down the final classification decision. This falls to the customs officer. (Lest you think that each officer has memorized the entire 99-chapter schedule—not! Teams of customs inspectors rove each port of entry, with various inspectors specializing in different types of goods.)

Payment and Liquidation

Now that your merchandise has been classified, it's on to the exciting phase of paying the piper, or in this case, the customs person. As with many assignments under government aegis, this is not always a simple, cut-and-dried operation.

Oh, it can be. Your entry summary and documentation can be accepted as submitted without any changes. In this case, you simply hand over a check for the amount of duty, or tariff, owed, and your merchandise or entry is entered as liquidated. This means, in essence, done, over, finished, complete. You and customs have figuratively shaken hands and closed the books.

In other cases, however, customs may send you notification that the classification is not correct and cannot be liquidated as entered after all. If the revised classification results in a tariff change in your favor, they'll send you a refund. Like their compatriot, the IRS, however, they can also decide on a change in their own favor, in which case you need to send them money.

Smart Tip

Don't wait for a last-minute shocker when you learn the import tariff. Make sure you've checked with your customs broker for an idea of what the HS number for your products will be before you bring them into the country.

If you don't agree with the change, you have 90 days to file a protest, which then goes on to review or, in some cases, to court. The entry is not considered liquidated until the final ruling.

Pack Up Your Troubles

Nothing makes customs inspectors happier than a shipment they can go through easily. So pack up your troubles and suggest to your exporter that he follow these customs tips:

- ○ Invoice merchandise in a systematic manner.
- ○ Show the exact quantity of goods in each box, bale, case, or other package.
- ○ Number each package (i.e., box three of four).
- ○ Put these numbers on the invoice next to the itemized goods in each package.

Charting Your Trade Route
Market Research

very business needs consumers for its products and services to, as the Vulcans so eloquently put it, live long and prosper. Now that you know what running an import/export business entails, you need to plan, or target, your market, and determine who your potential clients will be, which geographic areas you'll draw from, and what specific products or services you'll offer to draw them in.

This is a very important phase in the mega-trader building project. The proper market research can help boost your trading company into a true profit center, and the more research you do, and the better prepared you are before you officially open your doors, the less floundering you're likely to do.

This chapter, therefore, homes in on market research tips and techniques for the newbie importer/exporter. First up:

Tripping Manufacturers

Your target market—the customers you are aiming for—can encompass any product or service you can think up. Any manufacturer, supplier, importer, exporter, artisan, crafter, or retailer is fair game. You can go after companies that deal in heavy construction equipment or delicate jewelry, gourmet goodies or pet food, telecommunications or toys. The only essential requirement is that they want to sell their merchandise or buy someone else's.

This doesn't mean, however, that your best technique is standing at manufacturers' gates, tripping them as they walk to their cars after work each evening. Targeting by definition means homing in on a specific group.

If you have previous experience in a particular field, for example, you should seriously consider targeting that market first. You'll feel comfortable with the jargon and procedures so your sales pitch—and your initial sales—will go more smoothly and easily. As an added bonus, you may already have contacts in the field who can either become your first clients or steer you toward colleagues in that area.

Dan S. targeted the field of technology—specifically, software solutions for commercial use and computer cables—simply because he's worked in that area for more than ten years. He knows the field and feels comfortable in it.

Wahib W., too, began in a field he knew well, runway and navigational lights, then went on to other international construction projects,

Trader's View

Follow the lead of John L. in Brazil. Skip areas you just don't know. "We are able to provide good assistance in several fields except machinery and commodities of high volume, such as soy, oil, and sugar," John explains. "Both fields require very special knowledge and a big infrastructure."

importing railroad and telephone pole materials, and construction services, as well as other heavy equipment materials.

Where in the World?

Besides deciding what products you'll specialize in, you want to think about what countries you'll work with. Some traders start off with a part of the world they already know; others let their products be their guide to far corners of the globe.

Wahib W., raised in Egypt, found exporting to Egypt a natural. And for Peter P., who's of Ukrainian heritage and has a college minor in Russian, exporting to Russia was a breeze.

In Brazil, John L. works mostly with Brazilian companies locating and developing international business opportunities. Searching for leads for these clients takes him around the globe. "I have business relations with the entire world," John explains, "except Africa (excluding South Africa), Eastern Europe, Iran, Iraq, Cuba, Turkey, Nepal, Tibet, and other small places very poor in foreign trade."

In Germany, Michael R. counts only one area of the world where he hasn't done business. "[I have dealt] with all internationally interesting markets worldwide," he says, "except South America, as I don't speak Spanish."

Dan S. in New Jersey found his clients at a trade show in Manchester, England— one of his first prospects is English.

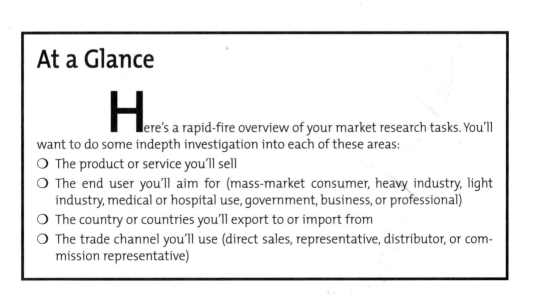

> **Tip...**
>
> ## Smart Tip
> Need information about a specific country? Get connected with every national embassy in Washington, DC, through The Electronic Embassy at www.embassy.org.

At a Glance

Here's a rapid-fire overview of your market research tasks. You'll want to do some indepth investigation into each of these areas:

○ The product or service you'll sell

○ The end user you'll aim for (mass-market consumer, heavy industry, light industry, medical or hospital use, government, business, or professional)

○ The country or countries you'll export to or import from

○ The trade channel you'll use (direct sales, representative, distributor, or commission representative)

▲

What's My Niche?

OK. You've narrowed the list of products you'll target. Now you'll want to find your niche, the unique angle that will set your business apart from—and above—the competition. This is where you can really let your creativity shine through.

You may decide to start as an export management company (EMC, remember?), seeking out buyers for domestic manufacturing firms, or as an export trading company (ETC), finding domestic sources willing to export. Or you might want to stick with the original Trader Sam formula, importing and exporting on your own as an import/export merchant.

In Florida, Lloyd D. positioned his company as both an EMC and ETC, depending on his clients' needs. "[As an EMC, we] work directly for a manufacturer, or his exclusive distributor/manager for international sales, as a marketing and screening provider," Lloyd explains, "and will search for and locate overseas buyers-for-resale and/or qualified distributors/sales representatives. [Our] objective is to function as an extension of [our] principal's in-house export sales efforts."

Under its ETC hat, Lloyd says, "[my company] performs in a fashion similar to that previously described, except for a diminished principal relationship, and business is typically conducted on a case-by-case or *ad hoc* basis. It is more a sourcing function for the buyer and the seller."

Starting from Me

Sources for finding import/export customers are abundant, advises Wahib W. But as an international trader, the trick lies not merely in what information you can find but in what you do with it. "Where do you want to be?" Wahib asks. "Which country do you want to go with? This is what you're targeting.

"I have to start from me," the construction projects exporter continues, "from what I can offer, what I can sell, or what I can do to make a profit. That's my niche."

As examples, Wahib offers slices of his own company's life: "I act sometimes as a buyer for a government, like a purchasing agent. Some companies want us to go and solicit projects for their product. So now we know there's a certain product we want to go and sell. Or we have a government in Egypt that wants telephone poles. I have the specifications, and I have to go solicit the manufacturer to make them for me. In that case, I can act as a prime or general contractor, and the American company will be the subcontractor. They sell to me, and I sell to the foreign government."

John L. in Brazil also has structured his business from the viewpoint of assisting clients rather than selling products. "My company," John explains, "is an international business services provider. We assist companies in locating and developing worldwide business opportunities."

In Germany, Michael R. describes his company's role this way: "[We are] a worldwide consultancy to SMEs [small- and medium-sized enterprises] that wish to increase their sales and profits by using the available world markets more successfully."

"Secondhand Rose"

Nearby in Belgium, Jan H. has focused his company on specific products, specializing in the worldwide import and export of new and used tires, secondhand vehicles and machinery, and—as in the Barbara Streisand hit "Secondhand Rose"—secondhand clothing.

In France, Bruno C. works with a broader range of merchandise. "We export a wide range of products, from protection and security products to computing products,"

The Whole Earth EMC

As your special niche, you might specialize in smaller manufacturers who haven't even considered exporting, or maybe providers of services—everything from bridge building to telecommunications—who have no idea how to go about it. For these people, you might promote yourself as a sort of Whole Earth EMC, a full-service company offering everything for the international product wanna-be. How about:

- ○ Finding, evaluating, and appointing dealers, distributors, and commission representatives in foreign markets
- ○ Providing all promotional support—advertising, marketing, and trade show exhibitions
- ○ Document and correspondence translation
- ○ Preparation of all agreements with foreign distributors
- ○ Preparation of all acceptances and approvals
- ○ Arranging financing
- ○ Overseeing all order-processing correspondence
- ○ Managing all shipping and documentation
- ○ Providing all after-market assistance

Bruno says. "We also export products such as plastic films and bags and some ferrous and aluminum products."

And in Atlanta, Peter P. attacked the specific merchandise target from yet another angle, acting as a sort of in-house EMC with a specific product line. "We are a Russian-based company," Peter explains. "We import goods into Russia and distribute them throughout greater Russia, primarily frozen foodstuffs. Our specialty right now is frozen meats. What the U.S. offices do here in Atlanta and in New York is oversee the procurement. We negotiate for the procurement of the product directly with Western suppliers, develop credit terms with them, and coordinate the logistics of getting the goods from the West, not only from the United States, but from North America and Europe as well as other parts of the world. We oversee the shipment of the goods sold to Russia on a CIF basis, delivered to the Russian port."

These strategies are all excellent examples of finding a unique angle, that special niche. You might want to formulate your business as an EMC for a particular type of merchandise or for a particular country. Or how about importing or exporting a full-spectrum line of merchandise, like garden tools and clothing, or artists' paints and papers?

> ### Trader's View
>
> Just how important is market research? Very, according to Belgian Jan H. "Know your product fully," the tire and clothing exporter advises. "Analyze the markets and supply situation. Know your customers."

My Mission: Trade

As an import/export newbie, you may start out by simply selling your clients' products in foreign markets. Acting as their representative, you'll transact business in their name for a commission, salary, or retainer and commission. But again, you need to research your market, find out what sorts of buyers are available, and know the types of goods they're buying. This is an extremely important step in setting up your international trade business and one that you cannot afford to overlook.

So how do you accomplish this task? Well, as long as you're hoping to export goods out of the United States, a mind-boggling array of resources is available at your fingertips. Because exports give the economy a big charge, our friendly government agents are happy to help you sell just about anything to foreign markets.

Arguably the largest clearinghouse of information for finding foreign buyers is the International Trade Administration (ITA), a division of the U.S. Department of Commerce. And the ITA's U.S. & Foreign Commercial Service (Hmm—sounds like the title of a James Bond film: "On Her Majesty's Commercial Service") is on permanent standby, alert and willing to help you. Its only mission is to help you develop and flex your export wings, which it does by providing some phenomenal services—everything from country-specific market analyses to trade leads to setting up and chaperoning personal meetings between you and interested foreign businesspeople. The US & FCS, which likes to call itself the more streamlined but less dashing "Commercial Service" these days, is one place where you can actually see your tax dollars at work, seemingly just for you.

According to the Commercial Service web site, the organization's goal is "to help U.S. companies export." Period. "In fiscal year 2006, we helped more than 69,000 exporters achieve more than $63 billion in export sales." The group employs trade specialists in 107 cities and more than 80 countries to help you meet your importing/exporting goals. Services include, according to the web site, "world-class" market research, trade events that will help you promote your product, introductions to buyers and distributors, and counseling and advocacy services.

While you're studying this section (you're not just giving it a glance and a promise, are you?), keep these resources in mind. You'll want to go back to them as your career moves along. They're terrific wellsprings not only for market research but for advertising, marketing, and promotional purposes as well.

Unfortunately, if you're hoping to sell foreign-made doodads in the United States, you'll have to find this information without help from the government. Don't despair—there are still plenty of resources for market research. See the "Up Close and Personal" section on page 109.

Unlocking Mysteries

A terrific source for export market research is the National Trade Data Bank (NTDB). Its motto? "Unlocking the mysteries of international trade." A powerhouse of world trade data, the data bank claims more than 40,000 separate trade- and business-related documents on file. You can access it through STAT-USA, a division of the Commercial Service at (800) STAT-USA or www.stat-usa.gov. Take advantage of it!

You can't miss with topics like:

- Export opportunities by industry, country, and product
- How-to market guides
- Demographic, political, and socioeconomic conditions in hundreds of countries
- And, as the Commercial Service says, much more! This includes comprehensive reports on the commercial environments of more than 100 countries through economic, political, and market analyses, foreign trade zone information, and so many market research reports that the list alone is pages long.

Tip...

Smart Tip
You'll find directories of Export Assistance Centers and worldwide Commercial Service offices on the Commercial Service web site at www.ita.doc.gov/cs.

Product Market Research Worksheet

Don't be befuddled by market research tasks. Use this handy worksheet—make copies and use one for each product or service you're considering. Then give each one a grade: Fantastic, Has Potential, or Not Such a Hot Idea. When you've completed several sheets, compare them, weed out the NSAHIs (you know—the Not Such a Hot Ideas), start working on the Fantastics, and keep the Potentials on file for future reference.

1. Name or description of product _____

   _____

2. What are the product's selling features? _____

   _____

3. Are there competitive products? If so, list them: _____

   _____

4. What are their selling features? _____

   _____

5. What is the sales potential of the product or service in my target market?

   _____

6. What are comparably priced goods going for in my target market? __

   _____

7. Who will be the end user of the product? _____

   _____

8. Is the population of potential end users large enough to substantiate sales? _____

   _____

9. Can I expand the market, or will I be taking a share of the existing market?

   _____

10. Is the existing market large enough to share? _____

    _____

11. Which elements have the most influence on potential customers or clients? Price, quality, brand name, "imported" cachet, service, credit terms, delivery terms, advertising, or marketing assistance? _____

    _____

    _____

Product Market Research Worksheet, continued

12. Where can I buy this product? _____

_____

13. Will I need to have it manufactured? _____

_____

14. If so, what is the turnaround time for manufacturing, and will this influence sales? _____

_____

15. What will be my cost for the product? _____

_____

16. What variables will affect pricing (special packaging or marking requirements, special shipping requirements as for perishables, other variables)?

_____

_____

17. What are the potential problems that will contribute to my price, such as end-user unfamiliarity with the product or service? _____

_____

_____

18. What are the potential benefits that can contribute to my price, such as high demand for the product or service? _____

_____

_____

19. What is the potential for licensing? _____

_____

Final grade

❑ Fantastic

❑ Has Potential

❑ Not Such a Hot Idea

Country Market Research Worksheet

Once you've done your product market research (or at the same time, if your market is intrinsic to product sales), move on to this worksheet. Again, use this handy checklist—make copies and use one for each country you're considering. Then give each one a grade: Fantastic, Has Potential, or Not Such a Hot Idea. When you've completed several sheets, compare them, weed out the NSAHIs (you know—the Not Such a Hot Ideas), start working on the Fantastics, and keep the Potentials on file for future reference.

1. Why does this country have potential for my product or service? _____

   _____

   _____

2. How can I gain exposure in this country? _____

   _____

3. Will I need to travel abroad to find markets, conduct research, and find distributors, or can I do this at home via phone and the internet? _____

   _____

4. Will I encounter language barriers or difficulties? _____

   _____

5. What cultural differences will I need to account for? _____

   _____

6. How will I handle them? _____

   _____

7. What is the economic climate (on a national level—unemployment rates, inflation, or depression; on a personal level—disposable incomes, spending patterns)?

   _____

   _____

Country Market Research Worksheet, continued

8. What is the sociological climate (urban and rural populations, literacy and educational levels, any special religious considerations)? _____

_____

_____

9. What is the political climate? _____

_____

_____

10. Will I experience any special shipping or handling problems because of geography or local customs? If so, what? _____

_____

_____

11. What trade channel will I use (direct sales, representative, distributor, or commission representative)? _____

_____

_____

12. How will I locate my trade channel people? _____

_____

_____

13. What are the country-specific problems that will contribute to my price, such as quotas, duties, or country regulations? _____

_____

_____

14. What are the country-specific benefits that can contribute to my price, such as duty-free or low trade barriers? _____

_____

_____

Final grade
❑ Fantastic
❑ Has Potential
❑ Not Such a Hot Idea

I'm ITA!

The U.S. government's International Trade Administration (ITA) is on a mission: Help American businesses compete in the world marketplace by:

○ Promoting and assisting American exports (and exporters)

○ Assuring American businesses of equal access to foreign markets

○ Empowering American businesses to compete against unfairly traded imports

The ITA has created four units to carry out this mission:

1. The *U.S. Commercial Service*, which provides business counseling to U.S. exporters

2. *Manufacturing and Services*, which provides information for U.S. exporters, policy makers, and trade negotiators through industry sector specialists

3. *Market Access and Compliance*, in which country experts provide market analysis to American businesses

4. *Import Administration*, which guards our U.S. economy from unfairly priced imports

---

Like everything else in life, however, this wealth of information is not free. A subscription to www.usatradeonline.gov goes for about $75 per month or $300 per year. You can set up an internet account with STAT-USA and access the information online any time you like.

Intelligence Agency

How about a sort of (not) for-your-eyes-only intelligence report on the countries of your choice? Check out *Country Commercial Guides*, which furnish every piece of information you could ever want to know, including political, economic, and market analyses. The complete set of guides are free for the viewing at www.usatrade.gov. Click on "Market Research," then "Market Research Library." Select "Country Commercial Guides," and the country of your choice from the drop-down list.

Remember those international intrigue movies where the hero works at an "intelligence desk" in a foreign country? Well, the Commercial Service has the same sort of chaps and

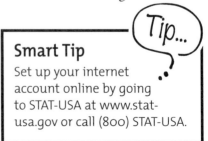

Smart Tip

Set up your internet account online by going to STAT-USA at www.stat-usa.gov or call (800) STAT-USA.

lassies toiling at U.S. embassies and consulates abroad, compiling in-depth reports on industries around the world. These *Country Commercial Guides* detail everything you could possibly want to know, including:

- Market potential and demand trends
- Market size and import statistics
- Competition
- Market access
- Regulations and standards
- Best sales prospects
- End users
- Key industry contacts

Again, these folks are pushing exports, not imports, so you're not going to find much useful information if you're looking to bring goods into the country. But if you have U.S.-made widgets you think the rest of the world will jump on, these guides are your friends.

Custom Tailored

Country Commercial Guides are not all the Commercial Service has to offer. Experts at its Export Assistance Centers will write up a *Customized Market Analysis* specially tailored to your product or service. This is a market research tool to make start-up entrepreneurs in other industries start salivating with envy. You choose your target country; specialists then conduct interviews with in-the-know local sources—importers, distributors, consumers or end users, and man-ufacturers of comparable products. In about 60 days, bingo! Your custom analysis is sent to your door. The cost for this service ranges from $1,000 to $3,000, depending on the country.

Smart Tip

Call (800) USA-TRADE for free export advice from government representatives any time.

If you just have a few specific questions about your market, you can also pay for Flexible Market Research, which runs you anywhere from $200 to $3,000.

You can order a *Customized Market Analysis* and determine cost specifics for your area of interest through your nearest Export Assistance Center. How do you find a center? Go to www.ita.doc.gov/uscs or call (800) USA-TRADE.

Up Close and Personal

The Commercial Service is not the only place to turn for market research informa-tion. You can find out a lot on your own by reading local, national, and international newspapers and trade publications, by surfing international trade sites on the internet (see Appendix for lists), and through the personal interview—talking to traders already at work in the field. These people can give you an insider's look at what works, what doesn't, and why.

Importers and exporters are not quite as accessible as professionals in some other industries. They're often abroad on business and when they're back in the office, they're on overload with catch-up work. But if you present yourself in a pleasant and courteous manner, they'll probably share their expertise with you.

You'll find international traders in your local Yellow Pages, in various industry associations (check out our Appendix for a list), and, of course, on the internet.

If you plan to conduct a phone or in-person interview, be sure you call first to schedule a short meeting at a time convenient to your interviewee. If you're approaching your subject via e-mail, write a short note explaining that you'd like to conduct a "mini-interview online" and would like the opportunity to submit some questions. It's professional courtesy to presume (correctly) that other people have busy schedules. Let your subject know the reason for the interview, about how much of his or her time you expect to take, and possibly even divulge a few of the questions you'll be asking. This will put them at ease about the interview and also get them thinking ahead.

Most people, once you get them going, are only too happy to talk about themselves and their businesses. Take advantage of this fact to learn what you need to know, but don't take unfair advantage of a trader's time or personal space. Courtesy will get you further than you might imagine!

Now, with all these caveats firmly in mind, check out the International Trader's Interview on page 113. Make copies and use it for phone or personal interviews or retype the questions for your e-mail interview.

Up Closer and More Personal

If you prefer to get even closer and more personal, you'll want to check out the Commercial Service's Matchmaker Trade Delegation program, the ultimate in dating services for the export-ready trader. For this one, you'll need to have your merchandise market research already complete and be ready to implement sales. Then you simply

What's in a Lead?

So what does a trade lead look like? A text advertisement or invitation. Check out these samples.

Company:	Car Hop Ltd.
Contact:	Ms. Daphne Denton
Position:	Head of Export
Business:	Car pennants and other designer car accessories
Address:	No. 1 The Groves, Greater Chestershire Industrial Estate, Chestershire
Country:	Great Britain
Phone:	011-44-181-000000
Fax:	011-44-181-000001
E-mail:	carhop@holiday.com

Car pennants from CAR HOP LTD. are the latest in auto accessories. Find your vehicle fast in a crowded car park with these colorful plastic banners that extend from the radio aerial. Pennants can be had in a variety of sport team logos, with city names, or personalized with your name, your girlfriend's or your dog's names. Any color, text, and graphics. Gift shops, clubs, service stations, and auto parts centres sell our products. Dealer inquiries welcome. Ask for our detailed catalog or inquire about your own designs. Also ask about your range of related CAR HOP accessories.

Date:	17 July 200x
From:	Spencer Avalon
Company:	Avalon Traders Ltd.
Phone:	(000) 000-0000
Fax:	(000) 000-0001
E-mail:	avalon@holiday.com
Subject:	Pine Furniture
No. Units:	2 x 40 containers
When:	Immediate

Buyer's Location: Asia
Seeks Products From: USA and/or Canada
Transaction Range: $50,000+
Business Activity: Resell to dedicated distributors
Frequency: 4x per year
Acceptable Terms of Sale: FCA/FOB/FAS
Acceptable Payment Terms: Letter of credit, at sight
Comments: Seller must ship within seven days of receiving letter of credit. Contact Spencer Avalon for full details.

contact the Matchmaker people and they do everything (and we mean everything) necessary to introduce you to the right business contacts at trade delegations that target two or three countries with strong sales potential for American products.

"The U.S. Department of Commerce staff will have completed all the legwork by the time you arrive in country," the Matchmaker people explain. "The hotel reservations, meeting facilities, interpreters, and appointment schedules are all arranged for you. All you have to do is arrive in country ready to interview your potential business prospects."

As a Matchmaker delegate, here is what you get:

- Market analysis of your merchandise or service
- Two days of prescreened business appointments in each country
- Indepth market and trade finance briefings by both American government and local experts
- "Logistical support," including hotel reservations, interpreters, and meeting rooms
- Embassy receptions and site visits (with selected Matchmakers)
- Counseling and follow-up from your local Export Assistance Center

The sites and topics of Matchmaker Trade Delegations are set up about two years in advance, so you have plenty of time to get your product or service research done before you make your "date." Here's a sampling of the sorts of topics and countries you'll find on the Matchmaker schedule:

- Health-care technologies in the United Kingdom, Italy, Spain, and Greece
- Architecture, construction, and engineering in India
- Sporting goods in Brazil and Chile
- Franchising in Italy, Spain, Portugal, and Greece

Star Treatment

As the ultimate in export dating services, the Commercial Service offers its Gold Key program for exporters who want more personalized service. While the Matchmaker service sends you globe-trotting with 10 to 20 other company representatives and sets you all up with a booth and display, the Gold Key option

> **Bright Idea**
> After the interview, always send a short thank-you note. This is not only simple courtesy but a way to set a nice tone for any future relations.

> **Smart Tip**
> You will find Matchmaker Trade Delegation Schedules for the next couple of years on www.usatrade.gov. Click on "Find Trade Events/Missions," then on "Domestic and Foreign Trade Events," then search based on your criteria.

International Trader's Interview

Company name: _____

Name and title of contact person: _____

1. What does your company do? Import, export, or both? _____
   _____

2. What types of products do you deal with? _____
   _____

3. Which products have you had the most success with and why? _____
   _____

4. Which products have you had the least success with and why? _____
   _____

5. What type of competition do you face? _____
   _____

6. What countries do you work with? _____
   _____

7. Where and how do you find most of your customers? _____
   _____
   _____

8. What is your trade channel? Do you use direct sales, sales representatives, distributors, or commission representatives? _____
   _____
   _____

9. Could you explain why? _____
   _____
   _____

Don't forget the thank you!

finds potential partners for you and you alone—in the country you want. (With the Matchmaker program, you must choose from pre-set country formats.)

The basic charge for an agent distributor search will set you back $250. If you want star treatment—a car, an office, a driver, and interpreter—the bills grow from there. All you need to bring is your product or service literature. "Gold Key," says an Export Assistance Center spokesperson in Florida, "is our best program."

Compass Points

Amazing as the Commercial Service's programs are, they're not the only points on the compass. You can find lots of other sources for market research and trade leads simply by traveling the internet. You will find many services out there with helpful information for newbie traders. Check out the following organizations:

- *World Trade Point Federation (www.tradepoint.org), a division of the United Nations.* On this site you can post a notice saying what sort of widgets you're hoping to import or export. You may also be able to find trade partners in the countries you've targeted.

- *Organization of Women in International Trade (www.owit.org).* This not-for-women-only site provides networking and educational opportunities.

No Wanna-Bes, Please

The Export Assistance Center is only interested in helping you if you're a serious trader. No dilettantes or wanna-bes need apply. "We work solely with export-ready manufacturing firms or export representatives who are already established," says a spokesman with a center in Florida.

Why? Too many would-be traders who don't do their homework (and probably haven't read this book). Nascent exporters are sent to their local SBDCs (Small Business Development Centers).

Of the exporters the Florida center works with, a wide variety of products are represented. Among the most prevalent:

- ○ Medical equipment
- ○ Computers, software, and peripherals
- ○ Telecommunications
- ○ Building products
- ○ Laboratory and scientific instruments

- *International Chamber of Commerce (www.iccwbo.org)*. This site offers information about conferences, an online bookstore, and lots of lofty discussion about international trade.

You can—and should—find lots more trade lead services just by searching the internet. Try conducting a search on the country you're interested in trading with as well as "chamber of commerce" and you should get a good start on finding market leads.

Since some of these sites are freebies while others, like Trade Compass, are not, check out several before committing yourself to a fee-based service.

7

The Armchair Trader
Working Online

Remember the book and subsequent movie, *The Accidental Tourist*? The story of a writer who pens travel books for business people who hate to travel made the character Macon Leary a living, breathing enigma. After all, how can a person who hates to travel write books about travel? Likewise for us, how can you really be an importer or exporter if you don't leave the couch? Can you forsake the plane, the steamship, the sleeper car for the Lazy Boy? You might be surprised.

All the Comforts of Home

Let's face it. Most beginning traders do not have it in their budgets to sail off to Africa in search of the latest handcrafted items or jet to France each November to sample the fresh bottles of Beaujolais Nouveau. Most traders starting out do their footwork on the information superhighway, not the Autobahn.

To really operate efficiently as an armchair trader, you simply must have all of the technological goodies your budget will allow and the savvy to keep them functioning on a regular basis.

A Trip to the Hardware Store

In addition to all of the day-to-day office equipment we'll discuss in Chapter 11, you need to put a special focus on your computer, fax, and internet components in order to trade at the speed of light. Or, at least at the highest speed your connection will allow.

Let's begin with hardware—your computer. For the purposes of setting up your virtual trading office, a laptop is key. Why? It will allow you to be mobile within your workspace, letting you to move freely about the office. If you work from home, a laptop can turn a sunny day stuck indoors chained to your workstation to a productive day of trading by the pool. And once you have that capital to sail off in search of the world's finest import goods, your office can effectively travel with you.

Styles and functionality of computers come in and go out of style faster than Paris Hilton's wardrobe, so try to shoot for a model with the most RAM and storage space available. One hundred GB hard drives are par for the course, and Windows XP or Vista operating systems are the norm for PCs, and the latest rev of OS X Tiger for Mac.

Most importantly, though, is your internet capability. Suck it up and get off those phone lines, or your trades will travel at the speed of a donkey. Invest the extra monthly fees to have a T1 or DSL internet connection. You might pay more upfront, but you will save money (in the form of time) on the backend. Also consider outfitting your new baby for wireless access. You'll find that you can log onto the internet from just about anywhere these days—cafes, libraries, bookstores, you name it. If you are not a technophile, fear not. Find a reputable techie (like the Geek Squad folks from Best Buy) to make it all happen for you. In less than a day, you can be flying through the online world at warp speed.

House Rules:
What Can You Do Online?

In a word, everything. Very few aspects of the trading world are exempt from internet availability. Though we strongly recommend the continued use of your fax machine (hardcopy just feels so . . . permanent), that doesn't mean it can't coexist with your e-mail.

Take forms, for example. Now, we have provided you with an arsenal of example forms in this book. But say you really don't want to deal with setting up and filling out your own forms for every single transaction. Hop online and check out the wealth of forms software and companies designed specifically to offer the service of import/export forms management. A simple Google search for "Export Forms" will spit out thousands of options from example forms from government agencies to shareware that you can purchase and manage yourself.

> ## Tip...
> ### Smart Tip
> Try a shareware service, such as EZ Forms at www.ez-forms.com/ezforms export.htm. For around $200, they provide you will most of the necessary forms you need to keep business moving along. Updates are available and output comes in PDF form so you can scan, fax, e-mail, etc. For an extra fee, EZ Forms will customize your forms and site license the shareware for use on multiple machines.

Most traders today are tech-savvy and will not only accept, but expect, the fact that you do the majority of your communications via e-mail, instant messaging (IM), and voiceover IP. They know it's relatively safe (you did install firewall and antiviral software, yes?), operates 24 hours a day, and is the cheapest form of international communication short of messages in bottles, which takes considerably longer to reach their recipients. E-mail is also easy to track and refer back to when you need confirmation of a discussion or item sent or received. Utilize an e-mail program with good storage space that allows for several folder structures so you can organize your communications as efficiently as possible.

BTW, IMHO You Should CYA on the B2B or Your Biz Will be DOA

Huuuuhh? No idea what that heading means? Probably no one over 20 does, or at least no one outside of the IM/Chat world. Internet slang is everywhere from the cell phone to the chat room. Thankfully, though, it hasn't quite made its way into the boardroom . . . so let's keep it that way. What may work for you when you IM your spouse to pick up the kids at school won't fly in the professional world. Though we're singing the praises of online communication—fast, cheap, efficient!—the need for the niceties cannot be ignored. Etiquette is not something reserved for debutantes dressed in white—it is an essential piece of the global business market.

When in doubt, refer to the rules your momma taught:

Always say "please." Always say "thank you." Don't bark orders in your e-mails and refrain from overly concise language, which can come off as rude.

Think before you react. If things are not going your way, hold off before you fire off a nasty e-mail telling that supplier in Germany just where he can stick his schnitzel. Wait. Breathe. If need be, set a timer for one hour and blow off some steam before you respond in anger or frustration.

Include a descriptive headline on all e-mails, particularly if some action is required. Be specific. If you wish to know the price of a specific Grecian urn and you need to know ASAP, don't just write "Grecian Urn" in the header. Instead, write "Action Requested: Need Grecian Urn Quote by Tomorrow." This way, your recipient sees the urgent request and you will be able to more adequately file the response e-mail.

If you do require an action by a specific date or time, say it (nicely) in the body text of the e-mail. Bold or highlight the information and time frame in which you need to know. Like this: **Please let me know the price of Urn #2423 by 5 P.M. EST on January 20.** Thank you.

Include a greeting and a closing, just like a real letter. You have time for this, trust me. Even when you are responding, put the person's name at the top and yours at the bottom instead of just firing off one sentence. To make life easier, create a signature within your e-mail program that will automatically sign for you on each e-mail. Make it personal, not rote. Instead of your name followed by your contact information, use a formal closing first, like "Sincerely," "My Best," or "Respectfully," then type your name and info. Nice never hurts.

Bright Idea

Check out more on e-mail etiquette—where else!—online at www.emailreplies.com. There, you will find information specific to sending replies. Also, check out our old pal Emily Post at www.emilypost.com. She's a modern woman with plenty of e-mail pointers.

Say What? Language Barriers

It goes without saying that as a business person, you know how to handle yourself around people. But what about people who don't necessarily speak your language?

Each country differs in how people (especially those in business) relate to one another. What is acceptable practice in the United States may be frowned upon in Asia. Just like any other cultural difference, the language we use in business communication can greatly affect the outcome of a business deal.

> ### Smart Tip
> Invest a few bucks in your "language barrier library." Pick up copies of an international business dictionary, basic English grammar guide, and basic phrase books for the countries you work with the most.

The best advice is to avoid using American slang or colloquial phrases. Your foreign trade partners will, in all likelihood, take what you say at face value if they are not familiar with the eccentricities of the English language. You and your trade partner in Asia are laughing via IM about something funny that happened at the dock and you type, "How funny! What a hoot!" The response will likely be, "I don't see an owl. What do you mean?"

On the other end of the spectrum, your foreign counterparts may speak English, but not as well as their native language. They may bungle some phrasing or confound you with the use of their own colloquialisms ("Bob's your uncle," as the Brits say, even when you know full well your uncle's name is Frank), so be patient and ask questions. If you don't understand something in a communication, confirm the meaning. Likewise, have patience if you are not being understood. And though you may consider yourself a walking, talking Strunk and White, do not correct your trading partners' online grammar skills unless they ask for your help. Try to always use correct grammar when you respond—set a good example for the Queen's English.

> ### Bright Idea
> Many YMCAs and community centers offer basic language courses for a fraction of the cost of online or language institute classes. You'll get the basics of phrasing down and some of the most common sayings. Worth your $40? *Si. Da. Oui.*

Maintaining a Presence

Web site or no web site? That is the question. And the answer is an overwhelming yes. Or, more accurately, why not? Web site creation and maintenance today are cheaper than ever. For the price of a Netflix membership, you can create and manage an online presence that will be available to possible clients all over the world. And no, you don't need to know a lot about web design or maintenance to make it happen.

WYSIWYG

Most web site design sites offer a "What You See is What You Get" (WYSIWYG) approach to design. Using templates created by the hosting company, you can simply enter text and post photos or images to your site, and change these as often as you like. You can choose colors, graphics, and fonts that best express your company and what it stands for.

Smart Tip

Tip...

You can search for domain names and receive alternate choices if your number one pick is taken at www.register.com. The site also provides links for web hosting, design, and other useful services.

While this option is great for beginners, keep in mind that it may not offer all the bells and whistles of your favorite online sites, like visitor counters, encryption, or e-biz capabilities. You do, indeed, get what you pay for. But, if you want a simple site with a few pages that tells who you are, what your company does, and how to reach you, this is the fastest, easiest, and most polished-looking way to do so for the absolute beginner.

DIY, or Better Yet, DIFM

You can also buckle down and learn all of the techie tricks for designing your own HTML or Flash web site, but why bother when, quite frankly, it pays to have someone more experienced do it for you. Instead of DIY, just say DIFM (do it for me).

For around $150 and up, you can have a professionally-designed web site that will have all the bells and whistles you want. For a monthly fee, most design companies can also arrange for hosting and online or phone tech support 24 hours a day, seven days a week. You will need to provide a script for each page you want on the site, guidance on buttons and links, and images or logos, but the geeks do the rest. In a few days, you get a slick-looking site that looks like it was designed by Picasso himself.

No matter what route you choose, you will have to pay to register a domain name for your company site. So, make it count. If the name of your company is already taken by another registered domain, try tweaking it a bit. For example, www.bobs africanimports.com may already be taken, but try www.bobsafrican.com, www.african imports.com, www.bobs-african.com, or www.bobs-african-imports.com on for size. You can also try adding on a different site type on the end, like .biz or .org.

Marketing to the World with One Click

Look beyond your own storefront for successful online trade marketing. After all, just hanging out your online shingle does not mean business will just walk in the virtual door. Like personal investing, you must build a diversified portfolio of online marketing and advertising to generate positive results.

Count Me In

The first marketing ploy is the easiest and cheapest—participate in online import/export communities. Whether you post frequently on Q&A message boards or record the online minutes for your local international business club, be a presence. There are points to be gained by simply "showing up." Remember, though, that you are representing your company at all times, so type accordingly. Some tips:

- *Project the positive.* You are the public face of your trading company, so act like it. If you feel the need to post something negative, think on it first, then do so in the most professional manner possible.

- *Become an expert exporter.* Offer quotes for news articles, write in to message boards as a professional exporter/importer with XX years in the business. Soon, you'll find yourself at the top of the Google listings.

- *Check that grammar.* You don't need to be Shakespeare to have good, solid, basic grammar skills.

- *Offer an exchange.* Provide a free online course to a group or association in exchange for online marketing to its constituents.

- *Maintain and update.* Keeping your own web site updated with the latest facts, figures, and contact information is a must. Online visitors notice that "last updated" ticker on the home page and associate it with the level of care you provide your business.

Hello, Neighbor:
Advertising on Import/Export Friendly Sites

Remember what your parents always told you: It doesn't hurt to ask. This is the case, too, with advertising. If an online site includes advertising, find out how you can jump on the bandwagon.

If you have any money in your budget for advertising, set some aside for online marketing in the form of purchasing e-mail lists and sending blasts, sending out press releases to trade news sites, and buying selective ad space.

Information firms abound on the internet, and they are all willing to sell you lists of possible contacts and clients. Beware, though, and do your research before you fall for a pyramid scheme that will only result in you losing $500 of your hard-earned coin. Instead, consult your trusted government business and trade sites and contacts to find out who's reputable and who's not in the information selling business.

Press releases are free to create (minus your personal labor cost) and free to send out to any organization, be it professional or news-oriented. Consider taking time once or twice a month to compile a press release about big news in your own company or about an industry trend on which you can comment about as an export/import expert. Create an address list within your e-mail management program so you can fire off that release with one click. Boom! You've accomplished several tasks—positioning yourself as an expert, reaching a free audience, saving time—in one shot.

> **Tip...**
>
> ### Smart Tip
>
> An effective online marketing tool is the creation of your own online newsletter. It can be created in a professional program, such as Quark Xpress or Adobe Photoshop, or a simple e-mail of information. Make it functional by including recent company news as well as industry news and tips. Add a button on your homepage for people to sign up for your FREE newsletter and—bang!—you've got a list of willing advertisers.

Howdy, Pardner: Co-Op/Partner Marketing and Advertising

Another way to reach the same markets is to find co-op avenues of marketing and advertising. In other words, find some reciprocity in your efforts.

Leave It to the Experts

If you want to leave the online marketing to someone else while you spend more time qualifying clients and actually selling or buying products, consider hiring a marketing firm to bear the weight of the task. Look to professional marketing associations for leads:

○ American Marketing Association: www.marketingpower.com

○ Direct Marketing Association: www.the-dma.org

○ Promotion Marketing Association: www.pmalink.org

○ eMarketing Association: www.emarketingassociation.com.

Many sites, whether those of groups and associations or of your foreign counterparts, advertise online. Rest assured that not all of (or even a majority of) this advertising is paid for in full. Rather, much of it appears thanks to a cooperative effort on the part of the advertiser and venue.

Perhaps an ad is paid for partially, and the balance of the bill is offset by offering reciprocal advertising on another site. Or, perhaps you can score an ad on a web site for 30 days from a trade partner if you offer them the exact same courtesy. Maybe your currency for advertising is free or discounted shipping on products, reduced fees, or an overall price break. There are only as many ways to think of co-op advertising and marketing as there are stars in the sky. You are only limited by imagination.

Several web sites offer guidance in your online marketing and advertising efforts. Good old www.export.gov is a solid starting point for basic marketing info. Trade Easy's web site (www.tradeeasy.com) offers marketing solutions to sellers in a buyer's market. And www.importexporthelp.com offers over 873 tools for trade marketing solutions.

The Trader's Trunk
Start-Up Basics

This chapter explores the bottom of the trader's trunk, those features that form the basics of the business, from company name, to legal structure, to permits.

Name That Business

Every business, like every child, has to have a name, and you should devote as much thought to choosing an appellation for your company as you would for your off-spring. After all, you plan to have your business baby around for a long time. You want a name you can be proud of, one that identifies it—and by extension, you—as worthy of your clients' confidence.

Because import/export is a more serious business than, say, pizza delivery or greeting card design, that sobriety should be reflected in your company name. This means, unfortunately for the more frivolous among us, that you can rule out names like Teddy Bear Traders or Ex-Cuse Me Exports.

Instead, your name should call attention to your expertise and efficiency. The terminally creative, however, can take heart. Noncutesy doesn't mean dull. Your name can—and should—deliver a snappy punch.

Howdy, Partner

One trader attacked the name problem from the standpoint of his vision of his company. "With Global Partners," he says, "we wanted to say that we're all partners, me and my clients and manufacturers. We all have to be partners to make it work."

When brainstorming your company name, keep in mind that, with a few exceptions, the people you'll target won't be using English as a native language. So take care with the words you choose. Colloquial or slang words or phrases sometimes aren't even clear to people in different parts of the United States; don't try to make things more difficult by pressing them on non-Americans. Everyone in the industry, on the other hand, easily understands international trade buzzwords like "global" and "overseas."

Sea to Shining Sea

Many importers and exporters incorporate the name of the region with which they trade into their business moniker—for example, Far East Imports or Amazon Traders. Or you might want to incorporate a geographic feature of your own region, such as Desert Traders if you live in Palm Springs or Sea-to-Sea Exports if your office is near a seaport. Or you might decide on a variation of your own name, like the owner of LND Export Management, who used his initials as the basis for his company name.

Whatever you go with, remember that you will be repeating your name every time you answer the phone. Sound out the title before you settle on it. Some names look great in print but are difficult if not impossible to understand over the phone. M&A Associates, for example, may seem like a keen name for partners Marty and Andrea, but when spoken, it sounds like MNA.

Business Name Brainstorming

List three ideas based on the geographic area you plan to trade with (i.e., Into Africa, European, Down Under):

1. _____

2. _____

3. _____

List three ideas based on the types of products you plan to trade, remembering not to limit yourself to one product alone (i.e., Arts and Antiques, Gourmet Goods, Image Imports):

1. _____

2. _____

3. _____

List three ideas based on a local feature (i.e., mountain, seaside, or historical reference like Alamo, or even a botanical feature, if that's what your area is known for or you like, such as magnolia, rose, or chaparral):

1. _____

2. _____

3. _____

After you've decided which name you like the best, have you:

❏ Said it aloud to make sure it's easily understood and pronounced? (Has it passed muster with your family? Have you had a friend call to see how it sounds over the phone?)

❏ Checked your local Yellow Pages to make sure the same or a similar name is not already listed?

❏ Checked with your local business name authority to make sure it's available?

Most callers rate about a C-minus in listening comprehension. No matter how clearly you enunciate, they aren't going to understand M&A. So save yourself hours of telephone frustration and choose something simple.

For some really good name ideas, check out the international trading firms in our Appendix. You'll want to make yours as individual as you are, but these will help start your creative gears turning.

The Fictitious Business Name

After you've decided on a name, you'll need to register it. Basically, registering your name means that you notify the proper authorities that you're doing business under a name other than your own. This is to let the public know that Tropical Trading Partners is owned by you, expert exporter.

The process varies in different regions of the country. In Florida, for example, you access the state government web site and click around until you finally call up the page about fictitious business names. You fill out a series of forms, swear you are who you say you are

Trader's View

Wahib W., the construction materials exporter, likes to call his company a "collective international sales group" because all the parties in a project must mesh their skills and interests to make the project successful. "You cannot just go and sell, sell, sell if nobody's interested," he explains. "It's not going to work. If you have a buyer and the manufacturer's not interested, you still cannot do anything."

Talking Trade

Where to start naming your business? How about with a lexicon of trader's lingo sure to set that international image in the mind of any potential client or customer?

Abroad	Global	Pacific
Atlantic	Inter-Continental	Passport
Caravan	International	Seven Seas
Cargo	Hemisphere	Trader
Compass	Mediterranean	Tropical
Earth	Overseas	Worldwide

and enter your credit card number. Eventually, you'll receive a letter confirming that you registered your name with the state. If you want a nice little certificate to frame and hang on your wall, you need to shell out extra bucks.

In California on the other hand, you file an application with the county clerk, then advertise your name in a "general circulation" newspaper in that county for four weeks. Once that's all said and done and you've paid the fee, you receive your statement of registration. Check with your city, county, and state government to find out what the story is in your state.

Beware!

Registering a fictitious business name doesn't necessarily guarantee that you're the only one in your area doing business under that name. You can check the fictitious names in your county or state to make sure your brilliant moniker isn't already in use, but someone else may register the same name after you do.

Your Skeletal Structure

To appease those picky IRS people, your business must have a structure. You can operate it as a sole proprietorship, a partnership, or a corporation, with variations thereof. Many international traders go with the simplest version, the sole proprietorship. You'll probably be starting out on your own, so there's no need to get complicated or expensive. You can always switch to another format later on if and when you take on partners and/or employees.

Beyond the basic structure for your company—the ones we've just discussed—various other international trade configurations exist. There's the joint venture, which is a sort of marriage or partnership between two distinct and separate companies—for example, yours and one in a foreign country. And there's the strategic alliance, an agreement between your company and another one to work toward a common goal.

Tip...

Smart Tip

Do not fear the behemoth that is the IRS web site. Yes, it's big, but surprisingly user-friendly. Find everything you need to know about small business tax issues at www.irs.gov/businesses/small. From deductible business expenses (ch-ching!) to applying for EINs (employer ID numbers), Big Brother has you covered.

Why would you want to form a venture with an overseas company? One reason is to get around trade barriers. If your company is part domestic in whatever country you're working with, you can skim around prohibitive tariffs and quotas. Another reason? You can form a team or network with an in-country company that already has effective trade channels in operation. And a third reason is to get into government-controlled infrastructure-type projects, like power plants or telecommunications.

Then there's the wholly owned subsidiary or branch, in which your company or your client's company becomes owner of a firm. You can encounter a spider's web of entanglements in international arrangements of this type because the host country often sets up all sorts of special rules, such as how long a "foreign" company (that's you) can own property or how much profit you can collect.

> **Bright Idea**
>
> The Commercial Service people and their compatriots at your local Export Assistance Center can help you set up a joint venture program.

So why would anybody want to open a subsidiary or branch abroad? As the Ferengi would say, "Profit." Emerging nations often offer hefty incentives to businesses from more developed parts of the world to vitalize their own economies by creating jobs and cash flow for their people. If you do your homework and check out every permutation of foreign business ownership laws, you're less likely to get stung by unpleasant surprises.

There's also the licensing or franchising type of business. With licensing, you give a foreign company or licensee permission to sell your or your client's trademarked product and in return, they pay royalties on their sales. Everybody recognizes the world's pre-eminent licensing products: anything stamped with the likeness of Mickey, Minnie, or their Disney cohorts. You might develop a gold mine in licensing characters developed by a client with loveable little chaps just waiting to be discovered.

> **Beware!**
>
> When brainstorming a business name, be careful not to fence yourself in with a moniker that may limit you later. If you're starting out importing Mexican pottery, for example, you may not want to call your company Mexican Pottery Imports—unless you're certain that's the country and product category you'll stick with. If you change direction down the line and decide to bring in jewelry from Jamaica or marbles from Majorca, you could find yourself with the wrong name in a different game.

With a franchise, you give your or your client's foreign buyer permission to sell your licensed products with your special sales or service techniques. The ultimate franchisor is, of course, that other Mickey: McDonald's. American food franchises traditionally do very well abroad, but there are scads of other franchises available or that you can put together yourself, from cleaning services to herbal retailers. All you need is your imagination.

Home Zoned Home

The international trade business puts wings on your feet in more ways than one. Because most of your business will be conducted long-distance via mail, phone, and the internet, you won't need to be available at set hours, as you would if you were running a retail establishment or restaurant. Since you will rarely have clients dropping in, except via a long-distance phone call, you will not need a receptionist, a lobby, or even meeting rooms. This gives you a lot of freedom as to where you locate your business—a business park, executive suite, or even at home.

If you plan on a home office, you should check into zoning regulations, even though a small or newbie international trader is not a business that's going to attract a lot of attention from local authorities. You won't need signage and you'll rarely have clients knocking at your door, so you won't need to worry about parking restrictions. But it's still a good idea to play it safe. Find out from your local city or county government whether any permits are necessary. While you're at it, check to see if you'll need a business license, which is usually an official-looking piece of paper you get in exchange for a nominal annual fee.

> ### Smart Tip
>
> Delve into Entrepreneur's online resource for franchises at www.entrepreneur.com/franchisezone. You'll find scads of information on the benefits and drawbacks of franchising as well as a directory of franchise opportunities.

Attorney with ELAN

Attorneys are like plumbers—you don't want to think about them until you need one. But as a business owner, you should have a good attorney on call, one who knows international trade. You'll want her to look over any contracts you write with manufacturers, representatives, or distributors, and to advise you on the fine points of foreign trade law. You won't need to call her every week, or even every month. But there's no point in waiting until you have a problem to try to establish a relationship and get help.

To get you off on the right foot and to answer any start-up questions, the Small Business Administration (SBA) and the Federal Bar Association have developed The Export Legal Assistance Network, otherwise known as ELAN. As an enticement to the red-tape-phobic would-be trader, the ELAN folks will sit you down with a volunteer trade attorney who'll answer all your questions—for free! After the initial consultation, you can either sign on with the volunteer as your permanent trade attorney or take your newfound knowledge and hit the road without a backward glance.

You can also find a reliable import/export attorney by asking for referrals from associates

> ### Smart Tip
>
> On your list of start-up contacts, don't forget your accountant and insurance agent. Both can answer important questions about structuring and protecting your new company.

Hello? Is Anybody Out There?

The Export Legal Assistance Network (ELAN) is a jumping-off point for traders with legal questions. National Coordinator Judd Kessler spoke to us from his Washington, DC office about the behind the scenes workings of the group.

According to Kessler, fear is one of the greatest obstacles for people interested in becoming a professional importer or exporter. One cause for this fear is lack of familiarity with legal issues, but, says Kessler, that is what ELAN is there for—to assuage those fears. A service of the Department of Commerce, ELAN has legal counselors in 70 cities who provide import/export legal service in addition to their daily legal pursuits. Since 1984, the group has performed free initial legal counseling sessions for both new and established traders. Kessler himself receives about four to five calls per month in regard to trade concerns, and his number one request for callers is to, "Please do your basic homework before you call. The basic stuff is very mundane. What do you intend to export and to which countries? How are you getting paid? Who is your local representative?" These are questions the caller should already know something about before contacting ELAN. And, says Kessler, above all, "Have a business plan in place." Kessler stresses that you only get one call, so prepare ahead to make it productive.

The ELAN lawyers hear many kinds of issues on the phone, from questions about foreign trade agreements to how to avoid risks, customs concerns, trademark registration, and more. A popular concern is in regard to legality of shipments: what can be shipped where, and how can it be done cheaply and legally. "If, for example, you are going to ship anything with military or dual [civil and military] use, be very conscious of export regulations and with terrorism concerns," says Kessler. His advice to make sure your product and the country it's heading to are on the up-and-up is to check with the web site for the Office of Foreign Asset Control (OFAC), part of the U.S. Department of Treasury. The group's Specially Designated Nationals List is "a list of people you should not do business with."

Kessler says ELAN has advised exporters of products ranging from liquid dispensing and bottle filling equipment (how did you *think* your Heinz 57 got in the bottle?) to scrap metals. One ELAN client, in the New York scrap metal biz his whole life, was contacted by a Russian exporter with scrap steel rails for sale. "There is quite a market abroad, especially to Korea and China for scrap metal," says Kessler. Hmmm . . . there's an idea for all you scrap guys. Who knows? Though law is his business and he worked in international development for the State Department for 17 years before becoming involved with ELAN, maybe Kessler's got a second career in trade lead coordination in his future.

in the field or your international banker, but with the ELAN program, what have you got to lose? Contact the network at www.export-legal-assistance.org or through the SBA's Small Business Answer Desk at (800) U-ASK-SBA.

The Details

We've given you a peek into the trader's trunk, the basic underpinnings of the business. Remember, however, that other licenses and fees can crop up, depending on what you're importing and exporting, to where and from whom. Do your homework. Make sure you understand what's necessary in each situation—look before you leap into that cargo hold. The more you know about running an import/export business, the better trader you'll be.

Trade Dollars
Figuring Your Finances

That old refrain "The best things in life are free" does not quite apply when you are starting a business. This chapter dips into the murky waters of budgeting, financing, and operating costs, and, like chlorine, clears them up.

Start-Up Costs

One of the many nifty things about an import/export business is that its start-up costs are comparatively low. You have the advantage of homebased-ability, which cuts office lease expenses down to nothing. Unless you're starting as a distributor, you can get away without purchasing inventory, which means no outlay of funds for pretty doodads to grace display spaces (you have no display spaces!). Your major financial outlay will go toward office equipment and market research expenses—and if you are like many moderns, you already have the most expensive piece of office equipment: a computer system.

But let's take it from the top. The following is a breakdown of everything—from heavy investment pieces to flyweight items—you'll need to get up and running:

- Computer system with modem and printer
- Fax machine
- Internet/e-mail service
- Software
- Market research and/or trade leads
- Phone
- Voice mail or answering machine
- Stationery and office supplies
- Postage
- Travel expenses for conducting market research on foreign turf

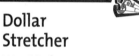

Dollar Stretcher

Want to keep equipment costs way down? Consider launching from a business incubator, where services, facilities, and equipment are shared among several businesses.

You can add all kinds of goodies of varying degrees of necessity to this list, and we'll cover them all in Chapter 11—which features a sort of shopping bonanza. For example, a copier is a plus. It's also nice to have bona fide office furniture: a tweedy upholstered chair with lumbar support that swivels and rolls, gleaming file cabinets that really lock, real oak bookshelves.

But let's consider that you are starting from absolute scratch. You can always set up your computer on your kitchen table or on a card table in a corner of the bedroom. You can stash files in cardboard boxes. It's not glamorous, but it'll suffice until you get your business steaming ahead.

Computing Computer Costs

The computer system is at the top of the list. It will allow you to access the myriad trade leads and market research materials available online, communicate with potential and established customers via e-mail (the quickest and cheapest method available), and generate stationery, invoices, certificates, and forms quickly, easily, and inexpensively. It's technically possible to start off without a computer system, but if you opt for this method, you're cutting yourself off from scads of valuable resources and asking to do things the hard way.

For a basic computer system that can have you surfing the internet within two hours after you buy it, you should allocate funds somewhere in the range of $2,000. We will go over the various permutations in Chapter 11, but this will give you a figure to pencil in for starters.

Fax Facts

Although you technically don't have to have a fax machine, just as you don't have to have a computer, your life as an international trader will run much more smoothly with one. You can shoot off and receive materials to and from clients, representatives, and distributors instead of waiting on both U.S. and foreign postal services. Sending a pro forma invoice, for example, has a lot more impact on a potential customer when it directly follows a request for information. You can purchase a basic plain-paper fax machine for as little as $100.

The Pep Talk

The gestation period for any business can be trying. Why? Because aside from money, you're investing a great deal of time, energy, and emotional intensity. You're pushing to get people interested in your service, from persuading manufacturers or artisans to work with you to finding foreign contacts to securing financing.

Going over all the details—especially the financial ones—with a magnifying lens and a critical eye is crucial to your success. You'll need to know how much shipping will cost, what commissions you'll need to pay, what commission you can take, and whether you can still make a profit.

Here's the keen part: With an import/export business, the risk is minimal. If you spend a nominal amount printing stationery and conducting all your research and then discover that your great idea wasn't so hot, you'll only be out your original nominal amount and no more. On the other hand, if you discover that your great idea is great—you have buyers and sellers flocking to your caravan—you can carry on knowing that your chances for success are terrific.

Nosing Around the Net

A good internet and e-mail service is a must for the international trader. With the power of the World Wide Web at your command, you can go anywhere on the globe instantaneously—access trade leads as soon as they're posted, communicate with clients and client wanna-bes in a keystroke, and garner market information from worldwide sources while seated at your desk. And it's cheap! Most Internet Service Providers (ISPs) run about $20 to $25 per month and give you unlimited access to the web and e-mail.

Smart Tip

Sending information by fax is more businesslike than calling with a list of figures. It's also far less expensive. The fax machine can place a call overseas at any hour of the day or night and transmit your message faster than you can—it doesn't have to spend time on formal greetings or chitchat before getting down to business.

The Skinny on Software

Software prices can vary radically, depending on which programs you buy and from whom. You won't need any special import/export programs, but you'll want a good, strong word processing program, a desktop publishing program, and an accounting program. Again, this is a subject we'll discuss in depth in Chapter 11. For start-up purposes, let's say that you'll want to allocate about $500.

Lead Me On

Like just about everything else in the international trader's world, the amount you'll pay for market research and trade leads is a variable, almost entirely dependent on you and your personal style. If you choose to go with the Commercial Service's STAT-USA program—the one with the trade leads and other market research information—you can pencil in about $75 per month or $200 per year.

Back to the noncommercial Commercial Service, the Gold Key Matching Service program pencils in at $250 to $1,000—or more, if you really want a lot of help. It's hard to pin a price tag on the Matchmaker program because costs vary with the countries involved, but as a thumbnail, you can figure between $1,500 and $3,000.

As you travel the internet, you'll find other trade lead services and sources of market research that may cost more or less, or nothing at all.

Dollar Stretcher

Use that e-mail service to contact customers abroad. Why place a pricey international call when you can send an e-mail message virtually for free?

Phone Fun

We assume that you already have a telephone, in which case you already know all about phone bills. You should, however, install at least one dedicated line for your business. You'll want one line for handling phone calls and another for your fax machine and ISP (internet service provider, remember?), unless you have cable. Computers and fax machines use phones the way teenagers do—when they're transmitting, no one else can possibly get through. So unless you want to risk having callers receive a busy signal or empty ring when you're sending or receiving quotes, leads, or other information, you'll want to have a separate line.

A cell phone will prove invaluable if you're out and about much, or even if you'd like to take a lunch without worrying about missing a call. You can have calls into your office forwarded to your mobile phone so you don't have to give business partners two different phone numbers. The monthly plan will vary depending on how you'll use the phone—how many minutes you expect to use, where you'll be when you use the phone, etc.—but you can count on about $60 a month.

Costs, of course, depend on how many fun features you add to your telephone service and which local and long-distance carriers you go with, but for the purpose of start-up budgeting, let's allocate about $25 per line. You'll also need to add the phone company's installation fee, which should be in the range of $40. Check with your local Ma Bell to determine exactly what these costs are in your area.

The Mechanical Receptionist

You won't always be available to answer your phone—often you will be traveling abroad, out interfacing with local suppliers, or running errands. During these times, you will need somebody or something to answer your phone. A Murphy's Law of business life is that people most often call when: a) you are not in your office, b) you are sitting down to a meal, or c) you're in the bathroom. Another business life law is that an unanswered phone is extremely unprofessional.

So you have two ways to go: the trusty answering machine or the phone company's exciting voice-mail feature. Both have pros and cons, which we'll discuss in Chapter 11. For estimating start-up costs, let's figure a basic answering machine at about $40 and voice mail at about $6 per month.

My Calling Card

Business stationery is as important to a savvy international image as a well-answered phone. To create that cosmopolitan identity—which will help sell your product or service—you'll need letterhead, envelopes, and business cards. There are lots of routes to take with all this stuff.

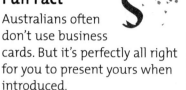

Fun Fact
Australians often don't use business cards. But it's perfectly all right for you to present yours when introduced.

Let's say, however, that to create the basics you can purchase blank stationery, including cards, and print them up yourself with a word processing or desktop publishing program. Or you can have a set of stationery and business cards inexpensively printed for you at a quick-print house, like Kinko's, or through Office Depot's in-house service. Either way, you should allocate about $75

Office supplies—pens, pencils, paper clips, mailing envelopes, reams of blank paper for designing brochures or catalogs, stapler, staples, letter opener, tape, printer cartridges—can be penciled in at about $150. This, of course, is if you start from absolute scratch, buying everything brand new for your business.

Stamps Around the World

Your start-up postage costs will be fairly low, but you will need to tally them. How much you spend depends a great deal on how much material you are mailing out and where on the globe you are sending it. If you are mailing lots of price sheets or brochures, your costs will be higher than if you do all price quoting by fax or e-mail.

Bright Idea
Request a free Business Information Kit, which contains international shipping tips and rate information, from the U.S. Postal Service by calling (800) ASK-USPS. Your kit will arrive— by mail, of course—at your door within five to seven business days after your call.

Check out the chart on page 143 to get an idea of the U.S. Postal Service's international charges; then we will take a look at some calculations. If you send five letters (simple brochure and price sheet) a day via air mail to prospective customers for 90 days and you average your air-mail rates at 70 cents, you will be spending $315 in start-up postage. This rate will, of course, vary according to your own market research plans.

Traveling Trader

This category, too, will vary tremendously according to how you choose to tailor your market research, your start-up costs, and, ultimately, your business life. Some traders are on the road more often than not, while others are basically armchair travelers. And, of course, when you do travel, your costs will vary depending on where you go, for how long, and whether you choose to spend your nights at the Ritz or the local youth hostel.

Sample International Mail Charges

The U.S. Post Office delivers airmail in four to seven days, Global Priority Mail in three to five days. Prices shown here are for a 1-ounce letter (a business envelope with four or five letter-sized pages = 1 ounce) and were based on mid-2007 figures. Call before you ship to get accurate prices.

Country	Airmail	Global Priority Small Envelope	Global Priority Large Envelope
Canada	.63	$4.25	$7.50
Germany	.84	$5.25	$9.50
Iceland	.84	$5.25	$9.50
Japan	.84	$5.25	$9.50
Mexico	.63	$4.25	$7.50
Thailand	.84	$5.25	$9.50

You may find that you can conduct all your market research from your desktop, or you may discover that for your particular product and style, you need to study the market up close and personal.

All that Jazz

Other expenses you'll need to plug into your start-up expense chart are business licenses, business insurance, legal advice, utility deposits, and all that jazz—the costs intrinsic to any company's invocation. Use the worksheet on 146 to pencil in and then tally up these costs and all the others we've discussed in this section. If you photocopy a couple extra sheets, you can work up several options, compare them all, and decide which will work best for you so you can arrive at your official start-up figure.

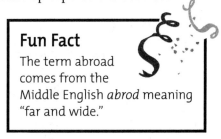

Fun Fact
The term abroad comes from the Middle English *abrod* meaning "far and wide."

Pricing Yourself

Now that we've determined how much it's going to cost you to get your business up and running, let's turn to the fun part—figuring out how much you can expect to make.

As an international trader, you are an intermediary in the buying and selling, or importing and exporting, transaction. Therefore, you have to determine not just the price of the product, but the price of your services as well. These two figures are separate yet interactive. Because you are a swimmer in the trade channel, the price of your services has to be added on to the product price, and that can affect its competitiveness in the marketplace.

Since the fee for your services will impact the success of the product, you may ultimately decide to change your pricing structure. You don't want to undercharge your client so that you can't cover your expenses and make a profit, but you don't want to overcharge and reduce the competitiveness of your company and the merchandise you represent.

Import/export management companies use two basic methods to price their services: commission and retainer. Normally, you choose one method or the other based on how salable you feel the product is. If you think it's an easy sell, you'll want to work on the commission method. If you feel it's going to be an upstream swim, difficult to sell, and require a lot of market research, you'll ask for a retainer.

A third method is to purchase the product outright and sell it abroad. This is a common scenario when you're dealing with manufacturers who would rather use you as a distributor than as a representative. You'll still market the product under the manufacturer's name, but your income will come from the profit generated by sales rather than by commission.

Start-Up Costs

Check out the start-up costs (the ones necessary to officially throw open your doors) on 145 for two hypothetical international trade companies, Cargo Bay Traders and Clipper Trading Service Co. Cargo Bay is a homebased company (office in the spare bedroom) run by an owner who's retired and decided to start out small with a minimum outlay. Clipper Trading Service, on the other hand, has rented a 900-square-foot office near the airport, purchased top-of-the-line equipment, and employed an administrative assistant.

Both companies are acting as representatives of the manufacturer and will receive compensation based on commissions. Cargo Bay is projecting an annual gross income of $68,400, while Clipper Trading Service is projecting $219,360. Neither owner will draw a salary; instead, they'll take a percentage of their net profits as income.

Sample Start-Up Costs

Costs	Cargo Bay Traders	Clipper Trading Service Co.
Rent		$1,900.00
Office equipment & furniture	$2,500.00	8,000.00
Market research/trade leads	175.00	3,000.00
Software	300.00	500.00
Phone	90.00	265.00
Utility deposits		150.00
Employee payroll		2,000.00
Grand opening advertising	100.00	500.00
Legal services	375.00	525.00
Postage	189.00	315.00
Internet service	25.00	25.00
Stationery/office supplies	50.00	150.00
Insurance	500.00	600.00
Travel		5,000.00
Miscellaneous expenses (add roughly 10% of total)	447.00	2,307.00
Total Start-Up Costs	**$4,751.00**	**$25,387.00**

Start-Up Costs Worksheet

Rent $ _____

Office equipment & furniture   _____

Market research/trade leads   _____

Software   _____

Phone
   (add $150 for a cell phone)   _____

Utility deposits   _____

Employee payroll   _____

Grand opening advertising   _____

Legal services   _____

Postage   _____

Internet service   _____

Stationery/office supplies   _____

Insurance   _____

Travel   _____

Miscellaneous expenses
   (add roughly 10% of total)   _____

Total Start-Up Costs $ _____

The Commish

Import/export management companies usually operate on a commission basis of about 10 percent. These fees are based on the product cost from the manufacturer.

With all these variables, estimating your commission might seem like a task fit for a professor of Boolean mathematics, but it's really not difficult. In fact, it's fun! (Adding up numbers is always more fun when it pertains to money in your pocket.)

Let's say you're working with English lawn chairs, which cost you $110 each. Here's what you do: First, take the price the manufacturer is charging for the product: $110. Now multiply $110 by 10 percent, which gives you a commission of $11 per chair.

So your product price at this point is $121 per chair ($110 + $11). To come up with the final price, you'll need to add other costs to this figure: any special marking or packaging, shipping, insurance, and any representative or distributor commissions that you'll pay to others in the trade channel, which we'll go over a little later. Once you've arrived at a final price, you'll check it against your competitors' prices (you did do your market research, right?). If your product's price is comparatively low, you can bump up your commission percentage.

For now, however, you can see that for every chair you or your trade channelers sell, you'll get $11. If you sell a thousand chairs, that's $11,000 for you!

Biting the Retainer

If the manufacturer can't discount her price sufficiently or if you feel that the product will be a tough sell, you'll want to ask for a flat retainer (the monetary kind, not the dental appliance kind). You'll pass all the costs of market research along to the manufacturer. By taking a retainer, you guarantee yourself a set income rather than one tied by commission to a "problem" product.

Trader's View

"Don't try to sell at [just] any rate," advises Bruno C. Make sure the commission you quote garners you a reasonable profit.

To determine what your retainer should be, you'll need to consider three variables associated with the performance of your services:

- *Labor and materials or supplies.* This usually includes your salary or estimated salary on an hourly basis plus the wages and benefits you pay any employees involved in the performance of the job. To determine labor costs, estimate the amount of time it will take to finish a job and multiply it by the hourly rate of your salary and that of any employees you might use. You can compute materials as a percentage of labor, but until you have past records to use as a guide, you should use 2 percent to 6 percent.

I Bill the Fees

Michael R., the German international trade consultant, makes a rule of working on a fee basis instead of on commission. Sometimes this is a retainer, sometimes a flat fee, depending on the kind of job—short term or long term—with a specific goal or offering of general support. "I bill my fees, even if relatively small," Michael says. "I do not work on a commission basis, as I would then have to concentrate on the products and not on [the client].

"I cannot—and do not want to—do everything because of the cost aspects," he tells potential customers. "But what I do I can arrange [to do with great flexibility]."

- *Overhead.* This variable comprises all the nonlabor, indirect expenses required to operate your business. To determine your overhead rate, add up all your expenses for one year, except for labor and materials. Divide this figure by your total cost of labor and materials to determine your overhead rate. Or use a rate of 35 percent to 42 percent of your labor and materials.

- *Profit.* And the end result is: After all labor, materials, and overhead expenses are deducted, profit can be determined by applying a percentage profit factor to the combined costs of labor and materials and overhead.

Trader's View

"Don't work for free," advises Brazilian John L. "Charge your clients for each step you do. In this way, prospective clients will respect you and see that you are a professional and not an IHEG (internet hunting everything guy)."

The Great Sock Caper

Sound like a job for that professor of Boolean mathematics? Not! Let's say, for example, that you're working with a manufacturer who wants to export self-laundering socks (walk in them and they begin to exude detergent). Since you're not certain the world is ready for this breakthrough, you decide to take it on a retainer basis. You figure it will take you a week to complete the deal: to arrange for the export of 530 dozen socks priced at $24 per dozen. To calculate your retainer, you begin by figuring your labor and materials cost—check out the chart on 151.

Then you calculate your overhead: all the nonlabor, indirect expenses required to operate your business. Divide this number by your Total Labor & Materials number. Until you have past expenses to guide you, you can figure that overhead will cost you

Playing Favorites

Which payment method pays off the best? Every trader has his own favorites. "We have sales representatives and we own subsidiaries in several countries," says Jan H., the Belgian tire and clothing trader.

"We sometimes use sales agents abroad," explains Bruno C., the French packaging exporter, "but so far it hasn't brought us [many] satisfactory and serious opportunities. We either sell direct to the 'final consumer,' who is a manufacturer, or directly to a wholesaler/dealer/trader."

In Brazil, John L., the international services provider, doesn't use sales agents at all. "Most of my clients are Brazilian companies looking for import/export businesses," he says. "I work based on a commission agreement. Most of my clients, however, pay me a monthly fixed amount to cover some current expenses, such as phone, fax, internet, and travel. When the project requires any detailed market survey, I charge the client for my working hours at a rate of USD 100 per hour."

from 35 percent to 42 percent of your labor and materials cost. You can raise or lower the percentage to suit your own operation.

Now add your overhead figure (in this instance, it's $445.53) to your labor and materials cost, and there's your Total Operating Expenses figure.

Most traders plan on making a net profit of 8 percent to 10 percent from their gross revenues. If you want to net 8 percent before taxes from the self-washing sock sales, you simply multiply your total operating expenses by a profit factor of 8.7 percent. If you consult the chart on 151, you will see that your net profit is $1,637.38.

Competitive Pricing

How you price your products is extremely important. The price has to be high enough to generate a scintillating profit yet low enough to be competitive in the foreign or domestic market you have chosen. This makes it essential for you to do your market research—finding the typical price range for selected merchandise in your target market and then comparing it against the manufacturer's price. Then you'll need to determine

Tip...

Smart Tip
Your profit factor should always be larger than the net profit you're aiming for. If you want to net an 8 percent profit, for example, make your profit factor 8.7 percent or 9 percent.

▲

Shot in the Foot

The retainer is a smart way to assure yourself of an income on those problem products. But it can also turn into an easy way to shoot yourself in the foot. If you do your job well and the product takes off, generating tons of sales, the manufacturer may start thinking in the following terms: She's supplying the product and paying all the costs to develop the market, and all you're doing is arranging sales, which is now dead easy. She may decide to ace you out of the picture by selling direct.

If, however, you've been working all along on a commission basis instead of on retainer, the manufacturer will probably view your commissions—which are costing her less than the retainer would—as adequate compensation.

This is not to say that the sour grape/retainer scenario will occur; the manufacturer may be delighted with what she's paying you until the end of time. But while you're considering which pricing route to take, keep this possibility in mind.

whether that price is competitive in the marketplace. If it's not, then you'll have to do one of the following:

- Ask the manufacturer or supplier for a better price
- Operate on a retainer-only basis with no commission
- Reconsider doing business with that manufacturer or supplier

Once you have determined the normal price range for comparable products and decided that you can add commissions and other markups to manufacturer's price and still be competitive, you can go buyer-hunting. (We will go over advertising and marketing in detail in Chapter 12.)

The Distributor Cap

Occasionally, you'll want to, or be asked to, act as a distributor of the merchandise. This means that you'll actually purchase the product from the manufacturer—usually at net wholesale prices, less a percentage for the manufacturer's sales overhead—and sell the merchandise: abroad, if you're exporting, or in the United States, if you're importing.

Tip...

Smart Tip
Pricing is often a case of trial and error until you come up with the magic number for both profit and salability. Don't get discouraged. Remember that if one price doesn't pencil in correctly, you can keep changing it until you come up with one that works.

When you're wearing your distributor cap (the sales kind, not the auto parts kind), every product you purchase from the manufacturer should be priced to cover:

- Its wholesale cost
- Handling costs (shipping, cargo insurance, tariffs, freight forwarder fees, sales rep commissions, and any other special costs the project or product requires)
- A proportionate share of your overhead
- A reasonable profit for you

If you've been paying attention so far, you'll have noticed that these are the same things we've talked about with every other form of pricing. Now to accomplish this, you have to apply a markup to the cost of the product, and this gives you your selling price. If the cost of the product, for example, is $5 and your selling price is $10, then your markup is $5 or 100 percent.

Leave the Light On

Let's say you are working with decorative frog-and-flower porch lights that you have bought from a company in Taiwan. You know they'll sell like hula-hoops in the '50s to trailer park residents all over the Sunbelt. The manufacturer is charging you $5 per light, or unit. Check out the chart on 154, and you'll see that your costs to

Figuring Your Retainer

	Hours	Rate	Cost
Labor*	40	$26/Hour	$1,040.00
Materials (2% of Your Labor)			20.80
Total Labor & Materials			$1,060.80
Labor & Materials			$1,060.80
Overhead (42% of Labor & Materials)	445.53		
Total Operating Expenses			$1,506.33
Total Operating Expenses			1,506.33
Profit Factor of 8.7%			131.05
Your Net Profit—Retainer			$1,637.38

* Labor cost is based on temporary help. If your employees are part time, add 15 percent for payroll taxes, workers' compensation, and other necessities. If your employees are full time, add 30 percent.

bring the lights stateside are $6.47 per unit. If you double this, selling each light for $12.94 at a markup of 100 percent, you'll be making $38,820 on the deal. This is good.

Remember, however, that you'll be selling the porch lights to retailers, who will also need to add their markup to make a profit. And there's no point in marking yourself right out of the ballpark. If you add a 100 percent markup and the retailer does the same, each light will now cost the trailer park resident, the end user, $25.88. And this price might now be too high to be competitive.

So you might want to lower your markup. If you make it 50 percent, your per-unit cost drops to $9.71 and you still make $19,410 on the deal. Still not bad.

That's Illuminating

Now let's leave those porch lights on and illuminate a few more facts about the money you can expect to make. It's much more difficult to determine a set yearly income for an import/export business than for other types of companies. If you're in the car wash business, for example, you're dealing with a predetermined service—cleaning vehicles—and while you can add or subtract waxes, vacuums, and air fresheners, the main thrust of what you're selling is not going to change.

In import/export, however, there are no fixed boundaries. (And isn't this one of the delights of the business?) Like Wahib W., the exporter in Maryland, you can be work-

---

No One Size

How much can you expect to pay your customs broker? There is no one-size-fits-all answer. "It's all based on what's entailed in the shipment," says Dale Wilson of DFM International, a customs brokerage. And how many variables there are.

However, you can expect to pay a base amount of about $130 per shipment, Wilson says, plus about $5 for each $1,000 the shipment is worth.

Expect to pay more if your shipment is subject to restrictions. If you have a food shipment, for example, your broker will have to deal with the Food and Drug Administration; if you're bringing in transmitters, he'll have to interface with the Federal Communications Commission folks. And if your cargo consists of several different types of furniture, like tables and chairs, each distinct piece will have to be categorized.

"If other agencies get involved," Wilson cautions, "the charges increase."

---

ing with railroads in one country one year and telephone poles in another country the next. You might export coffee go-cups in June and import lawn chairs in July.

Consequently, your profits and expenses will be different for each project. "We're up and down," says Wahib. "It's a long-term cycle. When you bid for a project, your expenses are low. But when you get a project, your expenses become five times higher." These expenses, of course, are offset by your profit, and since you've calculated them ahead of time, you're not likely to be smacked in the noggin by unpleasant surprises.

Smart Tip Tip...

Did you pick up that you are purchasing the porch lights Ex-Works? If so, you rate an A! If you didn't, here's your clue: Since you are paying inland freight to the port, ocean shipping, and marine insurance charges, we can see that you're taking delivery of the merchandise at the manufacturer's door, or at his "works." Hence, Ex-Works.

Baseline Expenses

Now that we've discussed the variable nature of the trader's operating expenses, let's back up a little. You will have some fixed expenses, ones that will form the baseline of your business and that you'll always have, no matter what you're importing or exporting. These, subtracted from your projected gross income, will tell the true tale of how much you'll be making.

We are going to assume once again that you'll be homebased, so we won't worry about expenses for office rent or utilities. We do, however, need to consider the following:

- Phone
- Postage
- Stationery and office supplies
- Travel
- ISP (internet service provider)
- Loan repayment

As we discussed in the start-up section of this chapter, phone service is a must in the import/export business. You'll need it not only to communicate by voice but—just as important, if not more so—to communicate by e-mail and fax. You can figure a base monthly charge of about $25 per line. After that, you'll have to decide how much you'll be using it and what parts of the world you'll be calling.

E-mail and fax are becoming the methods of choice for communicating with customers. John L. in Brazil says those are the options he uses. In Germany, Michael R. uses a combo plate of postal service, fax, telex (a telegraph that prints out typewritten

Figuring Your Markup

Manufacturer's Cost for 500 Dozen Frog-and-Flower Porch Lights	$30,000
Customs Broker's Fee	280
Inland Freight From Factory to Port	600
Marine Insurance	340
Ocean Freight From Keelung, Taiwan	6,000
Import Tariffs/Taxes	1,590
Total	$38,810

Divide your total costs of $38,810 by 6,000 (500 dozen) units. This gives you a per-unit cost of $6.47.

material), and e-mail, with e-mail playing a larger and larger role. Jan H., the tire and used clothing trader in Belgium, uses all three phone service methods: phone, fax, and e-mail.

"We used to communicate by fax," says Wahib W. in Maryland, "because it was very expensive by phone. Now we use the phone all the time because it's more affordable than it was before. Still, the highest bill I have is the phone."

If you choose the good old-fashioned method of picking up the phone and talking into it for your international dealings, your charges will be much higher than if you send faxes, which take only moments.

If you decide to communicate as much as possible by e-mail, your international calling charges are virtually nil. And your domestic charges (unless you live in a remote area with no local ISP access) are the same as for ordinary local calls. If you have unlimited local calling service, then your international service, via e-mail, is also unlimited.

Send Me a Letter

Your ongoing postage charges will also vary, depending on how much you rely on mail rather than on some type of phone service and where in the world you are sending material. What kind of material? Requests for catalogs from exporters, your own catalogs, brochures or price sheets to importers, introduction letters, and pro forma invoices, to name a few.

Feathers or Bricks

The freight forwarder's fees, like those of the customs broker, are not cut and dried. Prices are based on product, origin, destination, size, and weight. Air rates are usually based on either a per-pound or per-kilo weight or on the dimensional weight, whichever is greater. Dimensional weight is figured by multiplying length by width by height in inches and then dividing by 166 to arrive at the number of pounds. Why make it so complicated? The air carrier is compensating for the fact that a 48-inch square box of feathers, while weighing little, will take up more room than a 14-inch box of bricks.

Ray Tobia, president of Air Sea International Forwarding, emphasizes that it's difficult to give ballpark estimates but says you might use the following as a loose idea: Air charges from Newark, New Jersey, to London might run $2.20 per pound, while the same consignment from Los Angeles to London could cost $2.50 per pound.

Freight forwarders' ocean rates usually run per 20-foot or 40-foot container or, for loose freight, on a weight/measure basis—per cubic meter or per 1,000 kilos, whichever is greater. As another ballpark idea, Tobia suggests ocean costs of, say, New York to Sydney, Australia, at $175 per cubic meter and Los Angeles to Sydney at $125 per cubic meter.

Take a look at www.usps.com for an idea of U.S. Postal Service charges for a 1-ounce package or letter by Global Priority Mail. The postal service has lots of other options, including Express Mail and airmail. Its web site—which is amazingly easy to use and informative and has terrific graphics—comes complete with an International Mail Calculator. All you do is plug in the name of the country to which you want to send mail and the weight of your package, and the calculator comes up with prices for various types of postal services, including allowable size dimensions. And you don't even have to stand in line!

Paper Tiger

Once you have made your initial outlay for office supplies and stationery, your fixed expenses in this category should be fairly low.

Smart Tip

Call AT&T's General Business Resource Center at (800) 661-2705 to find out more about their international calling rates. You know how to do market research—check out the competition (like Verizon and Sprint), too!

Dollar Stretcher

Be environmentally and economically smart. Reuse that printer paper. Instead of practicing hoop shots into the trash with all those versions of letters, price sheets, and other printed materials that you decided you didn't like, set the pages aside. When you've compiled a tidy stack, load them back into your printer, and print on the blank side. Save your "good" paper for the final draft that goes out in the mail.

Staples last a long time, you can reuse paper clips, and unless you're planning some violent activity with your letter opener and scissors for which the police will bag them as evidence, you shouldn't have to buy another set.

Your main expense will be paper for your printer and fax machine and fine-quality paper for stationery and envelopes. (If you download even a portion of the myriad materials available on the internet, you'll become a paper tiger, ferociously feeding on printed matter.) You can refer to the office supplies shopping chart in Chapter 11 for prices.

Trip Tip

As we have discussed, your travel expenses will be entirely dependent on how you structure your business. Michael R. travels infrequently since he has built his company around consulting clients in his home country of Germany. In São Paolo, Brazil, John L. travels in-country once a month and abroad once a year, spending about ten days on each trip. And across the Atlantic in Belgium, Jan H. spends three to four days a week away from home in Europe and takes an average of eight four-day to ten-day intercontinental trips a year. Base your figures on the type of work and duration of travel you'll be doing.

Olé for Online Service

What praises have we not already sung for the internet service provider? As we have said (repeatedly), this is a must for the import/export business. It is also, in most cases, a fixed expense. ISPs generally charge a flat rate of $20 to $25 for unlimited monthly service, which gives you access to the internet and e-mail.

Paying the Piper

We have set aside a fixed expense called loan repayment. If you don't borrow money to start your business, you won't need to bother with this one. If, however, you finance your start-up costs through any means, you'll need to repay the piper. Here's where you pencil in whatever your monthly fee is.

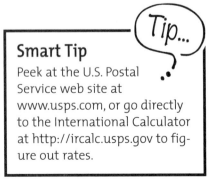

Smart Tip

Peek at the U.S. Postal Service web site at www.usps.com, or go directly to the International Calculator at http://ircalc.usps.gov to figure out rates.

Putting It Together

You can use the worksheet on page 161 to pencil in your projected income and estimated operating expenses. You may have many more expenses than the ones discussed here, such as yearly subscriptions to STAT-USA; trade shows or delegations and the travel expenses that go with them; employees and the workers' compensation and payroll costs that go with them; auto expenses; subscription fees for professional publications; butler and maid service (just

Comfort Factor

Finding a customs broker or freight forwarder is easy. You can find listings on the internet (go to a search engine, or look-up service, like www.dogpile.com or www.yahoo.com and type in your request), in the Yellow Pages, or you can ask other international traders for recommendations.

Finding the customs broker or freight forwarder who's right for you requires a little more work. Find someone you feel comfortable with and work toward an individual relationship so that you're dealing with a person you know and like within the company.

You'll want that person to not only be friendly but also knowledgeable and experienced. Find out how many years of experience she has in the business and how long she's been with this particular company. Then find out about the company:

- ❏ Does it handle customs brokerage and freight forwarding, or does it specialize in one of these transactions?
- ❏ Does it offer electronic interface (which speeds up operations considerably) with customs offices, or is everything handled on paper?
- ❏ How long has it been in operation?
- ❏ How many offices does it have, and where are they located?
- ❏ Don't forget to ask for references and then don't neglect to call those references and ask pertinent questions, like:
  - How long have they dealt with this person?
  - Have they had any problems? If so, what kind?
  - Would they recommend this person and company?

dreaming!); and pizza delivery or Chinese take-out costs. We've put in rent, utilities, employee, and insurance costs, but obviously, if these don't apply to you, don't worry about them.

Once you have calculated your estimated operating expenses, you can subtract them from your calculated earnings and—voilà!—you have a projected income/expense total

A Little Bit of Luck

Now that you have done all the arithmetic, you can determine just how much you will need to get your business up and running. And as a bonus, you can present all these beautifully executed figures to your lender to show him or her that your business is a good risk and that you will be able to repay your loan without difficulty.

Of course, one of the beauties of the import/export business is that its start-up costs are relatively low. So low, in fact, that some traders have let their first projects finance themselves.

Wahib W.'s business started from scratch. His salary with the mother company, from which his own firm took root, was $25,000. Then he got his first international trade project and his sales—and salary—took wing. "The first project was about $1.5 million," the Maryland trader explains. "The second was [about] $700,000. So that was helpful.

Murphy Stays Home

Our same hypothetical trading companies, Cargo Bay Traders and Clipper Trading Service Co., have thoughtfully provided sample projected operating income/expenses statements, which you can check out on page 160. You should keep in mind that although these figures are well in line with industry norms, so are figures that could be much lower (or higher).

The owners of these companies will have to work hard and smart to make sure that the infamous Murphy of Murphy's Law stays at home. They will carefully research their markets and products, diligently calculate all shipping tariffs and taxes, and keep a close eye on all their documentation. And they know that import/export is not a passport to overnight success; they don't expect to achieve these figures immediately.

You can do your own projected operating income/expense statement by using the worksheet on page 161.

"I don't want to say I'm lucky. You have to be somewhere to be lucky; luck doesn't come alone. As far as overhead, you can do export from anywhere you want. Even the phone bills are now cheap."

Romancing the Bank

Peter P., the Russian trade specialist, says his company also started with very little in start-up capital, but with a friend in the right place. "We had a principal owner who has a very strong relationship in the Russian banking system," Peter says. "As a result, he was able to secure for us a modest line of credit. Primarily, it was through my relationship with the suppliers in the West that we convinced them to begin doing business with us and supporting us. We had very little money in the bank. [But we had] a lot of luck and a lot of good grace."

You might want to consider financing through your bank or credit union. In this case, your start-up costs and income figures are extremely important. The bank will want to see all this, neatly laid out and carefully calculated. You will also want to show them all the statistics you can gather—for instance, the ones in this book—about the bright future of the international trade industry.

Ex-Im Bank

The Export-Import Bank of the United States (called Ex-Im Bank by those in the know) is a government agency on a mission to help finance the overseas sales of U.S. goods and services. What this means to you is that the Ex-Im people are standing by to help lend you working capital (assuming, of course, that you qualify). Again, the government is eager to help you sell U.S.-made goods abroad, so if you're exporting, this is another great resource for you.

To help support small-business exporters, the bank has developed several small-business programs:

- *Working Capital Guarantee.* This program guarantees 90 percent of the principal and interest on working capital loans made by commercial banks to credit-worthy small-business people who will use the money to purchase or produce American merchandise or services for export. You apply for a Preliminary Commitment, a sort of letter of credit from Ex-Im Bank, and then take it to your

> **Dollar Stretcher**
>
> Several credit companies offer airline miles, usually one for each dollar you spend. So while you're racking up expenses, you can also stack up air miles to be used toward your travels. For starters, check out American Express, Citibank, and Chase Manhattan. (See the Appendix for contact numbers.)

Sample Operating Income/Expense Statements

	Cargo Bay Traders	Clipper Trading Service Co.
Projected Monthly Income	$5,700.00	$18,280.00
Projected Monthly Expenses		
Rent		1,900.00
Market research/Trade leads	25.00	350.00
Phone service	100.00	560.00
Utilities		75.00
Employee payroll		2,000.00
Advertising	150.00	1,500.00
Postage	50.00	100.00
Insurance	90.00	90.00
Internet service	25.00	25.00
Travel		2,000.00
Miscellaneous Expenses (Stationery & office supplies)	10.00	50.00
Loan repayment		200.00
Total Expenses	$450.00	$8,550.00
Projected Income/Expense Total	$5,275.00	$10,140.00

Operating Income/Expense Statements

Projected Monthly Income $ _____

Projected Monthly Expenses

   Rent

       _____

   Market research/Trade leads

       _____

   Phone service
    (include $60 for cell phone service)

       _____

   Utilities

       _____

   Employee payroll

       _____

   Advertising

       _____

   Postage

       _____

   Insurance

       _____

   Internet service

       _____

   Travel

       _____

   Miscellaneous Expenses
    (Stationery & office supplies)

       _____

   Loan repayment

       _____

Total Expenses $ _____

Projected Income/Expense Total $ _____

own bank as an enticement to give you the best terms. The guarantee, which usually comes due in six months, can be for a single transaction or a revolving credit line.

Smart Tip

Contact Ex-Im Bank on the World Wide Web at www.exim.gov, or call it at (202) 565-EXIM.

- *Export Credit Insurance.* We'll go over this one in detail in Chapter 10. For now let's say that the program provides various policies to guard against a foreign buyer neglecting to pay you.

- *Direct Loans.* But not to you. Here the Ex-Im Bank will lend money to importers wishing to purchase American-made goods, thus indirectly helping your cause.

- *Guarantees.* Again, Ex-Im Bank is helping foreign buyers here and indirectly helping you as an exporter by covering the importer of U.S. goods or services against the political and commercial risks of nonpayment.

To qualify as American-made, the product or service must consist of at least 50 percent American content and must not adversely impact the U.S. economy.

In Your Pocket

Most entrepreneurs use a very exclusive source to finance their start-up expenses—family and friends. You may choose to go this route yourself. You'll have a lot less

Environmental Goodbody

The Ex-Im Bank was born in 1934 during the dark days of the Depression, when exports were viewed as a potential boost to our economic rehabilitation. After World War II, the bank helped American exporters in the reconstruction of Europe and Asia and took on the task of promoting trade between the United States and the Soviet Union.

Now that these missions have been accomplished, the bank has transferred much of its attention to emerging countries whose economies are, Ex-Im says, growing at twice the rate of the industrialized world.

The bank is also an environmental goodbody. One of its major goals is to increase exports of the environmental goods and services that are in great demand among those emerging nations.

paperwork to fill out, and you can let your financier share in the excitement as your business takes off. But remember that you'll still need to figure the repayment of borrowed funds into your costs and that you should treat your repayment agreement as seriously as you would any bank loan.

Another route many entrepreneurs take to obtain financing is through an entity as close as your back pocket—the credit card. Before you choose this option, take a look at your available credit balance and—this is important—at the annual percentage rate. Card companies frequently offer low, low rates as an incentive to sign up or use their service. Go with the one that offers the best rate for the longest period.

> ## Smart Tip
>
> **Tip...**
>
> To make the best possible impression on your banker, assemble your start-up materials in a professional-looking folder along with your desktop-published brochure or price lists. The more businesslike your company looks, the better.

Employees, Insurance, and Other Facts of Life

Depending on how much growth you envision for your business, you may never need employees. Or you may expand to the point where you can't do everything yourself—the point where you'll need to consider taking on assistants. Employees are another of those funny facts of life that seem to bring with them as many cons as pros. When you hire

help, you're not a swinging single anymore. You have responsibilities. Suddenly, there's payroll to be met, workers' compensation insurance to be paid, state and federal employee taxes to be paid. And work to be delegated.

Some people are born employers, finding it easy to teach someone else the ropes and then hand over the reins. Others never feel quite comfortable telling someone else what to do or how to do it.

One of the many perks of the import/export business is that you can accomplish a great deal without ever hiring anyone. You can easily start out as a one-man (or woman) band, handling all the tasks of your fledgling company yourself. You won't need help immediately. But as your company flourishes, you may one day find that you need: a) more hours in a day, b) to make great strides in the field of cloning, or c) to hire help.

Fun with Filing

A tremendous amount of the work in international trade involves correspondence, invoicing, and preparing documents. And as your company grows, you may discover that you can't have fun with filing and at the same time market your services to clients, arrange deals with representatives and distributors, and promote your clients' products.

When you reach the point where your paperwork and other daily grind tasks are cutting drastically into your marketing and customer service time (and you're walking around with coffee jitters and bags under your eyes from trying to do it all), you'll need to hire an administrative assistant. This valuable member of your new team can work on a part-time or full-time basis, depending on your needs.

You will want an organized and detail-oriented person who can think independently, someone who has a cheerful phone personality and manners, good communication skills, and a knowledge of the computer programs you use.

Your administrative assistant will free you to go out and market and service your accounts. This is good. But as you continue to grow, sooner or later you'll find again that you can't do it all yourself. You'll need to hire another team member, an account supervisor to help recruit and service accounts.

Trader's View

"My daughter, Isabelle, runs the office," says Jan H. in Belgium, "and I have three employees grading tires and loading and unloading containers."

The All-Star

Ideally, your new all-star will have a working knowledge of international trade, but this is not as important as enthusiasm for the sales and services your company offers. For starters, you'll assign him or her an account to service. Then, as he learns how your company operates and what services you offer, he can recruit his own accounts.

Depending on the size of the account, a person with extensive experience in international trade should be able to handle three to five accounts per year. If the accounts are small and don't need a lot of support, she may able to service more than that.

Since nobody works for free, and because salespeople in particular are best motivated by incentives, you'll want to provide your account supervisors (let's face it, by this time you have several) with either a draw-vs.-commission or salary-and-commission on their accounts.

Smart Tip

Tip...

You can protect yourself against former employees stealing your accounts by having every account supervisor sign a written employment contract containing a noncompete provision. You should consult your attorney for the finer points, but you can usually limit the competition from a former employee by both geographic area and time period.

What's the difference? In a draw-vs.-commission arrangement, you provide your employees with a draw, a set monthly income so that they can be assured of money coming in to pay the rent and feed the dog and cat. Any commissions they earn are offset against the draw so that they don't get actual money from the commissions until they've gone over the amount of the monthly draw. (If the draw is $500, for instance, and they earn commissions of $800, they receive $300 in commissions with the balance of $500 going to "repay" the draw.)

In a salary-plus-commission arrangement, you pay your employees a set monthly income, but in this case, any commissions they earn are added on to the monthly payment instead of being subtracted from it. So if their monthly salary is $500 and they earn commissions of $800, they get the whole $800 plus the salary.

Draw-vs.-commission is the best way to motivate your account supervisors to perform at peak efficiency. (The salary-and-commission method doesn't seem to dangle the same carrot.) Of course, if you have a particularly valuable team member, you might pay her on a salary-plus-commission basis. This will serve not only to express your satisfaction with her performance but will act as a terrific way to ensure that she stays with you instead of going off on her own and taking your accounts with her.

Standing on the Corner

How exactly do you set about finding the right team members? You could stand on the corner and holler until you attract the right person's attention. But here are some more practical suggestions for finding account supervisors:

- Place a classified ad in your local newspaper or, if you live in a smaller, less-urban area where import/export-trained people might be scarce, in a large metropolitan newspaper. You can entice potential account supervisors to your town with the benefits of living in your less-populated, low-stress part of the world.

- Recruit salespeople in related fields. If, for example, you export medical supplies, try headhunting in the domestic medical supplies or pharmaceutical sales arenas.
- Post an e-mail ad on the web sites of various international trade associations. (See the Appendix for a list of these.)
- Recruit at local colleges that offer courses in international trade. You can post an ad on the department's bulletin board or talk to professors about recommending graduating star students.

To find that gem of an administrative assistant, try these ideas:

Bright Idea

Even though English is the "international" lingo for business, you'll have a major advantage if at least one of your team members speaks the languages of the countries you're dealing with. It's a nice gesture toward foreign clients, it can help avoid potential linguistic misunderstandings, and it can go a long way toward helping you write effective marketing materials or correspondence, especially for the end user.

Happy Holidays

When you're recruiting team members, keep in mind an important bonus qualification: familiarity with the cultures of your target countries. Although not a must, this particular quality can be a big help to the international trader.

Did you know, for example, that in China, the New Year—celebrated in mid to late January—is a major holiday on a par with Christmas, Hanukkah, Thanksgiving, and the Fourth of July all rolled into one? Or that all commerce comes to a full stop for one week to one month? Or that in parts of Israel, everything shuts down for 24 hours on the weekly Sabbath? Or that during Ramadan, the Muslim holy month, everybody fasts between dawn and dusk?

A cultural pro on your team can fill you in on all these potential trading booby traps before you fall into them.

Of course, until the day when your team consists of more than one member—you—you should take the time to research these kinds of things yourself. There are several online sites that will tell you more about holidays the world over.

- Place an ad in your local newspaper.
- Recruit from local secretarial schools.
- Try headhunting from domestic companies engaged in products similar to the merchandise you sell.
- Recruit from freight forwarding or customs broker firms.

The Backup Brain

Hiring an employee is one of those take-a-deep-breath-or-hyperventilate steps. You're taking on an extension of yourself, someone who hopefully will become not just another pair of hands but a backup brain, a friend, ally, and member of your business family. How do you choose someone to fill all those shoes?

Your administrative assistant should be not just a desk jockey, a mindless drone at the computer keyboard and telephone, but an integral part of your team. You'll need to rely on him or her to field all the problems that might arise while you're out traveling the world. You'll want someone with the following skills and abilities:

Standard Operating Procedure

As a trader, you should become familiar with the ISO 9000—it's quickly becoming a fact of life among international companies. So are the QS 9000 and the ISO 14000. So what are these entities?

They're quality management systems devised by the International Organization for Standardization (yes, we realize the acronym should be IOS!) in Geneva, Switzerland, and they're rapidly becoming a common product requirement, especially in European Union countries but also in the United States and other nations.

If the product you're representing has an ISO 9000 certification, it can hold its head up among its competitors—it's been manufactured with quality, customer service, and the well-being of its own work force well in hand.

A QS 9000 certification is the next step up (the "more mature version," according to The ISO 9000 Network, a commercial certification group) and relates specifically to the automotive industry, while the ISO 14000 focuses on management of the environment.

For more information, you can contact the ISO Central Secretariat at www.iso.org or check with the National Institute of Standards and Technology at http://ts.nist.gov.

- *Analytical.* Can they think through a problem and arrive at a solution?

- *Oral communication.* Do they have a good phone personality? Can they communicate a problem? Resolve that problem? How's their vocabulary? Grammar?

- *Written communication.* Can they write an effective letter explaining, for example, a missing piece of documentation? Detailing the resolution? How's their grammar? Punctuation?

- *Detail-oriented.* Can they enter correct information on an invoice or lading document without transposing or scrambling it?

- *Able to take direction.* Can they follow directions? And can they do so without getting insulted or defensive?

- *Personality complements your own.* Some people work better with cheery chatterboxes; others go for the strong, silent type. If you hate interruptions, think twice about hiring that prattling prospect. On the other hand, if you want someone to talk with during the day, avoid those types who close their office doors and eat lunch at their desks.

Testing 1, 2, 3

Now test 'em out! Ask your prospect to:

- Write out a typical scenario in which the terms of a letter of credit cannot be completed for a fairly simple reason. (You be the judge.) You might use, for example, a case in which a certificate of origin has not been received from the exporter. Ask your prospect to solve the problem.

- Present a scenario of an importer who's worried because he hasn't received his merchandise; you are out of the country. Ask your prospect what she'd say over the phone and how she'd handle the problem.

- Have her fill out a few documents if she's familiar with import/export. How does she do?

- Have her whip up a sample piece of correspondence or enter checks into your accounting program if she's familiar with your computer programs. How does she do?

- Enter a column of numbers on a calculator. Does she add it up quickly and correctly?

Bright Idea
Why not hire from within? Your young-adult son or daughter might be just the person to fill that administrative assistant slot on a part-time basis. If things go well and he or she turns out to have a flair for the business, you can eventually train them to follow in your traveling footsteps as a potential account supervisor.

- Take a filing test. Can she stick papers in the right folders? Does she file alphabetically or by some strange method of her own?

After you have done all this, of course, you will want to read resumes, check references, and then use your own people skills. How do you feel intuitively about your candidate(s)?

Insuring Your Gems

Once you find those gems of employees, you will need to think about caring for them. Workers' compensation insurance laws vary among states; check with your insurance agent for details in your area. Workers' comp covers you for any illness or injury your employees might incur, from a paper cut gone septic to a back injury from lifting heavy file boxes to yellow fever contracted while out on a sales trip. (People can come up with a lot of strange complaints when money's involved.)

If your employees work in your home office and get injured there, your homeowners' insurance may refuse to pay on the grounds that it's actually a workers' comp case. Rather than making yourself a nervous wreck (incurring your own mental health claim) over all this, check with your insurance agent and then make an informed decision.

Thanks, Ex-Im

Thanks to the Export/Import Bank of the United States, you can purchase several types of export credit risk insurance specially designed for the newbie exporter and the SME (small- to medium-sized enterprise, remember?). These policies protect you against the possibility that your foreign buyer will decide not to pay you for either commercial or political reasons and therefore, the bank hopes, will encourage both you and your financial institution to take on higher-risk foreign markets. Your menu options are:

- *Small-business policy.* This multibuyer policy requires that you insure all your export credit sales with Ex-Im; it's designed to free you from the "first-loss" deductible of most commercial policies. To take advantage, you must have an export credit sales volume of less than $5 million in the last three years before application, your company must qualify as a small business under the Small Business Administration's definition of the term, and you must have been in business at least one year with a positive net worth. How do you find out if you qualify? Call the SBA's Office of Size Standards at (202) 205-6618 or check its web site at www.sba.gov/size.

- *Umbrella policy*. This policy boasts the same coverage and eligibility as the small-business policy above, but it allows you (as an EMC or ETC) to act as an administrator or intermediary between Ex-Im and your clients.
- *Short-term single-buyer policy*. This one, which covers a single or repetitive sale, is

Smart Tip — Tip...

For more information, click on the Ex-Im Bank at www.exim.gov/msbprogs.html or call (800) 565-EXIM.

for the exporter who doesn't want to insure everything with Ex-Im. A special reduced premium is offered to small businesses.

Miami Vice

You already know the importance of cargo insurance. To follow a piece of advice from the American Express people, "Don't let your merchandise leave home without it." The coverage of potential loss or damage (or both) far outweighs the cost of the insurance, which usually runs about 1 percent of the insured value, although this varies with the type of goods and method of shipping.

You'll want to purchase all risk insurance, which covers your cargo against everything except man's inhumanity to man—war, strikes, riots, and civil commotion—and inherent vice in the cargo. This has nothing to do with Miami Vice officers hiding in your containers but instead refers to another sort of freeloader, boll weevils in those gorgeous cotton blankets, for example, or e. coli on your Texas steaks.

You can guard against the battling humans risk by purchasing war and SRCC (strikes, riots, and civil commotion) riders, and you can also buy riders to protect against whatever form of inherent vice your particular cargo may face.

You might also want to consider general average insurance. This protects you in the event of someone else's cargo loss. Say the ship carrying your containers runs afoul of stormy weather. The captain decides to jettison a portion of the cargo to save the rest, and he dumps somebody else's stuff into the briny deep. Fine, you say. Not quite. According to maritime law, even though your merchandise has made it to port safe and sound, you can't take possession until you've paid for your share of the loss.

The Blanket Policy

Let's look at another scenario. Say the other party in your transaction has purchased insurance, for example, the exporter who's shipping to you CIF (cost, insurance, and freight, remember?), but you've got a funny feeling that his coverage is not too reliable. Not to worry. You can purchase a contingent policy, which is about half the price of regular insurance and will serve as backup insurance in the event of a catastrophe.

The Lost World

In the event of a cargo misadventure, you may feel as if not only your merchandise but your world has been lost. Cheer up. You insurance coverage should include enough to repay you for not only lost or damaged products, but for your extra time and trouble and those lost profits.

You should figure on insuring an additional 10 percent of the CIF value of your cargo. If your merchandise is worth $5,000, for example, and your ocean freight charge is $400, then you'll want to buy about $6,000 worth of insurance.

> $5,000 + $400 = $5,400
> $5,400 + $540 (10 percent) = $5,940 (rounded up to $6,000)

As a newbie trader, your best bet will be to purchase insurance through your freight forwarder, who has a blanket policy, or directly from the air carrier. As you grow, you may wish to purchase a blanket policy of your own, which will cover you for everything you ship over the course of a year.

Stormy Weather

Out on the high seas, your cargo may be subjected to rough and stormy weather. On the docks, it can be equally buffeted about by tough longshoremen. What can you do to protect it against becoming a marine insurance claim?

- *Pack with dock loading and unloading procedures in mind.* Your cargo may be slung around (or skewered) by anything from a forklift to a sling or net, and then, if it survives that, left outdoors to rot. "I've seen [places] where they store materials out on port decks after unloading ships or out on the airplane cargo tarmacs," says Dan S., the New Jersey trader. "They just leave the material out there with no covering over it. If you're not well-versed with a lot of these ports overseas and how they do things [and] you don't have the right packaging, you just lose a lot of material."

- *Pack to expect Mother Nature's worst.* Container loads can shift during heavy seas and storms. Someone else's cargo can smash into yours—or vice versa. A sea voyage may be good for a human's health, but it can be murder on merchandise. Think heat and humidity, salt air (which is incredibly corrosive), rain, and sea spray. When any or all of this gets into your containers, you can end up with rust, blistering, mold, mildew, and moisture damage.

Mark It Up!

The importer usually specifies export marks that should appear on the cargo for easy identification by receivers. These marks include the following:

- ○ Shipper's mark
- ○ Country of origin
- ○ Weight marking in pounds and kilograms
- ○ Number of packages and size of cases in inches and centimeters
- ○ Handling marks using international pictorial symbols (if appropriate)
- ○ Cautionary markings in English and the language of the country of destination (if appropriate)
- ○ Special labels for hazardous materials

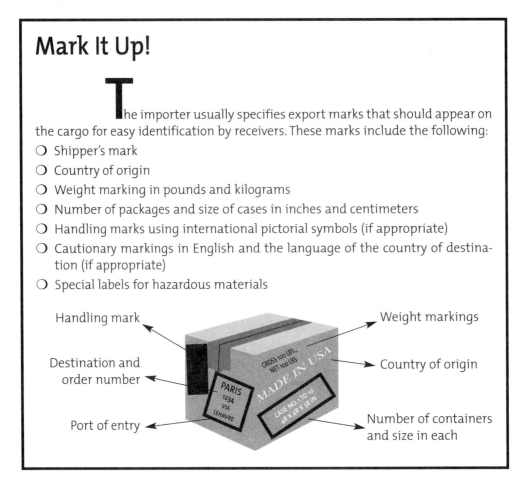

- Handling mark
- Destination and order number
- Port of entry
- Weight markings
- Country of origin
- Number of containers and size in each

GROSS 100 LBS., NET 100 LBS
MADE IN USA
PARIS 1234 VIA LEHAVRE
CASE NO. 1 TO 10 48 X 48 X 38 IN

- Pack to expect human nature's worst. Some people just can't resist somebody else's goods. Theft can be a problem, especially when containers are left on the docks for a long time.

With all these potential disasters in mind, pack smart. Use adequate packaging materials; make sure your merchandise is cushioned against blows. Waterproof everything possible. Have package exteriors shrink-wrapped. Use waterproof lining on interiors. Coat exposed metal parts on machinery, for example, with grease or some other rust arrester. Use heavy strapping and seals. Discourage theft by eliminating trademarks or content descriptions on container exteriors. (No need to stencil "solid gold bars" on the box!)

11

Inside the
Cargo Hold
Your Business
Equipment

Your office will hold your most basic cargo—
your computer, fax machine, and other business equipment.
With these tools, your operations will run smoothly, speedily,
and efficiently; without them, your company would be like a
small and rickety biplane trying to deliver merchandise while
your competition soars along in jumbo jets.

We've provided a handy checklist (see page 184) to help you determine what you'll need, what you already have on hand, and which of those in-stock items is trade-ready. Die-hard shoppers may want to rush out and buy every item brand-spanking new, but this may not be necessary. Some or all of these things might already be scattered around your home, just waiting to be put to use.

After you've read this chapter, run through the checklist and evaluate your stock. Is your computer trade-ready, or is it an antique that won't be able to keep up the pace? Does your answering machine take and receive clearly audible messages, or does it tend to garble crucial information? How about that printer? Can it produce professional-looking materials in short order, or does it take ages to spit out a solitary, quavery page?

Now, checklist in hand, let's take a whirlwind virtual shopping spree. Ready, steady, go!

Wait a second. Let's discuss something first. There's always the buy of a lifetime, and there's always the ultimate fancy-schmancy tip-top of the line. What we're looking for here are the low- and middle-of-the-road models.

Computer Glitterati

Your computer will be the luminary of your office setup, coordinating your invoicing, accounting, word processing, and desktop publishing activities—not to mention co-starring in all e-mail correspondence. In addition to any traveling you'll do as part of your market research, it will be your most important start-up purchase. If you already own a computer, you'll want to make sure it's capable of handling the tasks you'll assign it.

Your new computer should have the latest operating system so that documents from business partners read in English, not Egyptian hieroglyphics. To run your software properly, you'll need at least 64MB RAM, plus at least an 8GB to 10GB hard drive, a 24X or better CD-ROM drive and a 56 Kbps modem. You can expect to pay from $1,500 to $3,500 for a good name-brand computer with prices increasing as you add on goodies.

Purring Printers

A good printer is a must. You'll want to produce reports, charts, graphs, brochures, newsletters, thank-you letters, pay-up-or-else letters, contracts, statements, and sundry other materials, and they all need to look polished and professional. The materials you produce will be a direct reflection of your company. Shaky, faint, dot-matrix correspondence looks amateurish. Sharp, bold graphics and print give your business an aura of confidence and success.

You also want a printer that's fast. There's nothing quite like the frustration of waiting for material to trickle out of a slow-going printer. One page per minute can seem like one page per hour.

Fortunately, really hot-stuff printers are less expensive than ever before. You can purchase an LED, which virtually simulates the higher-ticket laser printer, or an inkjet, many of which can produce all the wonderful colors of commercial artwork. Color-capable models print more slowly than their black-and-white counterparts, but if you'll be creating lots of marketing materials, like brochures and newsletters, then color should be a consideration. You can expect to pay $250 to $500 for a color inkjet or laser printer.

> ### Bright Idea
> If you plan to travel a great deal, you might want to invest in a laptop computer, either instead of or in addition to your desktop model. A top-of-the-line laptop can do everything a desktop can, plus it can travel virtually anywhere, and you can even perch it on your knees on the plane.

Just the Fax

The fax machine, as we've discussed, is a must for the international trader. Along with e-mail, it's the method of choice for communicating quickly and clearly with clients, manufacturers, importers, and exporters around the globe. And don't forget faxing lunch orders to that deli down the street.

Fax machines can be purchased as combo fax/copiers, printers, and scanners. They can be slow when used as a printer, so be sure to check before you buy. Also, make sure the fax machine you purchase will print on plain paper. Most of the documents you receive will be keepers—correspondence, invoices, and the like that will need to go into your permanent files. The ink on thermal fax paper (that slick gray stuff) fades to near invisibility in a short time, thus negating any archiving attempts.

Soft on Software

A dazzling array of software lines the shelves of most office supply stores, ready to help you perform every business task—design and print your own checks, make mailing lists and labels, develop professional quality marketing materials, be your own attorney and accountant.

Most new computers come pre-loaded with all the software you will need for basic office procedures. If yours doesn't or if you have lucked into a stripped-down hand-me-down, you may want to look into the following programs. You'll need a word processing program, with which you can write correspondence, contracts, sales reports for your clients, and whatever else strikes your fancy. A good basic program, such as Microsoft Word, can be had for $85 to $220.

You may also want an accounting program, such as QuickBooks or Microsoft Money, to track your business finances. These are a sort of checkbook on CD-ROM and make record-keeping a breeze. You assign categories, such as office supplies and business travel, to the checks you write, and at tax time you print out a report showing how much you spent for what. Your accountant not only thanks you but gives you a discount for not having to wade through all your receipts. You can expect to pay $80 to $250 for your cyberspace checkbook.

Hello, Central

You'll probably have three telephone lines coming into your home, two of which will be for your office. Therefore, you'll want a two-line phone so you can put one on hold while you're answering the other. You can divide up the three lines any way you like: You might put your home line and your business line on the two-line phone, leaving the third line for your fax machine and modem. Or you might put the business and fax-modem line on the two-line phone, leaving your home line in the kitchen or den. The idea behind either of these choices is that you can call out on your home or fax-modem line (when it's not in use) and leave the business line for incoming calls.

> ### Bright Idea
> Purchase a greeting card program. You can customize not only the artwork, but the text or verse and matching envelope. Sending a personalized thank-you card to clients and customers, with the addressee's name embedded right in the message, makes a terrific impression. You can find professional-quality (and really fun!) greeting card programs in the $30 to $50 range.

Whichever option you choose, you'll want the telephone to have two lines that can be put on hold. This way, business callers can't hear you explaining to your children why they can't have a nose ring when they call you collect from the mall.

A speaker is also a nice feature, especially for all those on-hold-forever calls to your banker, attorney, insurance company, or whomever. Your hands are free to work up financial data on your latest export venture, your shoulders remain unhunched, and there's no earring jabbing you in the side of the head while you listen to Muzak and wait your turn.

You can expect to pay about $70 to $150 for a two-line speakerphone with auto redial, memory dial, flashing lights, mute button, and other assorted goodies.

Phone on the Go

If you spend much time outside the office (even if it's at the coffeehouse on the corner), a cell phone might be a good investment. And if you're one of those jet-setting trader types who scouts the globe in search of the next whiz-bang commodity, a cell phone is all but a must. When your shipment of Tibetan jewelry arrives, when that goat cheese order is about to go rancid—you'll know immediately and can respond in time to pick up your goods or save the deal. A cell phone costs $100 and up, and a

Dollar Stretcher

If you have a cell phone, you can avoid paying money for another land line and for voice mail. Ask your local phone company to forward calls to your cell phone. If you're on the phone or away from your desk—or if your computer is using the phone line for e-mail—calls into your land line will roll over to your cell phone. And if you don't pick up the cell phone, the phone will take the message for you.

monthly calling plan—depending on how much you want to yak—will run you between $30 and $80 a month.

Automated Answering Service

If you choose not to go with voice mail from your phone company, you'll need an answering machine. Unless you want to put your business greeting on your home machine and take the risk that your kids might erase messages to you, you should buy a separate machine for your office.

The models on the market now are digital, which, aside from the technical mumbo jumbo, means they don't have audiotapes to get knotted or broken. There are also all sorts of fancy gizmos with caller ID, speakerphones, cordless phones, and 15 kinds of memos, but a good basic model capable of answering your business line can be had for less than $40. For a snazzier model that can answer two lines, expect to pay about $150.

Vociferous Voice Mail

Voice mail is the phone company's answer to the answering machine, with a few nice twists. Like an answering machine, voice mail takes your messages when you're not in the office. If you have call waiting, a feature that discreetly beeps to announce an incoming call while you're already on the phone, and you choose not to answer that second call, voice mail will take a message for you. With voice mail, as with many answering machines, you can access your messages from a remote location.

Voice mail costs depend on your local Ma Bell and the features you choose, but you can expect to pay $6 to $20 a month.

Laugh at Lightning

You should invest in a UPS, or uninterruptible power supply, for your computer system, especially if you live in an area where lightning or power surges are frequent features. If you're a computer newbie, you may not realize that even a flicker of power loss can shut down your computer, causing it to forget all the data you've carefully entered during your current work session, or—the ultimate horror—fry your

Read All About It

The written word is a powerful learning tool. One of your first steps in your new venture should be to read everything you can, not just about the specifics of international trade but about starting a small business and marketing and sales techniques. Blitz the bookstore. Make an assault on your public library.

Your own business library should contain a variety of reference manuals. For starters, check out the following:

O *Building an Import/Export Business* by Kenneth D. Weiss, John Wiley & Sons
O *Import/Export: How to Get Started in International Trade* by Carl A. Nelson, McGraw-Hill
O *Export-Import* by Joseph A. Zodl, Betterway Books
O Any of the Barron's foreign language books, such as *Learn Italian the Fast and Fun Way* by Marcel Danesi, Barron's Educational Series

Don't stop with these. Immerse yourself in your subject. The more you know, the better international trader you'll be.

computer's brains entirely. With a UPS in your arsenal, you won't lose power to your system when the house power fails or flickers. Instead, the unit flashes red and sounds a warning, giving you ample time to safely shut down your computer.

Since you'll be spending a lot of time on the internet, you want to be sure that your UPS includes phone line protection. You can expect to pay $125 and up for one of these power pals.

Lightning Strikes Again

A surge protector safeguards your electronic equipment from power spikes during storms or outages. Your battery backup will double as a surge protector for your computer hard drive, or CPU, and monitor, but you'll want protection for those other valuable office allies: your printer, fax machine, and copier. They don't need a battery backup because no data will be lost if the power goes out, and a surge protector will do the job for a lot less money. If you have a fax machine, be sure the surge protector also defends its phone line. You can expect to pay $15 to $60 for a surge protector.

Cool and Calculating

What do calculators and telephones have in common? A numbered keypad and an important place on your desk. Even though your computer probably has a built-in calculator program, it helps to have the real thing close at hand. You can do calculations quickly, and you can even check your work if you have a paper-tape model. Expect to pay less than $15 for a battery-operated model and $25 to $75 for a plug-in calculator.

> ⚠️ **Beware!**
>
> Don't "enhance" your answering machine message with background music or a cutesy script. It's not businesslike. Keep it simple. Give your business name—spoken clearly and carefully—and ask callers to leave a short message and a phone number. Thank them for calling and assure them that someone from your office will return their call as soon as possible.

Paper Cloning

The copier is an optional item, probably the least important on the list, but as you grow, you may find it a necessary luxury. Keep in mind that you should never send a piece of paper out of your office unless you've kept a copy. You can always print two copies of every document you generate on your computer, keeping one as a file copy. But some forms, like the Shippers Export Declaration and other government-driven documents that you can't wring from your computer, demand a copier-made duplicate. Copiers range from less than $400 to $800 or more.

Step into My Office

Office furniture is another optional item. It's important that your work environment be comfortable and ergonomic, but if you're homebased, it's acceptable to start off with an old door set on cinder blocks for a desk and an egg crate for your files. When you're ready to make the big step toward real office furniture for that oh-so-professional look, you have a stunning array of possibilities to choose from.

> **Bright Idea**
>
> If you plan to send a lot of material by mail, you may want to look into a postage meter. This is a time saver in the lick-and-stick department, the standing-in-line-at-the-post-office department, and, with those envelope sealing gizmos, it can even protect against pesky paper cuts.

We shopped the big office supply warehouse stores and found midrange desks from $200 to $300, a computer work center for $200, printer stands from $50 to $75, two-drawer letter-size file cabinets (which can double as your printer stand) from $25 to $100, and a four-shelf bookcase for $70.

Equipment Expenses

To give you an idea of how much you can expect to budget, check out the costs of furniture, equipment, and supplies for two hypothetical import/export services, Silk Road Imports and Caravan Traders (see page 183). Silk Road, a homebased newbie with no employees except its owner, so far has made a net profit of $15,000. The fledgling business counts as its equipment resources an inexpensive computer system, an inkjet printer, and the basics in software.

Caravan, up and running for three years, makes its base in an office in an industrial park near the airport, has one full-time employee in addition to the owner, and has annual net profits of $200,000. Caravan boasts a top-of-the-line computer system for its owner, an inexpensive computer for its employee, a laser printer, a combo fax machine/scanner, a copier, and various publishing and marketing software programs that have caught its owner's eye over the years.

Office Supplies Shopping Mini-List

Computer/copier/fax paper	$_____
Blank business cards	_____
Blank letterhead stationery	_____
Matching envelopes	_____
10 x 13 envelopes	_____
Legal-sized envelopes	_____
File folders	_____
Return address self-stamper or stickers	_____
Extra printer cartridge	_____
Mouse pad	_____
Miscellaneous office supplies (pencils, paper clips, etc.)	_____
Extra fax cartridge	_____
Total Expenditures	$_____

Sample Office Expenses

Furniture, Equipment, and Supplies	Silk Road Imports	Caravan Traders
Computer system (including printer)	$2,050.00	$4,500.00
Fax machine	250.00	700.00
Software	380.00	550.00
Phone system	70.00	230.00
Cell phone	0	100.00
Answering machine	40.00	130.00
Uninterruptible power supply	125.00	250.00
Surge protector	34.00	34.00
Calculator	15.00	75.00
Copier	400.00	800.00
Desk	200.00	600.00
Desk chair	60.00	200.00
Printer stand	0	70.00
File cabinet	25.00	200.00
Bookcase	70.00	70.00
Printer/copier paper	25.00	50.00
Blank business cards	6.00	12.00
Letterhead	30.00	30.00
Matching envelopes	35.00	35.00
10 x 13 envelopes	14.00	28.00
Legal-sized envelopes	3.00	6.00
Address stamp or stickers	10.00	10.00
Extra printer cartridge	25.00	80.00
Extra fax cartridge	80.00	80.00
Mouse pad	10.00	20.00
Miscellaneous office supplies	100.00	150.00
Total Expenditures	**$3,842.00**	**$9,010.00**

The Trader's Office Checklist

Use this handy list as a shopping guide for equipping your office. It's been designed with the one-person home office in mind. If you have partners, employees, or you just inherited a million dollars from a mysterious foundation with the stipulation that you spend at least half on office equipment, you may want to make modifications.

After you have done your shopping, fill in the purchase price next to each item, add up the total and you will have a head start on the Start-Up Costs Worksheet on page 146!

❑ Windows XP or higher Pentium-class PC with
  SVGA monitor, modem, and CD-ROM drive $ _____

❑ Laser or inkjet printer   _____

❑ Fax machine   _____

❑ Software:

  word processing   _____

  desktop publishing   _____

  accounting   _____

❑ Phones, two or three lines with voice mail, or
  answering machine   _____

❑ Uninterruptible power supply   _____

❑ Zip drive (if not included with computer)   _____

❑ Surge protector   _____

❑ Calculator   _____

❑ Office supplies (see mini-list on page 182)   _____

Not on the critical list

❑ Copier   _____

❑ Desk   _____

❑ Desk chair   _____

❑ Filing cabinet   _____

❑ Bookcase   _____

  Total Expenditures $ _____

Chairs are a very personal matter. Some people like the dainty secretary's chair for its economy of space; others want the tonier high-back executive model. There are chairs with kangaroo pockets and chairs with pneumatic height adjustments. Prices range from $60 to $250.

The Stationary Suitcase

Whether you're a trader on the move, always flying from one exotic locale to another, or an armchair traveler who conducts most of his or her business from home base, you'll need a sort of stationary suitcase: a business office.

As we've explained, one of the perks of running an import/export business is that it lends itself ideally to the homebased entrepreneur. It doesn't require a high-traffic or high-visibility location and doesn't need to be in a trendy part of town. Although you may have an occasional client stop in, you won't need a mahogany-paneled office with a lobby and conference room, just a small and comfortable seating area. The only real space requirement is an area large enough for your desk, chair, filing cabinets, and perhaps a bookshelf.

It's convenient—you couldn't get any closer to your office unless you slept with your computer. It's economical—you don't need to spend money on leased space, extra utilities, transportation costs, or lunches down at the corner grill.

Dan S., the computer cable specialist in New Jersey, has his office at home. So do Lloyd D. in Florida and John L. in Brazil. "Of course, when necessary, I rent an adequate [warehouse] space," John says.

The Home Office

If you choose to be homebased, you can locate your office workspace anywhere in the house that's convenient, although ideally, you should have a dedicated office, a room that's reserved just for the business. You could locate this room in a den, a FROG (finished room over garage), the garage itself, or a spare bedroom. Keep in mind that whatever space you choose will be your workstation and command center.

If a dedicated office is not an option, you can also station yourself in a corner of the kitchen or at the dining room table. If you have a boisterous family, however, a cubby hole in your bedroom is likely to be much more conducive to quiet, clear thinking than a nook in the family room with the big-screen television blaring at all hours. Also remember that yelling into the phone over cartoon kerblams and pows! will not make you sound particularly professional to your customers.

The Tax Man Speaketh

Another advantage to the home office is the ability to write it off as a home business. The IRS will graciously allow you to deduct money from your income taxes if

Taking Inventory

OK. You've found some really terrific merchandise and decided to take it on wearing your distributor cap. You've taken title to the stuff—actually purchased it yourself—and are working with reps to sell it around the country. Great! Except that now you have inventory, stock that has to be stored somewhere and accounted for.

What to do? First, remember that your capital is tied up with your inventory. If you don't move your stock quickly, you're liable to run into that old business nemesis, the cash-flow problem. So try to have buyers lined up before you purchase the goods.

If you don't, start up an inventory system to ensure that you have enough stock on hand to supply your buyers but not so much that you're paying through the nose for storage space. Keep careful track of how quickly items are moving, determine how long it will take to replace them, and order new shipments accordingly. Do this at regular intervals so you can develop a better feel for how quickly items are selling and how long shipments take to arrive.

you're using a portion of your home as your income-producing workspace. You can deduct a percentage of expenses equivalent to the percentage of space your home office occupies. If, for example, you're using one room in an eight-room house, you can deduct one-eighth of your rent or mortgage plus one-eighth of your utility bills.

There is, of course, an if involved here. You can use this deduction if you're using this space solely as your office. If you've turned your spare bedroom into your office and you don't use it for anything but conducting your business, then you qualify. If, however, your office is tucked into a corner of the kitchen and you're still feeding people in there, you don't qualify for the home office deduction (unless you can convince the IRS that you order Chinese every night and the refrigerator is actually a file cabinet).

Growing Pains

As your business grows, or when you find yourself with stock to store—such as when you have your distributor cap on and have

Stat Fact
Looking to relocate to an "export friendly" state? As of 2007, California, Texas, Michigan, Washington, Illinois, and New York made up the largest percentages of US-exported manufactured products, according to a recent U.S. Census Bureau report.

purchased merchandise—you may decide that it's time to move up to outside or commercial office space.

Because the import/export business doesn't rely on client traffic or a prestigious address, any area that appeals to you and your pocketbook is up for grabs. Rick Casey, a realtor with Bay Properties in Panama City Beach, Florida, recommends going the office/warehouse route in an industrial park. If product storage is your only problem, Casey advises, you might also consider keeping your home office and renting space from a self-storage facility.

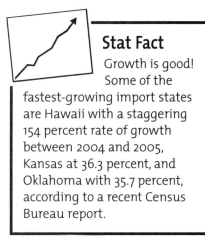

Stat Fact

Growth is good! Some of the fastest-growing import states are Hawaii with a staggering 154 percent rate of growth between 2004 and 2005, Kansas at 36.3 percent, and Oklahoma with 35.7 percent, according to a recent Census Bureau report.

If storage is not a concern for you but you want an office away from home, you might look for commercial space in other areas—but not in the retail arena. "You don't want to rent retail space when you're doing a service business," Casey says. "You don't need the high visibility." Or the higher prices.

Alternative Officing

If commercial office space isn't your bag, you might consider a more unconventional approach. Rent a house or apartment (provided you check the zoning laws first). If you already live in an apartment, you may choose to rent another unit in the same building to use as your office. You can walk to work. And the landlord may give you a package deal—or a finder's fee!

Or you can take a space over a downtown storefront. How about over a coffeehouse or doughnut shop or bagel bakery? What better incentive to get to work in the morning?

Organized and Efficient

If you prefer to have your coffee and croissant—and your office—in your home, it's important to remember that you're still a professional. Your work quarters, like you, should be organized and efficient. If at all possible, designate a separate room with four walls and a door. Aim for pleasant, quiet, well-lit surroundings. You are going to be spending a lot of time in this space, so you want it to be comfortable.

If you can't carve out a dedicated space, by all means take over a corner of another room. But consider it your permanent office. Clearing your work materials off the dining room table before meals is a definite drag.

Appropriate a desk or table that is large enough to hold your computer, keyboard, telephone, and pencil holder/stapler/etc. and still have enough room to spread out your working papers. A charming 19th century cherrywood secretary looks great but probably won't allow enough space for your market research, correspondence, and files, plus you and your computer. Don't skimp on elbow-room.

Your two main realms of activity will be marketing and administration. Make sure you have enough space to store account records and leads, both client and buyer, as well as reference materials. You can set up separate alphabetical file cards for contacts with suppliers, customers, sales representatives, and distributors, or you can use a system of folders in

Trader's View

In Belgium, Jan H. operates out of a 3,000-square-meter office/warehouse ("Don't ask me how much that is in square feet!" he says)—and has 10,000 square meters of space in outside storage facilities. For the nonmetric minded, that's a whopping 32,292 square feet of office/warehouse space and more than 107,000 square feet of outside storage space.

Home Office Worksheet

Use this handy worksheet to locate and design your home office.

List three possible locations in your home. Remember that you will have occasional guests. If your potential office space can't accommodate them, is there another home location where you can entertain?

1. _____

2. _____

3. _____

Make a physical survey of each location.

❑ Are phone and electrical outlets placed so that your equipment can easily access them? Or will you be faced with unsightly, unsafe cords snaking across the carpet?

❑ Measure your space. Will your current desk or table, or the one you have your eye on, fit?

❑ Do you have adequate lighting? If not, can you create or import it?

❑ Is there proper ventilation?

❑ What is the noise factor?

❑ Is there room to spread out your work?

which you keep copies of all correspondence and replies. Whichever system you choose, remember that you're in the business of matching buyers and sellers as well as producers and distributors, and that you must be able to access this information quickly and easily. It's no fun digging through the back of the clothes closet or running out to the garage every time somebody e-mails you with a question.

In addition to your marketing materials, you should also appropriate enough space for your administrative department. Accurate record-keeping is a must in any business, but even more so in import/export where documentation rules the day. You'll need at least one file cabinet to start with; you'll probably soon expand to two or more.

> **Beware!**
> Be sure to print and file hard copies of all e-mail correspondence that is sent to you and all missives you send to others. Keeping everything on your computer's hard drive may seem like a swell paper-saving idea, but if your computer crashes, you'll lose everything (including, temporarily, your mind). The same goes for computerized databases of customers, clients, distributors, and the like.

You'll also want a bookcase for your reference materials and a comfortable desk chair. If you have enough funds and room, a plump visitor's chair or sofa is a plus for those occasional business guests.

First Impressions

Even if your office is in your garage, your business still needs a professional image that tells potential clients and customers you're a savvy trader.

You can create this image on your own with desktop publishing. But as with deciding on a business name, be sure that the image you're beaming into the minds of buyers and clients is the one you want. Leave the over-the-top trendy or oh-so-cutesy images for other businesses. A logo featuring dancing skeletons with maracas won't quite cut it (although maracas do lend a Latin beat), and a cuddly teddy bear is not the best logo, either.

Your most important goal is to convey the impression of international trade efficiency and expertise. This is what you're selling. Have a friend or family member look over your designs before you commit to a print run of 500 cards or sheets of letterhead. Do they see typos? Amateurishness? Or do they catch the gleam of a business riding the waves of proficiency?

Likewise

If your office is in a commercial space, you'll need the same setup with plenty of room for all those files and your desk, chair, visitors' furniture, and a desk and chair for any employee(s) you may hire.

And let's not forget the electronics. Whether in a home or commercial office, your computer should occupy a place of honor away from dirt, drafts, and blinding sunlight. Ditto for your printer and fax machine.

In a commercial office, you'll also want that American office altarpiece, the coffee maker, and if you can provide a tidbit or two—a plate of cookies, for example, when you know guests are arriving—you'll go a long way toward cementing ties. Everyone appreciates a treat, and foreign visitors are usually eager to sample anything "American."

Of course, with a home office, you can still have coffee and cookies. Goodies are as close as your kitchen. So are all the other joys of home. And after all, isn't that one of the great perks of being able to work from home?

12

The Trader's Trumpet
Advertising and Marketing

As an international trader, your mission is sales—in two different but overlapping arenas: a) selling yourself and your company to clients as an import/export manager for their products, and b) selling the products themselves to representatives and distributors. Success in one of these arenas will contribute to your success in the other. Once you've established a favorable sales record with one client's goods, you'll have a track record with which to entice other clients. And, of course, each success will contribute to your own self-confidence, which will, in turn, lend that air of confidence to your negotiations with new prospects.

Chicken or Egg?

So which comes first, selling the product or yourself? In most cases, you'll need to sell your company first, because until you have a client's merchandise to represent, you're not going to get too far. Marketing your import/export management company involves two steps:

1. Convincing a prospective client that she has a product worth exporting
2. Persuading her to use your company as her export manager

Hunting for Exports

A surprisingly small percentage of domestic producers export their wares. So your marketing goal is to convince the huge remainder that they can increase profits by exporting—with your guidance—to specific target countries. You can accomplish this with direct mail and cold calls. If you're starting with imports, don't ignore this section—you'll work in basically the same manner.

Before you initiate contact with any manufacturer, you'll need to do some basic market research:

- What products are hot sellers in the domestic marketplace? Focus your attention on products that you know well or use yourself, or that are bestsellers in their market niches.
- Are these products hot sellers in your target countries?
- If not, are there situations or markets that would put these products in great demand if the products were available?
- Who manufactures these products?
- What is the selling price of each product—and of competing products or brands—domestically and in your target countries?

Direct-Mail Dazzle

Now you're ready to begin your direct-mail campaign. Choose one manufacturer of one of the products you have researched. Then call the company and ask for the name of the person to whom you will want to write. If the company is small, you will probably want the president or owner. If it's a larger concern, you might want to direct your letter to the vice president in charge of sales, the sales manager or the president or owner. By calling first to ask who the proper addressee is, you'll be assured of your letter reaching him or her instead of somebody else's wastebasket.

Armed with a name and title, write your letter, taking care to address the following points:

Smart Tip

Remember that your job will be easier if you approach manufacturers of products you know and believe in.

- Introduce yourself and your company.
- Briefly outline the potential of the overseas market.
- Outline the product's potential within that market.
- If possible, explain why and how your company, out of all others, will be able to position the product best. For example, if you have experience with like products, be sure to say so.
- If you already have contacts with foreign distributors, explain that you have foreign reps for overseas sales.
- Ask for a personal meeting to further discuss the possibilities.

Check out the sample letters on pages 194 and 195—one for the newbie with no experience in the product and one for the newbie with a background in the field.

Once your first letter is in the mail, sit down and write another one to another potential client in another product line, and then another, until you've exhausted your first set of preliminary market research products. It's best not to start with two clients that have the same type of products because if they both respond, you'll have to sell

Attracting Customers

International traders rarely use print ads to attract customers. Instead, they take advantage of the trade lead sources we've explored in Chapter 6 and throughout this book. But if you live in a trade-rich area, like Miami, you might choose to advertise in your local Yellow Pages, where hopeful manufacturers or vendors can look you up in a snap.

If you decide to go with a phone directory ad, look over the ads of your competitors and then go one better. Make yours stand out from the crowd with clever copy that tells what you do—for instance, products or regions in which you specialize—and why you excel.

▲

Sample Direct Sales Letter #1—Newbie with No Experience

Gum Tree Trading Company

123 Eucalyptus Lane
Sea Terrace, CA 92000, USA

July 5, 200x

Mr. Murray Mulch
President
Mulch Products Inc.
456 Tea Tree Street
Sea Terrace, CA 92000

Dear Mr. Mulch:

How would you like to exponentially increase your company's sales and expand your market with a minimum of time, trouble, and expense?

Sound impossible? It may not be. As owner of Gum Tree Trading Company, I am currently researching the profitable sales of mulch in the European market. As you may know, organic garden products are very popular in Europe, with sales continuously on the rise. I am familiar with your company's mulches, and after preliminary research, I believe they have tremendous export potential in this area.

To complete my research, I will need pricing information, any brochures and marketing information that you can offer, and a few sample bags of mulch, which I will send on to my foreign representatives.

If we find that we can sell your products profitably in Europe, we will handle all export details from shipping to distribution to securing payment. This is a terrific opportunity to increase your sales with little cost or risk to your firm. I will call you to discuss this exciting program in further detail.

Very best,

Andrea April

Andrea April
Gum Tree Trading Company

AA/ta

(000) 000-1234 (phone)—(000) 000-4567 (fax)
e-mail: GumTree@Holiday.com

Sample Direct Sales Letter #2—Newbie with Experience

Gum Tree Trading Company

123 Eucalyptus Lane
Sea Terrace, CA 92000, USA

July 5, 200x

Mr. Murray Mulch
President
Mulch Products Inc.
456 Tea Tree Street
Sea Terrace, CA 92000

Dear Mr. Mulch:

How would you like to exponentially increase your company's sales and expand your market with a minimum of time, trouble, and expense?

Sound impossible? It may not be. As owner of Gum Tree Trading Company, I am currently researching the profitable sales of mulch in the European market. As you may know, organic garden products are very popular in Europe, with sales continuously on the rise. I am familiar with your company's mulches, and after preliminary research, I believe they have tremendous export potential in this area.

To complete my research, I will need pricing information, any brochures and marketing information that you can offer, and a few sample bags of mulch, which I will send on to my foreign representatives.

If we find that we can sell your products profitably in Europe, we will handle all export details from shipping to distribution to securing payment. **With more than ten years of experience in garden product sales, I am confident that my company can sell your mulches.** This is a terrific opportunity to increase your sales with little cost or risk to your firm. I will call you to discuss this exciting program in further detail.

Very best,

Andrea April

Andrea April
Gum Tree Trading Company

AA/ta

(000) 000-1234 (phone)—(000) 000-4567 (fax)
e-mail: GumTree@Holiday.com

in competition with your own clients, which is both difficult and unfair. But once you've exhausted your first line of attack (and if you haven't achieved success), you can go back and try another client in the same product line.

Now wait a week or ten days. If you haven't heard from your first target manufacturer, give him a call. Ask to set up a meeting in his office to discuss your plan. Then call the next manufacturer and the next. If you're not familiar with sales, you may find this portion of the

Dollar Stretcher

If you can, target manufacturers within driving distance of your home office. This will keep your travel costs to a minimum.

I Wanna Sell Checklist

When you contact the manufacturer for the first time, you won't know whether you'll be able to handle her merchandise profitably. You'll have to find out its import or export price and then set up additional market research to determine how much sales potential you can realize from the product. So how do you accomplish this?

❑ Take one of the products you've already researched, one you know well and believe in or one that's a bestseller in its market niche.

❑ Contact the manufacturer and explain that you would like to sell her product abroad. Tell her you'll need to conduct some market research so you can find out all you can about the product, including cost, the trade channels she engages in, whether her company can provide any advertising assistance, what size orders she can fill, and how long it will take to fill orders.

❑ Perform a pricing analysis. How much can you sell the product for in a targeted country? What type of commission can you add? Can you keep the price competitive? Don't forget to figure your shipping costs, tariffs, and other operating expenses.

❑ Locate distributors or sales reps. Do they think they can sell the product at this price?

❑ Once you're satisfied that there's a viable market for the product, formulate an initial marketing plan.

❑ Get back to the manufacturer to work out the details and draw up a preliminary contract.

program a white-knuckler. Don't be nervous! You're legitimately offering these people a terrific opportunity. Not everyone is going to bite (not everyone can recognize a great deal when it jumps up and grabs them), but not everyone is going to turn you down, either. A "no thank you" now and then is part of the game.

(Cold-) Calling all Clients

Cold-calling, so-called because you call a potential client "cold," without any warming up by prior contact, is an alternative to the direct-mail approach. The good news is that if you're calling locally, it's usually cheaper than direct mail. The bad news is that it requires much more perseverance to be effective. The other good news, however, is that, done properly, a cold call can be much more effective than direct mail.

Before you make your first call, be sure you know what you want to say and how you want to say it. Some experts recommend writing out a sort of "script" that you can follow during the course of your call. This is a good starting-off exercise to help plan your spiel, but be aware of the fact that following a script has its drawbacks. The main one is that the person you're calling doesn't know he's supposed to be following the script, too, and when he gets off track, so do you.

A better idea is to discuss your marketing plan with everybody you can get to listen: your spouse or significant other, your parents or children (if they're old enough), your friends and even your obnoxious brother-in-law. Each time you tell somebody your ideas and the reasoning behind them, you're rehearsing for that cold call to a potential client. And each time someone raises an objection or points out a flaw (here is where the obnoxious brother-in-law comes in handy), it's an opportunity for you to either overcome the objection or revise your plan to compensate for the flaw. Then when you make your actual cold calls, you're well-versed in all sorts of responses. You know your stuff!

Check out the sample cold-call script on page 198. Don't try to follow it to the letter, but use it as a jumping-off point. And don't forget to communicate your enthusiasm!

Sample Cold-Call Script

Andrea: Hi, I'm Andrea April with Gum Tree Trading Company. We've been researching sales of organic mulch in Europe, and we think your products will sell very well there. May I take a few moments of your time to discuss this with you?

Mr. Mulch: I don't have time now.

Andrea: I understand. When would be a good time to call you back?

Mr. Mulch: I am really not interested. Wait a minute. Why do you think our products will sell well? Where in Europe?

Andrea: Europeans are much more environmentally conscious than we are, and they're also very into gardening, so organic products like yours are big sellers. We are seeing sales increasing by X percent annually, especially in Great Britain. We are also looking at France and Germany as excellent target markets.

Mr. Mulch: So why are you calling me?

Andrea: Because we would like to sell your products for you in Europe. We're an export management company. Are you familiar with this type of firm?

Mr. Mulch: No.

Andrea: Well, we will handle all the export details, from shipping to distribution to arranging for letters of credit, so you will be expanding your company's sales, your market, and your brand-name visibility at little cost to you.

Mr. Mulch: So what's the catch?

Andrea: None. We'll take a commission on our sales, but since this will come out of profits you would not have realized before this program, you'll still be way ahead of the game. And, of course, we'll have to complete our research before we can promise a deal. I will need you to provide me with pricing information, any brochures and marketing information you've got, and a few sample bags of mulch, which I'll send on to my foreign reps.

Mr. Mulch: You have people in England?

Andrea: Oh, yes. And in France and Germany as well. How about if I stop by your office later this week? I can show you our preliminary research, and we can discuss the program further.

Mr. Mulch: Europe, huh? I never thought about it. Sure. Let me have my secretary set up an appointment.

Desperately Seeking Imports

We've talked about how to find export products to send abroad. But what about imports? How do you go about finding goods to bring stateside? You have several options:

- Travel abroad on an import search mission.
- Wait for foreign manufacturers to contact you.
- Attend trade shows.
- Contact foreign embassies' trade development offices.
- Contact the U.S. Department of Commerce's International Trade Association.
- Track down leads on the internet and in trade publications.

Now, let's tackle these options one at a time.

Dear Manufacturer

eep these tips in mind when writing your direct-mail pieces:

○ *Try writing as if you're speaking to a friend.* You want your letter to sound professional, of course, but stiff and stodgy doesn't create interest. Keep it peppy!

○ *Insert a few details about the potential client's product and why the product will sell well abroad.* This lends credibility by demonstrating that you've done your homework. You know and understand the field at home and in your target market.

○ *Have you spelled the potential client's name and his company name correctly?* Goofing here will instantly telegraph that you don't know what you're talking about and/or that you don't pay attention to details.

○ *Do you have everything else spelled correctly, and is your grammar and punctuation fine-tuned?* If you're not a whiz at these things, hit your word processing program's spelling and grammar check key. After that, have someone who is a whiz look over your letter. (Electronic spelling and grammar checkers don't catch every error.)

○ *Remember to stick to the point.* Don't let your words wander.

The Travel Log

Traveling abroad is, in most people's minds, the most delightful of all these options. It's not always practical in terms of time, money, or other commitments you may have, such as your day job or family, but it's not a must, either, so don't fret if you can't manage it.

The big plus is that you can view foreign products in a realistic setting, checking out what sells where, why, and for how much. You

Beware!

Conventional imports, like the Swiss watches and Japanese electronics we've already mentioned, can be too high-profile for the newbie. Instead set your sights on something less established.

may know here at home, for example, that Swiss watches and Japanese electronics are top sellers, but so does everybody else. This knowledge is not necessarily going to shoot you to the top with a new and exciting product. But if you travel in Mexico, for example, you'll see that everybody on every street corner is savoring paletas, frozen Popsicle-type treats made with fresh fruit and cream. If you put this person-on-the-street observation together with your own domestic observation that smoothies—fresh fruit and yogurt frozen drinks—are the rage, you might decide that paletas could be a good import.

If you're interested in general merchandise, traveling in search of goods can be the best way to garner immediate results. As in domestic exporting, there are many manufacturers out there who have never considered selling their products in the United States, even though the market may be extremely profitable. And the most effective way to find these companies is through field research.

But keep this caveat in mind: Don't limit yourself by looking only at what products you want to import. Consider also what kinds of strategies you'll use to make your profits. Are you more interested in importing products with brand-name identities, or do you lean toward low price and high volume?

If you're going the low-price/high-volume route, you'll want to focus on countries that are low-cost-goods producers, like China, India, and Mexico. Because these

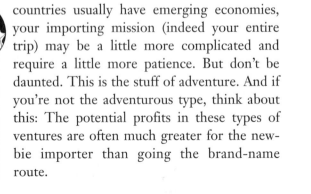

Trader's View

Jan H., the Belgian tire and clothing trader, gets most of his customers from one main source—hard work—which he breaks down into travel, trade shows, business magazines, and the internet.

countries usually have emerging economies, your importing mission (indeed your entire trip) may be a little more complicated and require a little more patience. But don't be daunted. This is the stuff of adventure. And if you're not the adventurous type, think about this: The potential profits in these types of ventures are often much greater for the newbie importer than going the brand-name route.

Just Call Me

Traveling in search of products to import is fun and lucrative, but experienced importers also rely on manufacturers contacting them. This method has two important bonuses: 1) You don't have to go anywhere to search for merchandise, and 2) you don't have to persuade anybody to export their merchandise. If they are contacting you, you know they are interested.

If you're brand-new to international trade, of course, this option is probably not going to do you much good because no one knows you're out there to contact. But as your company grows, as you make contacts all over the world, you'll find that other companies will come to you—often sooner and more frequently than you might imagine.

Not all your calls for help will come from manufacturers with a product to export. You'll also receive calls from importers seeking a particular U.S. product—sometimes merchandise with which you have no familiarity. Where do you go to fulfill their requests? One terrific source is the *Thomas Register of American Manufacturers*, a database of products and companies that boasts more than 700,000 manufacturers and distributors from 28 countries with 11,000 product categories. Access the register for free at www.thomasglobal.com.

Singles Dances

Trade shows are a terrific way to meet foreign manufacturers, distributors and representatives. Like church-sponsored singles dances, everybody there is in attendance for the purpose of attracting somebody else. So get out there and mingle!

Foreign trade shows or fairs, set up by foreign governments to showcase their own manufacturers, are held to tempt you, the potential importer. You'll have to travel abroad to attend some shows. Others come to you (or rather various locales in the United States). Call the embassy or consulate of the country you're interested in to find out when and if they have trade shows scheduled and where.

Dan S., the New Jersey trader, attended his first trade show in Manchester, England, and was delighted with the results. "I was able to get

Two-Way Street

Remember that you're on a two-way street—just as you're looking for merchandise to import, those foreign manufacturers and EMCs (export management companies) are seeking U.S. representation (that's you). Remember, too, that the foreign companies out seeking American reps will probably be looking at several companies. You'll have to convince them that yours is the one to go with. How?

○ Your knowledge of the product or field

○ Your sales contacts

○ Your sales track record; until you have a track record, use:

○ Your enthusiasm for the product

seven customers who were interested in what I was offering to sell," Dan says. "One of them saw my cables and said, 'You've got what I need, and I've got something that you need.'"

Toothpicks to Tires

While you're making those calls to consulates and embassies, ask for their trade development office. Many countries and geographic regions sponsor offices where you can find specific information on manufacturers of everything from toothpicks to truck tires to fur coats. Often a single phone call is all it takes to get a long list of suppliers eager to do business with American importers. Don't be shy—these people are on the job just to match you with a supplier back home. Let them get to work!

The U.S. government's International Trade Association can also help you locate various trade groups and development agencies that will help you find specific kinds of manufacturers or suppliers.

Trader's View

Dan S. came away from his first trade show feeling that it had been a very positive experience. But he's keeping his optimism guarded. "I never set my sights 110 percent," Dan says. "I sort of leave it at about 80 percent. With international trade, you're entering into another realm of business, done much differently than in the States."

Bounty Hunting

Like a good bounty hunter, you'll want to explore every avenue. Don't forget the many terrific online trade lead sites. For starters, check out:

- TradeNet at www. tradenet.com
- wtn-de.com at (guess where?) www.wtn-de.com
- National Trade Data Bank at www.stat-usa.gov
- Trade Key at www.tradekey.com

If you find something you like, send them a letter expressing your interest (see page 204).

Selling Yourself

You've located foreign manufacturers or suppliers whose products have U.S. sales potential. Now you have to sell them on the idea of entering the American marketplace and convince them that you're the person to usher them in. How do you do this? Basically, the same way you'll pitch domestic manufacturers, with a direct-mail campaign. Only in this case, you'll do better to think of it as a direct fax letter. Although many traders rely on international mail, unless you're sending to regions or countries with highly developed infrastructures, such as Western Europe or Canada, you'll be much more assured of your missive reaching its destination if you send it by fax.

In your letter, outline the various opportunities available in the United States for the product and highlight that you'll handle all import logistics with little cost to the manufacturer. Check out the sample letter on page 207. Notice that this letter is very similar to the domestic one, with two exceptions:

1. We've addressed the owner of the company as Monsieur (abbreviated M.) instead of "Mr." Even though the letter is in English, this little touch shows that you know something about the French language and that you've taken the care and courtesy to address M. Picard in his own tongue.

2. We've checked to make sure we've eliminated any slang that may be confusing to non-natives.

International Call

Follow up in a few days with another fax. Think of the follow-up as a firm but gentle nudge, an opportunity to strengthen your position and demonstrate real interest in

> ## Trader's View
> "Don't think having a good product alone will boost sales!" cautions German Michael R. "You have to do marketing and set aside a corresponding amount of time for that [task]."

Sample Trade Lead Response Letter

Treasure Bay Traders
789 Seekers Cove
Sea Terrace, CA 92000, USA

July 5, 200x

Mr. Nigel Owens
Managing Director
Sterling Frames Ltd.
62 Gosham Street
Chipping Huntbridge, Sussex, England

Dear Mr. Owens:

We are responding to your trade lead, which we viewed with great enthusiasm on the International Trade Data Network. We are very interested in importing fine English interior design products such as your sterling silver frames. Our research shows a great demand for this type of product in the American market and, although we are a newer trading company, we are positioning ourselves as a leader in European interior design imports.

Please send us your current catalog and best export prices, along with any samples you feel would help us promote your products. Please feel free to contact me to discuss any questions you may have.

Very best,

Eric Williams

Eric Williams
Treasure Bay Traders

EW/ta

(000) 000-1234 (phone)—(000) 000-4567 (fax)
e-mail: TreasureBay@Holiday.com

importing the merchandise. Check out the sample follow-up letter on page 208. Remember that part of your task is to convince the potential client that your company is the best one for the job, so you have to supply a reason for this. If you can't claim, as Andrea does in the sample letter, that you're experienced in interior design (or mulch or whatever) sales in the United States and Europe (or wherever), then come up with something else. Maybe you're only experienced in the United States so far. That's fine! That's where you'll be selling. Maybe you're not experienced yet, but you've done a great deal of research. Fill that in instead. Use your creativity!

If you know the potential client speaks English or if you speak his language, try a phone call instead of a fax. Just remember: When calling non-native English speakers, talk a little slower and a lot more clearly—most people tend to mumble or slur speech, which makes it difficult for foreign ears to comprehend.

The Marketing Plan

Whether you're planning on exporting or importing, be prepared to present your prospective client with a marketing plan. If the manufacturer is close to home, you'll naturally present it in person. If she's overseas, you may still have to (make that get to) arrange a personal visit to close the deal. If you feel strongly enough about the product's U.S. potential, the trip will be worth the time and expense.

To prepare your marketing plan, you'll need the information you've already asked for: pricing, product brochures or literature, and samples. If your prospect balks at supplying these materials, tell her that you'll need them to further explore the market potential and develop a presentation for her, outlining the market strategy you plan to pursue.

Once you have the materials in your office, sit down and figure out every possible expense you'll have so that you can arrive at your sales price. (Take another look at Chapter 9 for a review of how to do this.) Then, if you've already been in contact with distributors or representatives, find out if this price will sell in their market. If you don't have any reps yet, you'll need to locate one (see "Pursuing the Perfect Rep" section) and determine if he can work with that price. Assuming the answer is yes, you've got a viable product.

Now write out your marketing plan, which should include the following:

> **Tip...**
>
> ## Smart Tip
> To make an international call, dial the international code, 011, followed by the country code, the city code, and then the local number. You can find the country and city codes in your local phone book. To make sure you're not making that call at midnight your client's time, check out time zones for hundreds of international cities at www.worldtimeserver.com.

Money Talks

If the merchandise you're interested in isn't branded (doesn't carry a brand-name), copyrighted, or otherwise restricted in some way, perhaps your best profit potential lies in acting as an import merchant. You'll purchase the goods outright and then sell them to your own distributors. Provided you have the necessary capital and marketing power, your contact with the foreign supplier will be geared more toward negotiation. Ask that all relevant information, such as price and terms of quote and financial requirements, be in written form.

If you're serious about buying, most foreign suppliers will be eager to talk. But make sure the price quoted will give you enough room to make an acceptable profit. And when you're ready to buy, be prepared for a letter of credit. Virtually every overseas supplier will want one, especially if you're a first-time customer.

- *Target.* Which country or countries will you or your representatives sell in? Why are these markets viable? Include positive market research information and be sure to assemble it in a clear, concise, easy-to-digest format. This is where your desktop publishing programs will shine—you can make charts, graphs, and tables interspersed with facts, figures, and text.
- *Sales.* Explain at what price you'll sell the product, give your annual sales forecast, your fee structure, and the profits the manufacturer can expect.
- *Marketing.* Briefly touch on any special marketing or promotions for the product, for example, foreign or domestic trade shows or any local advertising your reps will do.

We Now Present

Your presentation package must look professional. Use those desktop publishing programs and your own creativity to develop the following elements:

- Your marketing plan
- Your company brochure with a current client list (when you have one)
- A personal resume highlighting any background relevant to the product or to sales or international trade

Now make up a cover page with the title *Export Marketing Plan for Mulch Products Inc.* (or whatever company) centered about one-fourth

Beware!
Your exact distribution and marketing plans are your trade secret. Don't give your prospect anything but a general outline. Let him rely on you!

Sample Foreign Sales Letter

Gum Tree Trading Company

123 Eucalyptus Lane
Sea Terrace, CA 92000, USA

July 5, 200x

M. John Pierre Picard
Picard & Fils et Cie
456 Rue des Matins
75007 Paris, France

Dear M. Picard:

How would you like to exponentially increase your company's sales and expand your market at almost no cost?

Does this seem impossible? It may not be. As owner of Gum Tree Trading Company, I am currently researching the profitable sales of European mirrors in the United States. As you may know, these interior design products are very popular in America. I am familiar with your company's high quality mirrors, and after preliminary research, I believe they have tremendous export potential.

To complete my research, I will need pricing information, any brochures and marketing information that you can offer, and a few sample mirrors.

If we find that we can sell your products profitably in the United States, we will handle all export details from shipping to distribution to securing payment. This is a terrific opportunity to increase your sales with little cost or risk to your firm. I look forward to hearing from you soon to discuss this exciting program in further detail.

Very best,

Andrea April

Andrea April
Gum Tree Trading Company

AA/ta

(000) 000-1234 (phone)—(000) 000-4567 (fax)
e-mail: GumTree@Holiday.com

Sample Foreign Sales Follow-Up Letter

Gum Tree Trading Company

123 Eucalyptus Lane
Sea Terrace, CA 92000, USA

July 5, 200x

M. John Pierre Picard
Picard & Fils et Cie
456 Rue des Matins
75007 Paris, France

Dear M. Picard:

I am writing to follow up on the fax I sent last week. My company is very interested in representing your fine mirrors in the United States. I would like to repeat that this is a terrific opportunity for your company. We would purchase directly from you and handle all export details ourselves.

We are experienced in interior design product sales in the United States and in Europe. I will call you to discuss this exciting program.

Very best,

Andrea April

Andrea April
Gum Tree Trading Company

AA/ta

(000) 000-1234 (phone)—(000) 000-4567 (fax)
e-mail: GumTree@Holiday.com

of the way down the page. A few inches below it, center your company name. You can put your logo below this if you've designed one. Put this package in a folder or binder. You'll find several styles to choose from at just about any office supply store. Make sure the one you go with looks stylish and professional—a good choice would be the kind with a black plastic and metal slide and a clear plastic cover through which your cover page will be visible.

> **Beware!**
> Make absolutely certain everything in your marketing plan is spelled correctly and is grammatically correct. Typos and grammar goofs will make you look amateurish and inattentive to detail.

Take a Meeting

Arrive at the presentation looking as sharp and professional as your marketing plan. Even if you live in a casual area where shorts and T-shirts are the norm, put on a power suit. Be prompt—tardiness is a sure way to put the kibosh on your chances for success. It demonstrates that you don't have a lot of respect for your prospective client and that you're not very efficient, neither of which is going to make you a golden boy or girl in the eyes of your target person.

Once behind the target's office door, you'll present your pitch. Be sure to cover:

- your fee structure
- how cost-effective exporting the product can be
- the potential returns the manufacturer will realize
- any costs involved to export the product, i.e., any special labeling or marking, export packing

Good News/Bad News

Pitching yourself as a sales representative who's working on commission, you probably won't be able to close a deal on the first or even second call. As an alternative, you may want to offer yourself as a distributor. The good news here is that it's easier to convince the manufacturer to go with you—he doesn't have to put out money for commissions or anything else except a few samples. The bad news is that buying the product yourself will add a sizable amount to your start-up costs. If you strongly believe in the product, however, and you have the funds (or can get a loan for them), this is one way to position yourself in the trade channel.

Remember that your angle is:

- Exporting opens additional markets to the manufacturer at very little cost to him.
- You'll handle all logistics, from shipping through documentation to the securing of payment and documentation.
- All he has to do is fulfill the orders you'll bring in and prepare them for shipment.

Shake on It

After your brilliant sales presentation, your prospect is anxious to shake on the deal and get exporting. Close by having him sign a sole representative contract, which you've already had your attorney draw up, and which you've cleverly brought along. This contract should cover the various guidelines of the agreement, including:

- Responsibility for promoting the product
- Territory
- Method and times of commission payments
- Handling methods required for letters of credit
- Any necessary product modification
- Annual sales forecasts

Getting the Product Out

You've successfully landed a client with a perfect product to sell and you've determined which countries you're going to sell it in. Now comes the next phase of the game—getting your product into the marketplace and generating those sales. This is a biggie. Even if your business organization is rock-solid, you're not going to earn a cent if the product sits on the proverbial shelf.

While import sales are essentially a hands-on affair, including cold-calling and meeting with retailers and wholesalers, export sales are much more difficult to organize—after all, you're dealing in foreign territory. This is why exporters often rely on foreign sales representatives or distributors. How you decide to set up your distribution network depends on what you're selling and how closely you want to be involved with sales.

You don't have to hire anybody—lots of exporters run the whole show themselves. But if you do decide to go with a rep, remember that these people will represent your client and his product to everyone in the trade channel down to the end user. And since you are the manufacturer's representative, your rep's performance will be a direct reflection on not only the client and the product, but on you and your company as well.

Loose Lips

Remember the old World War II adage "Loose lips sink ships"? Don't offer too many specifics when you're presenting your marketing plan, for two reasons:

1. *You're giving away trade secrets.* Although most of your prospects will be earnest and honest, there's always that one somebody who's not. If you tell all, this person may feel that he has no reason to work with you. You've explained your entire strategy, so now he can go out and do the same thing himself.

2. *Keep 'em hooked.* Your presentation should be something like the teaser on your favorite TV show, the one that airs before the opening credits. Its purpose is to hook your interest so that you'll stick with the program. Yours is to get your potential client excited about your program and to feel that if he sticks with you, he'll see exciting results. If you spill all the beans, you'll lose this advantage.

So—assuming you're going to hire sales help—which specific conduits in the trade channel will be most effective for you?

The three most common options for the export management company are:

- Sell direct to foreign markets (hire your own people to work in the country as sales representatives).
- Hire a commission representative or representative company.
- Work with a distributor.

The best trade channel options for the importer are:

- Manufacturer's representatives
- Distributors
- Retailers

> ## Trader's View
> Make sure everything is spelled out in clear terms. Bruno C., the French trader, cautions, "Be very precise in terms of your contract."

Selling Nozzles

Before we go any further, let's slip back into the trade channel and review the various conduits:

- *Representative.* This is a person who can work alone or as part of a company with various reps on board; she makes sales calls for you to wholesale or retail buyers.

Show Off

Your brochure is a terrific sales and marketing tool. Use it to give a brief explanation of what your company does and the tremendous benefits your clients will receive when they export through you. You may want to include a client list (when you have one) as well as some significant items of appeal to your prospects, like your experience in specific markets and/or products and a brief synopsis of your company's overall performance. If you can include a testimonial or two from current clients, so much the better.

Keep it short and sweet. Graphics design is most effective when your text is surrounded by a fair amount of blank space. If you cram too much information into the relatively small area of a brochure, you lose your audience's attention at first glance.

When she's solicited a sale, she passes it on to you. In most cases, you then send the merchandise directly to the buyer. A typical representative's commission is 5 percent of the cost of the goods, but this varies slightly from one part of the world to another and from product to product.

- *Distributor.* A company that buys your goods and resells them to a retailer or other representative for further distribution through the channel until the product reaches the end user; a distributor—who determines his own sales price for your product—may wait until sales have accumulated before buying the merchandise, or he may purchase the merchandise upfront and warehouse it, thus acting as a wholesaler. You won't have as much control as you would with a representative, but you will not have as many worries because the distributor will handle all advertising, promotions, returns, and customer service.

- *Manufacturer's representative.* This is a salesperson who specializes in a specific product or line of complementary products, for example, home electronics (televisions sets, radios, CD players, and sound systems). He often provides additional product assistance, such as warehousing and technical service. He can work alone or as part of an agency or "stable" of reps, in which case each rep

> **Tip...**
>
> **Smart Tip**
>
> When seeking a representative, compare before you choose and aim for one who's familiar with sales in your product arena. This way you're assured that she already has valuable contacts in the industry, contacts it could take an outsider years to achieve.

divides his selling time among the various products promoted by the agency. This allows you to field a regional or national sales force without expending any capital. The downside, however, is that since these people carry a variety of product lines, yours may end up at the bottom.

> **Smart Tip**
>
> Distributors should be placed under contract with specific clauses ensuring that they maintain adequate facilities and personnel to service the product.

- *Retailer.* The ultimate distributor who sells to the end user

- *Direct sales.* An anomalous offshoot of the trade channel direct sales can work for products with a very limited market in which each sale is substantial. If you're selling jet engine nozzles, for example, you can easily send out your own reps to pitch jet engine manufacturers—there aren't all that many out there. When you make a sale, you'll probably be assured of repeat business—there aren't too many nozzle suppliers, either. But for most products, the markets are so large and complex that this method is just not feasible.

Pursuing the Perfect Rep

Finding the perfect sales rep is just as important as finding that perfect manufacturer and product. Since some reps are better than others at pitching different types

Exclusively Yours

In your negotiations with the manufacturer, ask for exclusive distribution rights, at least for the area you'll be selling in. Many companies look for three-year exclusive rights at first, with the stipulation that this right is renewable each year thereafter. If you're selling products for a manufacturer who doesn't have any U.S. sales yet, you may think this is not a problem—but it can be. Once you do your job and the product is selling like mad, another importer may come along, approach "your" manufacturer and undercut your prices. So ask for an exclusive contract right from the beginning before you have competition to worry about.

If the manufacturer is afraid to give you a three-year exclusive, try negotiating. You can sign an agreement, for example, stipulating that if you sell X amount of product within a specified time period, you'll retain exclusive rights.

Trader's View

A distributor acting as a wholesaler, buying your imported merchandise and warehousing it before accumulating sales, is sometimes called an import house.

of products, the trick lies in choosing one that best complements your particular type of merchandise. If you plan to sell in more than one corner of the world, you may need to locate several representatives. If your target countries are all in close proximity, however, you'll do better to find a distribution company or rep that can handle them all.

So where do you find these perfect people? If you're talking exports, for starters, go back to Chapter 6 and take another look at the wonderful services offered by the ITA's Commercial Service, including the Agent/Distributor Service and the NTDB. Other foreign rep sources include:

- Freight forwarders and customs brokers
- Trade associations in the countries you are targeting
- Foreign consulates, embassies, and trade offices
- American chambers of commerce abroad
- International Yellow Pages (which you can find on the internet)
- International trade publications

Sources for domestic distributors and representatives include:

- Domestic trade associations, publications, and journals that cover your product's industry
- Referrals from your international banker
- Manufacturer's Agents National Association (see the Appendix for contact information)
- Your local phone directory or directories for target cities all over the United States
- U.S. and state trade centers

Interview Kit

After you've compiled a list of reputable distributors or representatives, the real work begins: choosing the best one for your company and products. Interview your prospects with as much care as you'd take to interview prospective employees. A good place to start is with a sort of interview in a kit, a three-part packet consisting of a one-page fact sheet, product literature, and a questionnaire. You should prepare a packet for

Bright Idea

You might consider mail order as a distribution source for your imported product. For all the details, order up Entrepreneur Press' *Start Your Own Mail Order Business*.

each client and have enough printed so that you can pop them in the mail or pass them out as the need arises.

The fact sheet should outline your client's commission structure, agreement policies, and company information so that each prospective rep has a snapshot of who he'll be dealing with and what he can expect as compensation. The questionnaire, which you'll ask prospects to fill out and return to you, is designed to elicit as much pertinent information as you could possibly need. Check out the sample on page 216.

Once you receive a prospect's questionnaire, make sure you check references. Find out if other companies that deal with this rep are satisfied with the relationship. Delve into what size territory the rep is most capable of covering—you don't want one with a tendency to bite off more than he can chew.

> ### Smart Tip
>
> If a prospect doesn't return the questionnaire, call or fax him with a friendly nudge. If you still don't receive a response, cross him off your list. A person who doesn't take the time to respond to a potential associate is probably not going to take the time to do a good job, either.

Persistence Pays!

What's it really like out there in the international trader's hot seat? How does it feel to knock on virtual doors around the world? For Bruno C., it's an exciting but bumpy ride. "I use different written elements as well as the international business opportunities you can find on different internet sites," the French trader explains. "So far, the results are quite a disappointment since I often compete with some very large companies and holdings that have their own agents nearly everywhere on the globe. On the other hand, when I get in touch with some companies interested in importing, I:

1. Don't receive any answer in spite of some repetitive relaunchings.
2. 'Arrive' too late because of my labor of gathering information for a proposal. It sometimes takes a lot of time and is sometimes impossible to find in spite of the incredible wealth of internet material.
3. Receive a rejection of my offer.
4. Receive a fax or letter that thanks me for the quotation and informs me that they won't need me for some time because they're [developing] the company.
5. Persist and—sometimes—IT WORKS!!!

Product Representative Questionnaire

Name _____

Company name _____

Address _____

_____

Phone number _____

E-mail address _____

1. What import products do you handle? _____
_____
_____

2. What export products do you handle? _____
_____
_____

3. Where do you make the majority of your sales? _____
_____
_____

4. How do you prefer to work (as distributor, sales rep, manufacturer's rep)?
_____

5. What territories do you cover? _____
_____

6. What commission would you feel comfortable with? _____
_____

7. Do you work on your own, or do you have a company? If so, how many branches and salespeople do you have? _____
_____
_____
_____

Product Representative Questionnaire, continued

8. Please list pertinent bank references, including address, phone number, and contact person: _____

_____

_____

_____

9. Please list at least three client references, including address, phone number or e-mail address, and contact person: (Use reverse for more, if necessary.)

a. _____

_____

b. _____

_____

c. _____

_____

10. May we have some details on your professional history if you work on your own, or on your company history?

Number of employees: _____

Years in business: _____

Annual sales: _____

Assets: _____

Liabilities: _____

Net worth: _____

11. Please list any other information you feel would be helpful to us in considering you to represent our client:

_____

_____

_____

You should now meet your prospect in person. You can find out if you really click, and you can size up the way he handles himself in a one-on-one situation rather than on paper. If you're in two different countries, however, and your budget simply won't stretch for an in-person meeting, be sure to conduct a phone interview.

> **Tip...**
>
> **Smart Tip**
>
> Granting the rep exclusive rights is a good way to give her a start-off perk and develop that winning relationship.

Sign on the Dotted Line

When you've decided which reps you want on your team, it's time to sign on the dotted line. You need a written agreement or contract to clarify their responsibilities and duties as well as yours. We strongly advise that you consult an attorney familiar with international law—especially as a newbie—since you might overlook details that could turn into Excedrin headaches down the line.

The specific details of each agreement will vary from one situation to another, but they should all include these types of basics:

- *Responsibilities of the distributor or representative and your responsibilities.* Make sure these are clearly delineated and spelled out. This will be a legally binding contract.

- *Term of contract.*

- *Compensation.*

- *Any bonus or incentive programs.*

- *Territory.* Does the distributor or rep have exclusive or nonexclusive rights to the territory? This is an important consideration. Most reps prefer to have exclusive rights to market your product in a given territory.

- *Pricing.* This is often the most significant variable determining sales success. Price your product carefully, neither too high nor too low. Remember that your representative will earn a specific percentage, while a distributor will buy at the prevailing wholesale market price.

- *Warranty and returns.* Who's responsible for returns or repairs? What is the policy? This can be a critical section of your agreement, depending, of course, on what you're selling. Also consider whether you'll need product liability insurance.

- *Does the rep have the right to use trademarks, patents, and copyrights in advertising?* Make sure the product doesn't require or infringe on any of these intellectual property rights.

- *Marketing and advertising.* Spell out who's responsible. Remember that you or the manufacturer may have to defray some of these costs.

- *Record-keeping.* Both parties should keep sales and other pertinent records and reserve the right to examine each other's documents.
- *Language.* What language in the agreement is legally binding?
- *Contract termination.* Give yourself an out. If the rep fails to meet certain requirements, for example, a minimum number of sales within a specified period, you can terminate the contract.

At 'Em Advertising

Although your main concern is finding buyers to distribute the product abroad or domestically, you don't want to drop your responsibility for further promoting the product. Ultimately, your success depends on how well the product sells to the end user. Some products may not require advertising, for example, imported handcrafts that sell in specialty stores and boutiques. Others, like certain food products or even organic mulches that may face stiff competition in the marketplace, may benefit from advertising campaigns.

Advertising is a major expense. The distributors you deal with and their distributors or reps along the trade channel may not have much in the way of advertising budgets. These people will also probably be dealing with several product lines in addition to yours, which means they may not be spending the ad dollars they have on your merchandise. In such a scenario, you may want to initiate a cooperative advertising program with the manufacturer.

Co-op advertising will not only reduce your distributors' advertising expenses but will also promote your client's product. It's a cost-efficient and effective way for both the manufacturer and retailer or distributor to reach their target markets.

Although co-op advertising policies differ among manufacturers, most are written so that the manufacturer pays a portion of the advertising costs and supplies the retailer with material to include in the ad whether it's print, radio, or television.

Banana Peels

You may need to give your manufacturer some major guidance in his advertising campaign. An ad blitz that takes this country by storm may fall flat or even backfire in another country. The annals of international trade are filled with horror stories of novice companies

Smart Tip

Tip...

Make sure your agreement contains a clause outlining what happens if you and your rep disagree about the terms of the contract. Most such contracts stipulate arbitration by the International Chamber of Commerce.

who slipped on figurative banana peels because they didn't understand the cultures of the countries they were selling in.

Make sure you, your manufacturer, and his advertising agency take these kinds of issues into consideration:

Bright Idea

Clever, consumer-friendly tags add to the buyer's perception of a product's value. Artisans who sell at crafts shows and gift boutiques, for instance, have found that a piece that carries a tag describing the artist and the craft will sell for a higher price than one with no tag.

- *Language.* Don't try to translate things literally. Some slang and colloquialisms have no direct translation; others transmogrify into something ridiculous, rude, or both. When you translate, make sure your words are grammatically correct.

- *Cultural taboos.* In many countries, particularly Islamic ones, states of undress that we may think look alluring in advertising art will come across as lewd, lascivious, and possibly even illegal.

- *Colors and symbols.* Colors mean different things to different peoples. White is the color of mourning in China; in some tropical countries, green implies danger. The thumbs-up sign is rude in Australia, and in Argentina, the OK sign (thumb and index finger inscribing a circle) has lewd connotations.

- *Educational levels.* In emerging countries where literacy levels are low, print ads are not going to get you very far. Try another media instead.

Look for the Label

Another way to either slip on a banana peel or tap dance to the top is through labeling. Although almost every product imported into the United States by law requires a "made in wherever" label, not every product needs a fancy or informative one. Those French mirrors, for instance, may not need any supplemental verbiage, while the organic mulch will probably benefit from a bag that extols its environmental virtues.

You'll have to decide how important labeling is based on each product and the country it's being sold in, although it can always be a benefit. You'll want to impress upon your clients that this is a terrific way to build goodwill and additional advertising among both dealers and consumers. You'll have to let them know that they may need to have their labels translated and reprinted into the target language. They may also have to convert sizes and measurements to the metric system so local consumers can understand them.

Labels also serve to let the consumer know how to use and care for the product. Informative labels increase sales of better-quality products. And this helps small manufacturers with a superior product overcome some of the effects of extensive advertising by larger competitors.

Cruise Control

"**W**e don't have an advertising budget," says Peter P., the frozen-foods trader. "As a company, we have two approaches. We can develop a private-label proprietary business for our group, or we can offer our services as a distributor and market and advertise global companies, like Procter & Gamble, that want to sell their product in Russia.

"We can say, 'Here we are. We're a distributor. We know Russia,'" Peter explains. "'We've got distributors around the country, and we can put together a marketing proposal for you. Here's what it's going to cost. Are you interested?'"

"People bite," the Atlanta-based trader says, "and then we run the program, control the pricing, control the process to the end user. We get our advertising support directly from the companies whose products we're advertising in Russia.

Public Relations Patter

Once you land your first clients, you should continue to promote yourself to them and to new prospects and your community through public relations. You can use materials garnered from your brochure, your copious market research, and your own import/export experiences to publish articles in pertinent industry association journals or to give talks for local business associations. Remember that word-of-mouth is a powerful advertising tool. Each person who reads your article or hears you speak is a potential client.

Join industry organizations, as Peter P.'s company did. "As a company that's interested in agribusiness," Peter says, "we do some public relations in Washington. We are [also] members of a few organizations, one being the USA Poultry and Egg Export Council, known as USAPEEC [pronounced yoos-a-peek]."

How about going live on the air? Volunteer yourself for a local radio station's "business time" chat show. Listeners can call in and ask questions about international trade.

If you are aware of a promotional event in town where you think industry manufacturers or suppliers might show up, say, at an industry-specific charity event, offer to help. If the event is in aid of an environmental cause and your services are green—you are selling or distributing environment-friendly products, for example—you can point this out. The main benefit of attending these events is that you can meet potential clients, shake their hands, and become a familiar face. Then when you call on

▲

Hand in Glove

Don't forget that your manufacturer will have to do some specific marking and labeling to meet government and shipping regulations, ensure proper handling, and help receivers identify shipments. Also remember that certain products that fall under regulatory guidelines must be clearly marked as such.

If you're importing latex gloves, for example, that have not been approved for medical use, you can't use the description "exam gloves" in any way. If you do, the Food and Drug Administration folks will hold your shipment until you change each inner box and outer carton to read "industrial use" or "general purpose." Your customs broker will be able to tell you about these sorts of regulations, but it's your responsibility to forward the information to your supplier.

them, you will have a common ground. You can say, "Remember me? We met at the Save the Spotted Owl Charity Picnic."

Service that Customer

In international trade, your customer service procedures fall into three categories: representatives, retailers, and end users. Like everything else in import/export, these categories overlap. By servicing one, you'll be helping the others. And the best way to do this is through dealer assistance programs. Here you supply your representatives with a variety of informational aids and materials. One set is designed to help the rep land the account:

- Catalogs
- Price lists
- Sales letters
- Any perks you can think up, like in-store posters or sample merchandise giveaways

The next set of materials is designed to help the retail customer sell to the end user:

- Product management aids
- Display aids and ideas
- Stock control plans
- Sales promotion kits

Web Presence

Many traders, including John L. in Brazil, Michael R. in Germany, and Dan S. in New Jersey, have their own web sites. "To be present on the web is a key point for any small business," says John—and with good reason. In the year since he launched his site, the Brazilian trader has signed on several clients who found his company through a web search.

In Germany, Michael went with a web presence for two reasons. "I wanted to be found worldwide," he says, "and to give others general information so as not to answer every question again and again."

And it's worked. "This year I made about 40 percent of the turnover of a normal year [just from the web site]," Michael explains of the site he's had for almost two years. "I suggest that every international trade client set up a site."

"It's quite amazing how much power the web contains," says Dan. Plug into the power yourself. You can create your own site, as Michael and Dan did, or, like John, you can hire a web designer.

Aside from these kinds of materials, your customer service program should emulate that of any domestic program. Your reps need to know that if they or someone further down the trade channel has a problem with the product, the manufacturer will take care of it. In instances where you're acting as a distributor and you've purchased the product outright, you'll either have to handle after-market problems and servicing yourself or write some kind of servicing into your contract with the manufacturer.

Bright Idea

Use your experience to teach others, a terrific way to get your name used in connection with the term "expert." Give an international trade seminar at a local college. Or, like Wahib W., lend advice to local manufacturers you're not interested in representing. "We were an advisor on the phone or if we had time, we showed them how to do it [just] to be friendly," he says. It all helps!

More Trade Dollars
Effectively Controlling Your Finances

Whether you are a chronic number-cruncher or one of the finance-phobic, you'll want to give your company periodic financial checkups. "Why?" you ask. "I already did all that math stuff in the start-up chapter." That was the pre-flight exam for the wonderful cargo carrier that's your business. When you've gone through all the checks and safety precautions of starting up and your fledgling operation is in full flight, you'll want to conduct periodic safety checks to make sure your business is as healthy as you imagine.

If there's a problem, you'll find out before it becomes critical. For instance, if you discover that your commission fees barely cover your travel expenses, you can change gears and raise your commission rate before signing another client at the same too-low rate. You can also take measures like depending more on faxes than international phone calls, cutting back on travel, or axing those gorgeous but expensive 95-color brochures from the print shop in favor of those churned out by your own printer.

Financial checkups don't have to be negative. They can give you a rosy glow by demonstrating how well you're doing—possibly even better than you expected. If you've been saving for a new printer or market research trip, or if you're hoping to take on an employee, you can judge how close you are to achieving that goal.

Making a Statement

An income statement, also called a profit-and-loss statement, charts the revenues and operating costs of your business over a specific period of time, usually a month. Check out the income statements on pages 228 and 229 for two more hypothetical import/export services, Trade Winds Imports and Fair Trade Exports. Trade Winds handles $684,000 worth of business annually, while Fair Trade breezes along with $2,193,600 of annual business.

Trade Winds, a one-man band, is owner-operated and has its home base in the guest bedroom. Fair Trade has one full-time employee, an administrative assistant, and makes its base in a 900-square-foot downtown office. Neither owner draws a salary; they both rely on a percentage of the net profit for their income.

Both companies operate on a commission basis, with the owners taking their compensation from pretax net profits.

You'll want to tailor your income statement to your particular business. To make the statement really right, you'll need to prorate items that are paid annually, such as business licenses, tax-time accounting fees, or Stat-USA subscriptions, and pop those figures into your monthly statement. For example, if you pay an annual Stat-USA fee of $175, divide this figure by 12 and add the resulting $14.58 to your subscriptions expense. Use the worksheet on page 230 to chart your own income statement. You'll be surprised how much fun finances can be!

Sad Experience

One issue that can vitally affect your finances is the extension of credit to your customers. Virtually any business beyond the level of street vending is forced into making credit-term decisions early on. As an international trader, you'll find yourself faced with those same decisions. As you start out, however, a large part of the problem will be lifted from your shoulders by virtue of the letter of credit. Since the tried-and-true L/C is an intrinsic part of the import/export world, your customers will take it for granted. This is how they pay you—upfront through the international bank.

But as your company grows and you and your customers get to know each other, they may begin to ask for credit terms. Sometimes it's difficult not to extend credit. Your customer may want to purchase exactly what you want to sell in an amount that's too sweet to resist. But he also wants 60 days credit before he pays. How you respond is up to you. In Belgium, Jan H. accepts only L/Cs and one other form of payment. "Due to many, many sad experiences," he says, "[I take] cash or irrevocable letter of credit only!"

In Germany, Michael R. accepts several different payment forms. "If the customer is buying merchandise, we agree for [starters] on a secure payment by L/C and/or bank draft," Michael explains. "Later we take payment as per an agreement or contract to be made. With bigger businesses, we may take financing in various percentages."

If you choose to extend credit, remember that any time you do, you're allowing your customer to use your money interest-free. This can be a good way to extend goodwill and build customer loyalty, but it can also be a good way to lose your shirt. Make sure that your cash flow can cover the credit period before you say OK. And make as sure as you can that your customer can come up with the funds when due.

How do you do this? By any one of several means:

- Ask your banker to investigate.
- Order a report from a service like Dun & Bradstreet, which has more than 100 million business records on file.
- Request a World Traders Data Report from your local U.S. Department of Commerce district office.

Banking Buddies

From your first import/export venture, you should get used to thinking of your bank as a buddy—after all, you're going to be working with the folks down at the branch a lot as you fulfill letters of credit. Your international banker should also be able to help you:

- Locate new overseas markets
- Develop data on the business climate in the country to which you're planning exports
- Introduce you by mail or phone to banking and trade contacts abroad

Smart Tip

Why not just ask the customer to fill out a credit report? In some countries, such a request is considered rude.

▲

Trade Winds Imports Income Statement

Income Statement
For the month of July 200x

Monthly Income

Gross sales	$57,000.00	
Cost of sales	50,160.00	

Gross Monthly Income   **$6,840.00**

Monthly Expenses

Rent	$ 0.00
Phone/utilities	168.00
Postage/delivery	39.00
Licenses/taxes	279.00
Employees	0.00
Benefits/taxes	0.00
Advertising/promotions	507.00
Legal services	108.00
Accounting services	165.00
Office supplies	86.00
Transportation/travel	450.00
Insurance	143.00
Subscriptions/dues	17.00
Miscellaneous	100.00

Total Monthly Expenses   **$2,062.00**

Net Monthly Profit   **$4,778.00**

Note: Cost of sales refers to the cost of the product as well as all documentation required to complete all trade transactions.

Fair Trade Exports Income Statement

Income Statement
For the month of July 200x

Monthly Income

Gross sales	$182,000.00	
Cost of sales	155,380.00	
Gross Monthly Income		**$26,620.00**

Monthly Expenses

Rent	$1,143.00	
Phone/utilities	192.00	
(add $60 cell phone charge)		
Postage/delivery	110.00	
Licenses/taxes	731.00	
Employees	2,011.00	
Benefits/taxes	302.00	
Advertising/promotions	1,462.00	
Legal services	192.00	
Accounting services	366.00	
Office supplies	137.00	
Transportation/travel	1,280.00	
Insurance	292.00	
Subscriptions/dues	37.00	
Miscellaneous	325.00	
Total Monthly Expenses		**$8,640.00**
Net Monthly Profit		**$17,980.00**

Note: Cost of sales refers to the cost of the product as well as all documentation required to complete all trade transactions.

▲

Income Statement Worksheet

Income Statement

For the month of _____

Monthly Income

Gross sales _____

Cost of sales _____

Gross Monthly Income $_____

Monthly Expenses

Rent _____

Phone/utilities _____
   (add $60 cell phone charge)

Postage/delivery _____

Licenses/taxes _____

Employees _____

Benefits/taxes _____

Advertising/promotions _____

Legal services _____

Accounting services _____

Office supplies _____

Transportation/travel _____

Insurance _____

Subscriptions/dues _____

Miscellaneous _____

Total Monthly Expenses $_____

Net Monthly Profit $_____

Note: Cost of sales refers to the cost of the product as well as all documentation required to complete all trade transactions.

- Provide letters of introduction and letters of credit for you when you're traveling abroad
- Provide credit information on potential overseas buyers
- Establish your good credit when someone checks up on you
- Advise you on export regulations
- Exchange currencies
- Assist in financing exports
- Collect foreign invoices, drafts, letters of credit, and other foreign receivables
- Transfer funds to other countries
- Lend credit assistance to your foreign buyers

Smart Tip

Tip...

Remember that your local bank, especially if you live in a rural area or small town, may not handle international affairs. You may have to go further afield. But don't neglect this important aspect of your new business.

Add finding a compatible banker to your start-up to-do list; then start interviewing, either by phone or in person.

Interviewing bankers gives you the opportunity to establish a relationship. And the closer your relationship with the bank manager or other executive, the better your chances of getting loans and special favors when you need them.

The fact that you're a newbie with a small start-up account is not a drawback. You're offering the bank the prospect of major future transactions; it doesn't hurt to cite examples from your projected income statements and market research. And don't

Oh, Pick OPIC!

The Overseas Private Investment Corporation, affectionately known as OPIC, is a U.S. government agency that provides project financing, investment insurance, and a variety of investor services to 150 emerging-economy countries around the globe. OPIC encourages American overseas private investments to generate domestic exports and create jobs. With assets of over $6.2 billion and fund balance of over $874 billion in investments, OPIC concentrates heavily on SME projects. The number of SME projects increased 104 percent between 2003 and 2004, and grew to 83 projects in 2005. Demand is expected to increase exponentially in the coming years.

As with any government entity, paperwork abounds, but if you're thinking of exporting services or working on large projects, you should give OPIC an electronic jingle at www.opic.gov or call the agency at (202) 336-8690.

forget the inherent glamour and adventure of international trade. If you were a banker, wouldn't you find your business more interesting than, say, dry cleaning? Choose a banker who's excited about your company; then let him share in the excitement of developing it.

Play Money

As an international trader, you'll often deal in other currencies besides U.S. dollars, so you'll need to develop an awareness and appreciation (or depreciation) of world currencies. Anyone who has traveled outside the United States finds out almost immediately that a dollar isn't always worth a dollar. Its value changes from country to country and from day to day according to U.S. and other national economies.

Whenever you discuss prices with your clients, customers, or anyone else in your trade channel, you'll need to think about the currency exchange rate. Since this rate constantly fluctuates, and since you may have to alter your prices to reflect the current rate, this adds an exciting tactical aspect to the import/export game.

Let's say, for instance, that you are working with Norwegian goods, and the dollar goes down in relation to the krone. If you're importing from Norway, this will make you groan because you'll now have to pay more in dollars to purchase the merchandise. But if you are exporting to Norway, this same news will put a smile on your face. The devalued dollar will cost less in the land of the fjord, so you can either lower your price, which will please your customer, or you can maintain your price and take a higher profit.

So as an international trader, it behooves you to keep your eye on currency rates. When the currency rate swings one way, you might want to import; when it swings the other, you can think export. Or you might make it a general rule to import goods from emerging-economy countries whose currencies are always weak in relation to the U.S. dollar (you can buy more for less), and export goods to countries with economies that are generally stronger than ours, such as those in Western Europe.

> **Bright Idea**
> Consider a bank with a home office in a country you will be working with. If you're exporting to Japan, for example, you might go with a bank like Sumitomo. If you are exporting to Germany, how about Deutsche Bank? Foreign banks with U.S. branches can often speed the opening of L/Cs and sometimes offer better lending terms.

See Spot Transact

Sometimes you'll be responsible for exchanging foreign currencies into U.S. dollars, which generally comprises two types of transactions:

- *The Spot Transaction.* This involves the sale of U.S. dollars and the purchase of foreign currency (or the reverse) for immediate delivery, or on-the-spot delivery. For instance, if you sell merchandise to a company in Japan, you'll quote your price in either U.S. dollars or yen. Now the exchange rate may change before the deal is complete, but you've already set your price. This is where your tactical ability comes in (or a crystal ball, if you have one). If you quote the price in dollars, the Japanese company assumes the risk of a change in rates because it will have to pay the dollar value no matter what, and this change may or may not be to its benefit. If you quote the price in yen, you're the one assuming the risk. On the date of payment, you have the bank change the yen to dollars (or buy dollars with the yen). If the yen is weaker, you lose a percentage of your profits, but if the yen is stronger, you gain profits.

Smart Tip

Sneak a peek at daily foreign exchange rates per the Federal Reserve Bank of New York at www.ny.frb.org. Look for "Markets", select "Foreign Exchange" and click on "FX Rates" for the latest exchange.

Money by Another Name

Country	Name of Currency
Australia	dollar
Canada	dollar
Brazil	real
India	rupee
Japan	yen
Malaysia	ringgit
Mexico	peso
New Zealand	dollar
Norway	krone
South Africa	rand
South Korea	won
Thailand	baht
Venezuela	bolívar

▲

- *The Forward Transaction.* If you don't have a crystal ball and don't want to sit around worrying about whether the exchange rate will go up or down, you can purchase the foreign currency at the time you make the deal. If you quote your price in yen, you immediately purchase the yen from the bank at the rate that coincides with your price quote. This way both parties are free of risk. But don't dismiss that crystal ball—if the foreign currency increases in value, you'll have lost an extra percentage point of potential profit.

> ## Smart Tip
>
> It's usually easier to find a buyer if you agree to accept payment in her currency. If you become a currency rate watcher, you should be able to spot trends and set your price according to what you predict the exchange rate will be when the deal is completed.

The Tax Man Cometh

When you earn all those bounties with your cleverly predicted exchange rates, someone will be queuing up for a piece of the action: Uncle Sam. If your budget allows, you should engage an accountant. You probably won't need him or her for your daily or monthly concerns, but it's well worth the expense to have someone in the know at the reins when April 15 comes around, or for those rare-but-Panicsville questions that come up now and again.

Your tax deductions should be about the same as those for any other small or homebased business. You can deduct a percentage of your home office so long as you are using it solely as an office. These deductions include all normal office expenses plus interest, taxes, insurance, and depreciation (this is where the accountant comes in handy). The IRS has added all sorts of permutations, including that the total amount of the deduction is limited by the gross income you derive from the business activity minus all your other business expenses apart from those related to the home office. And you thought that new board game you got for Christmas had complicated rules!

Basically, the IRS doesn't want you to come up with so many home office deductions that you end up paying no tax at all. If, after reading the lowdown, you're still confused, consult your accountant.

Trader's View

When you travel in Europe, you'll often come across the VAT, or value-added tax. This tax is tacked onto both domestic and imported products in European Union (EU) countries.

Driving Miss Trader

What else can you deduct? Business-related phone calls, the cost of business equipment and supplies (again, so long as you're truly using them solely for your business), sub-

Innocents Abroad

Traveling's half the fun of international trade. But make sure you're not an innocent abroad. Plan your itinerary carefully to make your trip as personally and professionally profitable as possible. To make every moment count, combine several business activities:

- ○ Find new clients and reps
- ○ Reinforce your relationships with current clients and reps
- ○ Evaluate your competition
- ○ Update your market research

Set up meetings before you leave home so you're assured that the people you want to see will be available. And, as always, do your homework. Will you be arriving in a country during a holiday or festival when offices will be closed? Research local customs.

Several web sites can give pointers: Check out Executive Planet at www.executive planet.com for extensive information on 30-plus top U.S. trade partners. Going Global (www.goingglobal.com) has great tips on 24 of the countries you'll most likely trade with. And don't forget the Country Commercial Guides at www.ita.doc.gov/cs. These sites will let you know country-specific "intelligence" on anything from which gestures are improper to how fashionably late to arrive for dinner to tips on small talk.

---

scriptions to professional and trade journals, and auto expenses. These accrue when you drive your trusty vehicle in the course of doing business or seeking business. In other words, you're chalking up deductible mileage when you motor out to your clients' offices to pick up samples or present marketing plans, or when you take a spin to the bank, the freight forwarder's office, or down to the docks with documentation.

It's wise to keep a log of your business miles. You can buy one of several varieties at your local office supply or stationery store, or you can make one yourself. Keep track as you go. It's no fun to have to backtrack at tax time and guesstimate how many miles you drove to see how many clients how many times during the year.

> **Bright Idea**
>
> If you're planning to take an international business trip, check into the Worldroom web site at www.worldroom.com for links to bargain airfares, currency exchange rates, hotel databases, weather, and time difference.

Let Me Entertain You

You can deduct entertainment expenses, such as wining and dining a client during the course of a sales pitch or hosting potential reps at a coffeehouse. Hold onto your receipts and keep a log of all these expenses as well. (If you're entertaining at home, have your clients or prospects sign a guest book.)

You must have a business-related purpose for entertaining, such as a sales presentation. General goodwill toward your fellow professionals doesn't make it, so be sure your log contains the reason for the partying.

Planes, Trains, and Automobiles

When you travel for business purposes, you can deduct airfares, train tickets, rental car mileage, and the like. You can also deduct hotels and meals. And you can even—under certain circumstances— deduct recreational side trips you take with your family while you're traveling on business. Since the IRS allows deductions for any such trip you take to expand your awareness and expertise in your field of business, it makes sense to take advantage of any conferences or seminars that you can attend.

While we're on the topic, if you don't already have a U.S. passport, apply for one now. Processing can take weeks. And keep your passport current. Some countries will deny you entry if you have six months or less left until your passport expires.

> **Tip...**
>
> ## Smart Tip
> The Internationalist web site at www.internationalist.com provides scads of fabulous travel information for the international businessperson—including banks and law firms by country, and overseas conferences.

14

Fair Winds or Foul Seas

Most people succeed in the import/export business by following the tried-and-true business methods of persistence and plain old-fashioned hard work, with a healthy dose of optimism liberally sprinkled throughout. All the raw talent in the world doesn't change the fact that becoming an international trader involves a lot of work. Rewarding and sometimes exhilarating work, but darn hard work nonetheless.

Hopefully after reading this book, you know that becoming an international trader is not the same as becoming an overnight success. It takes lots of market research, loads of planning, hours of financial calculations, sore knuckles from knocking on virtual doors, and the abundant application of creativity to land that first client, and more of the same to land the ones that follow.

Ring of Contacts

When the international traders interviewed for this book were asked about their best and worst experiences in the business, they gave—not surprisingly—some very honest responses.

"There are many [best] experiences," says Jan H. in Belgium, "but I have a nice feeling in my 30 years in business of having built a ring of contacts around the world, many of whom are personal friends, all business put aside."

In Germany, Michael R. tackles the question from two angles: his 24-plus years as a trader and his 16-year tenure as an international trade consultant. "Everything always went smoothly," he says, "and from the [standpoint of] my consultancy, my system of looking at markets simply works perfectly and has brought most clients between 30 percent and 80 percent rise in turnover per year."

But the import/export life doesn't always flow smoothly. Michael's worst experience involved a letter of credit from a customer in Thailand. "We were about ten days late in supply due to unforeseen circumstances," the German consultant recalls. "Although the contractual agreement said the customer had to change the date, he refused. So we had to fake the documentation to be presented to the bank in time for getting the money from the L/C. Then we shipped afterward, having the money already."

In São Paulo, Brazil, John L. ran into a similar case of a customer not keeping his word. "My worst experience," John says, "was one that did not happen! It's a joke. My worst moment happened when I had to get some television tube replacements from a Chinese maker. We had agreed on a 1.5 percent defective rate. In reality, the rate was 4 percent. So the maker was supposed to refund me the difference. After six months of negotiations, I had to lie, saying that if he would refund me, I would place another order."

Trader's View

The secret to success? Maintaining the highest business standards, according to Russian trade expert Peter P. "Professionalism is very important, especially in an emerging market," Peter says. "It's very important no matter who you deal with."

But not everything went badly. "My best experience was in the pet shop field," the Brazilian continues. "I located a source of aquarium supplies for a Brazilian company. The profit margin for my client was more than 600 percent."

For Lloyd D., as well, his best experiences come from being able to hand his clients golden eggs. "[It's] fulfilling our commitment with our principal to convert a simple inquiry into an actual sale," the Florida-based export manager says. A worst-case experience is the opposite. "[It's] when a prospective buyer, after several months of back-and-forth, suddenly disappears from the radar screen, without explanation, while we assume he has probably gone to a competitor."

And in France, Bruno C. relates, "So far, I haven't had a worst experience. Nonetheless, nearly every week I have very bad experiences when I get an answer from a potential client who says they are not looking for the product any more, or that they just need very small quantities, or that they possibly [won't] need our products [for another] three or more months. Since our products sometimes act as a complementary part of a finished product, this can occur because they haven't finished installing the production line.

"The inexistence of a 'worst experience' is certainly due to my short experience [in the business]. Anyway, I have got plenty of time. I'm in no hurry to live such an experience.

"Every significant contract is a best experience. A very best experience, for example, is when you have been working from three months to a few years on a really important contract. You haven't received any news from your potential client for a few months and then, suddenly, you receive an order."

When You Believe

If you are the type of person who can handle these sorts of highs and lows, then you will probably thrive in the world of international trade. If not, you may discover during your company's first year of life, or beyond, that the business isn't for you. You may feel that instead of being blown along by fair winds, you're at peril in foul seas.

Whether or not you're earning money, the success of your business is contingent on a happiness factor. Because it's a lot of work and a lot of responsibility, you may discover that you'd be just as happy—or more so—working for someone else. And that's OK. With everything you have learned you'll be a great job candidate.

None of the people interviewed for this book, from a green-as-can-be newbie to a veteran with more than 30 years' experience,

> **Trader's View**
>
> "Try not to be discouraged too fast or by a setback," Bruno C. counsels. "Practice sports and try to go out from time to time to [get away] from all your preoccupations."

seem to have any intention of packing it in. Rather, they seem to have a sense of being a part of the world, a philosophical outlook that lets them see all of us on this globe as part of a whole.

Michael in Germany sums it up best. "Do not just rely on a given home market," he says. "We are living in the world, but we all need the other ones. Be open to people, but don't lose your own thoroughly prepared idea. Cooperate with others. Don't just rely on yourself; others can open markets that you will never have reached on your own."

And Wahib W., the native Egyptian, says, "Work on [doing your job] all the time. It's a continuous process, doing it every day with the belief that you're going to succeed."

This seems to be the common denominator of all the international traders who so generously helped with this book: winning attitudes. If you go into this business with the right stuff—a willingness to work hard, to learn everything you can, the confidence to promote yourself and your business, and the drive to succeed—chances are you will.

Appendix
International Trade Resources

They say you can never be rich enough or young enough. While these could be argued, we believe you can never have enough resources. Therefore, we present for your consideration a wealth of sources for you to check into, check out, and harness for your own personal information blitz.

These sources are tidbits, ideas to get you started on your research. They are by no means the only sources out there, and they should not be taken as the Ultimate Answer. We have done our research, but businesses do tend to move, change, fold, and expand. As we have repeatedly stressed, do your homework. Get out and start investigating.

Associations

The American Association of Exporters and Importers, 1050 17th Street NW, Suite 810, Washington, DC 20036, (202) 857-8009, www.aaei.org

The Federation of International Trade Associations, 1900 Campus Commons Drive, Suite 340, Reston, VA 20191, (800) 969-FITA, www.fita.org

▲

International Chamber of Commerce, 38 cours Albert 1er, 75008 Paris, France, 011-33-1-49-53-28-28, www.iccwbo.org

The International Federation of Customs Brokers Associations, 55 Murray St., #320, Ottawa, Ont. K1N 5M3, Canada, www.ifcba.org

International Organization for Standardization, www.iso.ch

International Small Business Consortium, 3309 Windjammer St., Norman, OK 73072, www.isbc.com

World Trade Centers Association, 420 Lexington Ave., Suite 518, New York, NY 10170, (212) 432-2626, www.wtca.org

Books

Building an Import/Export Business, by Kenneth D. Weiss, John Wiley & Sons Inc.

Exporting, Importing, and Beyond, by Lawrence W. Tuller, Adams Media Corp.

Export-Import, by Joseph A. Zodl, Betterway Books

Import/Export: How to Get Started in International Trade, by Carl A. Nelson, McGraw-Hill

Importing into the U.S., available at www.customs.ustreas.gov

Selling to the World, by L. Fargo Wells, McGraw-Hill

Any of the Barron's foreign language series, such as *Learn Italian the Fast and Fun Way*, by Marcel Danesi, Barron's Educational Series

(Note: Check out the International Trade and Business Bookstore at http://tradecenter.ntis.gov for the U.S. government's collection of international trade books, which you can purchase online.)

Credit Cards with Air Miles

American Express, (800) 528-4800, www.americanexpress.com

Chase, (888) 269-8690, www.chase.com

Citibank, (800) 627-3999, www.citibank.com

Customs Brokers and Freight Forwarders

Air Sea International Forwarding Inc., 400 Perrine Rd., #408, Old Bridge, NJ 08857, (732) 727-8020, www.airseaint.com

Serra International Inc., 75 Montgomery St., #300, Jersey City, NJ 07302, (201) 860-9600, www.serraintl.com

Credit Reports

Dun & Bradstreet, (800) 234-3867, www.dnb.com

Forms

Unz & Co., 201 Circle Dr. N, Suite 104, Piscataway, NJ 08854, (800) 631-3098, (732) 868-0706, www.unzco.com

Helpful Government Agencies—Import/Export

Bureau of Industry and Security, Outreach and Educational Services, 14th St. & Pennsylvania Ave. NW, U.S. Department of Commerce, Washington, DC 20230, (202) 482-4811, www.bis.doc.gov; Check BIS' Web site for Western regional addresses and phone numbers.

Business Information Service for the Newly Independent States (BISNIS), U.S. Department of Commerce, USA Trade Center, Stop R*BISNIS, 1401 Constitution Ave. NW, Washington, DC 20230, www.bis nis.doc.gov, (800) USA-TRADE

Canine Enforcement, www.cbp.gov/xp/cgov/border_security/canines/canine.xml

Export Assistance Centers around the country can be found on the Commercial Service web site at www.ita.doc.gov/uscs or by calling (800) USA-TRADE.

Export-Import Bank of the United States (Ex-Im Bank), 811 Vermont Ave. NW, Washington, DC 20571, (202) 565-EXIM, www.exim.gov

The Export Legal Assistance Network (ELAN), www.export-legal-assistance.org

Foreign Agricultural Service, U.S. Department of Agriculture, 1400 Independence Ave. SW, Washington, DC 20250, (202) 720-7420, www.fas.usda.gov

International Trade Administration, 1401 Constitution Ave. NW, Washington, DC 20230, (800) USA-TRADE, www.ita.doc.gov

Overseas Private Investment Corporation (OPIC), 1100 New York Ave. NW, Washington, DC 20527, (202) 336-8799, www.opic.gov

Shipper's Export Declaration (U.S. Census Bureau, Foreign Trade Division), (301) 457-2238

Showcase Europe, www.buyusa.gov/europe/

Small Business Initiative (Export-Import Bank), www.exim.gov/products/special/small bus.cfm

U.S. Commercial Service, 1401 Constitution Ave. NW, Rm. 3802, Washington, DC 20230, (202) 482-2000, www.trade.gov/cs

U.S. Census Bureau, Foreign Trade Division, U.S. Department of Commerce, U.S. Bureau of the Census, 4700 Silver Hill Rd., Suitland, MD 20746, mailing address: Rm. 2179, Bldg. 3, Washington, DC 20233-6700, (301) 457-3041, www.census.gov/foreign-trade/www/abtftd.html

U.S. Customs Service, 1300 Pennsylvania Ave. NW, Washington, DC 20229, (202) 354-1000, www.customs.ustreas.gov

U.S. Department of Commerce, 1401 Constitution Ave. NW, Washington, DC 20230, (202) 482-2000, www.commerce.gov

Helpful Related Government Agencies

Agricultural Marketing Service, 1400 Independence Ave. SW, #3071-S, Washington, DC 20250-0201, (202) 720-5115, www.ams.usda.gov

Animal and Plant Health Inspection Service (APHIS-USDA), 12th and Independence Ave. SW, Washington, DC 20250, (202) 720-3861, www.aphis.usda.gov

Bureau of Alcohol, Tobacco, and Firearms, Import/Export, 650 Massachusetts Ave. NW, Washington, DC 20226, (202) 927-7760, www.atf.treas.gov

Business Information Kit, (800) ASK-USPS

Center for Biologics Evaluation and Research, 1401 Rockville Pike, #200N, Rockville, MD 20852-1448, (800) 835-4709, www.fda.gov/cber

Center for Devices and Radiological Health, 1350 Piccard Dr., HFZ-210, Rockville, MD 20850, (800) 638-2041, www.fda.gov/cdrh

Center for Food Safety and Applied Nutrition, 5100 Paint Branch Pkwy., College Park, MD 20740, (888) 723-3366, www.cfsan.fda.gov

Centers for Disease Control and Prevention, 1600 Clifton Rd., Atlanta, GA 30333, (404) 639-3311, www.cdc.gov

Drug Enforcement Administration (DEA), Mailstop AES, 2401 Jefferson Davis Hwy., Alexandria, VA 22301, (202) 307-1000, www.usdoj.gov/dea

Environmental Protection Agency, Ariel Rios Building, 1200 Pennsylvania Ave. NW, Washington, DC 20460, (202) 272-0167, www.epa.gov

Federal Communications Commission, 445 12th St. SW, Washington, DC 20544, (885) 225-5322, www.fcc.gov

Federal Trade Commission, 600 Pennsylvania Ave. NW, Washington, DC 20580, (202) 326-2222, www.ftc.gov

Food Safety and Inspection Service, 1400 Independence Ave. SW, Washington, DC 20250, (202) 720-9904, www.fsis.usda.gov

International Mail Calculator, http://ircalc.usps.gov

ISO 9000 Information, http://ts.nist.gov (click on "search," then type in ISO 9000)

National Center for Import/Export, (301) 734-8364 (for animals)

National Institute of Standards and Technology, Public Inquiries Unit, 100 Bureau Dr., Stop 1070, Gaithersburg, MD 20899, (301) 975-NIST, www.nist.gov

Office of Codes and Standards (DOE), 1000 Independence Ave. SW, Washington, DC 20585 (800) DIALDOE, www.energy.gov

Office of Engineering and Technology, 445 12th St. SW, Washington, DC 20554, (202) 418-2470, www.fcc.gov/oet

Office of Hazardous Materials, 400 Seventh St. SW, Washington, DC 20590-0001, (202) 366-8553, http://hazmat.dot.gov

Office of Nutritional Products, Labeling, and Dietary Supplements, 5100 Paint Branch Parkway, College Park, MD 20740, (301) 436-2373, www.cfsan.fda.gov/label.html

Office of Regulatory Affairs, 5600 Fishers Ln., Rockville, MD 20857, (888) INFO-FDA, www.fda.gov/ora

Office of Size Standards, 409 Third St. SW, Washington, DC 20416, (202) 205-6618, www.sba.gov/size

Plant Protection and Quarantine, Import and export, www.aphis.usda.gov/import_export.index.shtml

U.S. Consumer Product Safety Commission, Office of Compliance, 4330 East-West Hwy., Bethesda, MD 20814, (301) 504-7923, www.cpsc.gov

U.S. Department of Agriculture, 14th St. & Independence Ave. SW, Washington, DC 20250, (202) 720-2791, www.usda.gov

U.S. Department of Energy, 1000 Independence Ave. SW, Washington, DC 20585, (800) DIALDOE, www.energy.gov

U.S. Department of Health and Human Services, Secretary's Office, 200 Independence Ave. SW, Washington, DC 20201, (202) 619-0257, www.hhs.gov

U.S. Department of Justice, 950 Pennsylvania Ave. NW, Washington, DC 20530, (202) 514-2000, www.usdoj.gov

U.S. Department of Transportation, 400 Seventh St. SW, Washington, DC 20590, (202) 366-4000, www.dot.gov

U.S. Department of the Treasury, 1500 Pensylvannia Ave. NW, Washington, DC 20220, (202) 622-2000, www.ustreas.gov

U.S. Fish and Wildlife Service, 1849 C St. NW, Washington, DC 20240, (800) 344-WILD, www.fws.gov

U.S. Food and Drug Administration, 5600 Fishers Ln., Rockville, MD 20857, (888) 463-6332, www.fda.gov

U.S. Nuclear Regulatory Commission, 11555 Rockville Pike, Rockville, MD 20852-2738, (301) 415-7000, www.nrc.gov

U.S. Postal Service, (800) ASK-USPS, www.usps.com

U.S. Small Business Administration, International Trade, 409 Third St. SW, 8th Fl., Washington, DC 20416, (202) 205-6720, www.sba.gov

International Trade Directories

Croner Publications, 10951 Sorrento Valley Rd., #1D, San Diego, CA 92121-1613, (800) 441-4033, www.croner.com

Magazines and Publications

Export America, offered through the Department of Commerce, www.ita.doc.gov

The Journal of Commerce, 33 Washington St., Newark, NJ 07102, www.joc.com

Tradeshow Week, 5700 Wilshire Blvd., #120, Los Angeles, CA 90036-5804, (323) 965-5300, www.tradeshowweek.com

Market Research

Economic Bulletin Board (EBB), see address and phone for STAT-USA below, (800) STAT-USA for subscriptions

Foreign exchange rates from www.x-rates.com

International Trade Data Network, www.itdn.net

National Trade Data Bank, see address and phone for STAT-USA below; www.stat -usa.gov

STAT-USA, HCHB Room 4885, Department of Commerce, 14th St. & Constitution Ave., Washington, DC 20230, (202) 482-1986, (800) STAT-USA, www.stat-usa.gov

Thomas Register of American Manufacturers, Thomas Publishing Co., 5 Penn Plaza, New York, NY 10001, (212) 695-0500, www.thomasregister.com

Miscellaneous International Business Web Sites

AT&T Phone Service, General Business Resource Center, (800) 661-2705, www.att.com

The Electronic Embassy, www.embassy.org

FedEx, (800) GOFEDEX, www.fedex.com

Seminars and Workshops

The American Association of Exporters & Importers, 1050 17th St. NW, Washington, DC 20036, (202) 857-8009, www.aaei.org

The Federation of International Trade Associations, 1900 Campus Commons Dr., Suite 340, Reston, VA 20191, (800) 969-3482, www.fita.org

Unz & Co., 201 Circle Dr. N, Suite 104, Piscataway, NJ 08854, (800) 631-3098 or (732) 868-0706, www.unzco.com

(*Note*: Check with your local community college or university. It may sponsor seminars and workshops, too.)

Successful International Trade Businesses

Global Partners Inc., 303 Second St., Suite D, Annapolis, MD 21403, (410) 626-1515, www.globalpartnersusa.com

Intyre, Jan Herremans, Veldstraat 21a, B-9220 Hamme, Belgium, 011-32-52-481136, www.intyre.com, e-mail: info@intyre.com

LND Export Management, Lloyd N. Davidson, 749 SW Watson Pl., Port St. Lucie, FL 34953-6340, (772) 336-0139, e-mail: lnd@lndexportmanagement.com

Michael Richter, MBA, Drehergässle 5, DE-88499 Daugendorf, Germany, 011-49-7371-93210, www.MichaelRichter-Marketing.de, e-mail: michael@michaelrichter-marketing.de

Sociètè Corindus, Bruno Carlier, Ave. Gabriel de Clieu, 76 370 Derchigny Graincourt, France, 011-33-2-35-19-36-44, e-mail: corindus.france@wanadoo.fr

United Network International Trading (UNIT), John Laurino, Rua Albuquerque Lins 574, ap 172, São Paulo, SP 01230-000, Brazil, 011 (55-11) 3826-9435; www.laurino-lopez. com.br, e-mail: john@laurino-lopez.com.br

Trade Leads

National Trade Data Base, www.stat-usa. gov

TradeNet, www.tradenet.com

(*Note*: Check out the U.S. Department of Commerce's Trade Information Center at www.ita.doc.gov/td/tic for a list of dozens of trade lead sites.)

Glossary

Absolute quota: limit on the amount of a product that can be brought into a country during a specified time period.

Advising bank: the seller's or exporter's bank in a letter of credit transaction.

Agent: salesperson who pitches a product to wholesale or retail buyers but does not take title to the product.

Air waybill: bill of lading from an air carrier.

Andean Trade Preference Act (ATPA): legislation granting duty-free product entry for designated Andes-mountain region nations.

Anti-Dumping Act: U.S. legislation designed to counteract the practice of dumping.

APHIS: acronym for Animal and Plant Health Inspection Service, a division of the Department of Agriculture.

Applicant: the buyer or importer in a letter of credit transaction; also called an opener.

Assist: a tool, mold, engineering drawing, artwork, or other item that assists in the assembly and sale of the product.

ATA carnet: an international customs document allowing duty-free entry for goods, such as product samples; also called a carnet.

ATPA: see Andean Trade Preference Act.

Available at sight: letter of credit term meaning the funds will be paid as soon as the conditions of the L/C are met.

BEM: big emerging market; in other words, an emerging nation with great export potential.

Beneficiary: the exporter or seller in a letter of credit transaction.

Bill of lading: a receipt from the ship, air, or trucking line showing that it has the merchandise.

BIS: see Bureau of Industry and Security.

BISNIS: International Trade Administration's acronym for its Business Information Service for the Newly Independent States.

Bonded warehouse: warehouse or other storage area within customs territory where imported goods can be stored without paying a duty.

Branded product: one that carries a brand name.

Bureau of Industry and Security (BIS): U.S. government agency that administers exports.

Caribbean Basin Initiative: a plan under which designated Caribbean countries are granted duty-free entry for certain products.

Carnet: see ATA carnet.

Cash against documents: see Collection draft.

Cash in advance: payment term meaning the importer pays for the goods before they are shipped.

CBI: see Caribbean Basin Initiative.

Certificate of manufacture: document verifying that the merchandise has been manufactured and fulfills the general product requirements.

Certificate of origin: form verifying the product was manufactured in the country of origin.

CFR: see Cost and freight.

CIF: see Cost, insurance, and freight.

CIP: see Cost, insurance, and freight paid to.

Clean bill of lading: one in which no discrepancies or problems with the goods have been noted.

Clean draft: draft to which no documents are attached.

Clean on board bill of lading: see Clean bill of lading.

Collection documents: shipping documents or records.

Collection draft: agreement in which buyer takes title to the shipment once it reaches its final destination and pays for it there.

Commercial invoice: finished version of the pro forma invoice.

Commercial Service: see US & FCS.

Commission agent: an intermediary commissioned by a foreign firm searching for domestic products to purchase.

Commission representative: foreign independent sales representative.

Commodity control list: a listing of potential export items subject to BIS export controls.

Compact of Free Association (FAS): legislation granting duty-free entry to certain products of the Marshall Islands and the Federated States of Micronesia.

Conference line: association of ocean freight carriers with common shipping rates and conditions; also called ocean freight conference.

Confirm: letter of credit term meaning the bank guarantees payment as long as the conditions of the L/C are met.

Consular invoice: document demanded by a country, along with a fee, before it will allow entry of merchandise.

Consularization of documents: practice of paying a fee at import to have entry documents stamped as legal; also called legalization of documents.

Consumption entry: customs entry for goods intended for immediate resale.

Cost and freight (CFR): shipping term meaning the exporter has the goods transported to the port or airport and loaded onto the carrier, and pays the shipping charges to the destination.

Cost, insurance, and freight (CIF): shipping term meaning the exporter pays all costs, including insurance and freight, to the product's destination.

Cost, insurance, and freight paid to (CIP): same as cost, insurance, and freight, except that the exporter pays for delivery to the importer's door and retains title up to that point.

▲

Contingent policy: an insurance policy that backs up the regular policy in the event of a catastrophe.

Country-controlled buying agent: foreign government agency or quasi-governmental firm charged with locating and purchasing products.

Customhouse broker: see Customs broker.

Customs broker: individual or company licensed by the Department of the Treasury who acts as the importer's agent for the product's entry into a country; also called customhouse broker.

DAF: see Delivered at frontier.

Date of expiry: the date the letter of credit expires.

DDP: see Delivered duty paid.

Dealer assistance program: a program in which the importer or exporter provides sales representatives with product information aids and materials.

Delivered at frontier (DAF): shipping term meaning the exporter pays ground transport freight costs to the border, where the importer takes title.

Delivered duty paid (DDP): shipping term meaning the exporter takes on all costs, including customs duties, to have the goods delivered to the importer's door.

Dimensional weight: a value of the cargo that considers its weight and volume.

Discrepancy: letter of credit term meaning a problem in fulfilling the L/C's conditions.

Distributor: a company that buys an imported product and then sells it to a retailer or other agent; also called a wholesale distributor.

Dock receipt: document verifying that the merchandise has arrived at the dock.

Documentary credit: see Letter of credit.

Draft: banking term meaning the buyer's order to pay the seller.

Drawback refund: a refund on duties paid on imported merchandise that is processed or assembled for re-export.

Dumping: the practice of flooding a market with an imported product that's far cheaper than a comparable domestic one.

Duty: import tax.

EAR: acronym for Export Administration Regulations.

EBB: Economic Bulletin Board, a trade service of the U.S. Department of Commerce.

ECU: see European currency unit.

ELAN: the Export Legal Assistance Network, developed the Federal Bar Association and the Small Business Administration.

EMC: see Export management company.

Entry for consumption: see Consumption entry.

EU: see European Union.

Euro: see European currency unit.

European currency unit: a standard monetary unit for the 15 nations of the European Union; also called an ECU or a euro.

European Single Market: another name for the European Union.

European Union (EU): a single nontrade barrier marketplace formed by 15 Western European nations.

Evidence of right to make entry: a bill of lading or air waybill submitted to the port-side customs office.

Ex-Im Bank: the Export-Import Bank of the United States.

Export management company (EMC): a business that handles export operations for a domestic company.

Export trading company: a business that exports goods and services or provides export-related services.

Ex Dock: shipping term meaning the importer takes title to the product at the export dock.

Ex Ship: shipping term meaning the importer takes title to the product at the ship before it departs.

EXW: see Ex Works.

Ex Works (EXW): shipping term meaning the importer takes title to the product at the exporter's or manufacturer's "works," or factory.

FAS: see Compact of Free Association; can also be a shipping term—see free alongside ship.

FCA: see Free carrier.

FOB: see Free on board vessel.

Foreign distributor: a foreign merchant, similar to a wholesale distributor in the United States, who buys for his or her own account, then distributes the product.

Foreign trade zone (FTZ): a warehouse or other storage facility in which imported goods can be stored or processed without having to pay duties.

Formal customs entry: one in which the merchandise is valued at $2,000 or more.

Forward transaction: term used when foreign currency is purchased at the time an export price is quoted.

Foul bill of lading: one in which a problem with the goods has been discovered.

Free alongside ship (FAS): shipping term meaning the exporter will have the goods loaded onto the ship or air carrier, where the importer then takes title.

Free carrier (FCA): shipping term meaning the exporter loads the goods onto the truck or other carrier at his works, where the importer takes title.

Free on board vessel (FOB): shipping term meaning the exporter loads the goods onto the ship or vessel, where the importer takes title.

Freight forwarder: individual or company that acts as the exporter's agent for product export.

FTA: see United States-Israel Free Trade Area.

FTZ: see Foreign trade zone.

Full set: shipping term referring to the three original bills of lading traditionally issued and signed by the captain.

GATT: see General Agreement on Tariffs and Trade.

General Agreement on Tariffs and Trade (GATT): international agreement designed to reduce trade barriers between countries.

General average insurance: covers the holder against general cargo loss on board ship as opposed to covering only the holder's merchandise.

General order (G.O.): goods considered abandoned by customs and put into a bonded warehouse.

G.O.: see General order.

Harmonize: to develop a single or matching system of tariffs.

Harmonized Tariff Schedule of the United States: listing of all U.S. tariffs.

Immediate transport entry: customs entry for goods to be shipped to another location for customs clearance.

Import/export merchant: a businessperson who purchases goods directly from a domestic or foreign manufacturer, then packs, ships, and resells the goods.

Import quota: a limit on the quantity of a particular product that can be brought into a country over a specified period of time.

Incoterms: International Chamber of Commerce terms that are a worldwide standardization of shipping terminology.

Independent line: shipping line not allied with an ocean freight conference.

Informal customs entry: one in which the imported goods are valued at $2,000 or less.

Inherent vice: damage that could arise due to the nature of the goods being shipped.

Inspection certificate: document certifying the quality, quantity, or conformity of the product.

Insurance certificate: document confirming that marine insurance has been provided and indicating type of coverage.

Intellectual property: a product that has been patented, trademarked, or copyrighted and is protected by law.

Irrevocable letter of credit: a letter of credit that cannot be rescinded by the buyer, or importer.

ISO: International Organization of Standards.

ISO 9000: international quality management certification.

ISO 14000: international environmental management certification.

Issuing bank: see Opening bank.

ITA: International Trade Administration; a division of the U.S. Department of Commerce.

Joint venture: a partnership between two or more companies.

Lading: freight or cargo.

L/C: see Letter of credit.

Legalization of documents: see Consularization of documents.

Letter of credit (L/C): document issued by a bank per instructions from an importer authorizing the exporter to draw payment after fulfilling terms set out in the document; also called a documentary credit.

Liquidate: to complete a customs entry.

Manufacturer's representative: an independent salesperson who operates out of an agency that handles an assortment of complementary products.

Most favored nation: see Normal trade relations.

NAFTA: see North American Free Trade Agreement.

Negotiable bill of lading: same as "To order of shipper," meaning the bill is not consigned specifically to the importer.

Normal trade relations: trading partner status with the United States allowing standard duties on goods (formerly known as most favored nation).

North American Free Trade Agreement (NAFTA): agreement among Canada, Mexico, and the United States to phase out all trade barriers over a 15-year period beginning in 1994.

NTDB: National Trade Data Bank; a world trade database available through the U.S. Commercial Service.

Ocean freight conference: see Conference line.

OEM: original equipment manufacturer.

On board bill of lading: document that confirms the cargo has been placed on board the vessel.

On consignment: payment term meaning the importer pays for the goods after he's sold them.

On deck bill of lading: document used when the goods must be transported on deck, as with livestock.

Open account: payment term meaning the importer sends payment to the exporter or seller when he receives the goods.

Opener: see Applicant.

Opening bank: the customer's, or importer's, bank in a letter of credit transaction; also called an issuing bank or an originating bank.

OPIC: the Overseas Private Investment Corporation, a U.S. government financing agency.

Order bill of lading: negotiable bill that must be endorsed by the shipper before it's handed over to the bank.

Order notify bill of lading: similar to an order bill of lading except that the importer and sometimes the customs broker must be notified when the ship reaches port.

Originating bank: see Opening bank.

Packing list: document detailing the number of items in shipment, how they are packed, serial numbers, weight and dimensions; also called a packing slip.

Packing slip: see Packing list.

Pro forma invoice: a price quotation in the form of an invoice.

QS 9000: international quality management certification for the automotive industry.

Retailer: the last conduit in the trade channel that sells the product to the consumer.

Revocable letter of credit: a letter of credit that can be rescinded by the buyer, or importer.

SED: see Shipper's Export Declaration.

Shipper's Export Declaration (SED): document required by the U.S. Census Bureau for all export shipments in excess of $2,500.

Sight draft: a draft payable when the merchandise arrives at the dock.

Sight letter of credit: letter of credit paid immediately upon fulfillment of the terms.

SME: small or medium enterprise.

Spot transaction: the sale of domestic dollars and the purchase of foreign currency, or the reverse, for immediate delivery, or on the spot.

SRCC: marine insurance term meaning strikes, riots, and civil commotion.

Standby letter of credit: an L/C that's set in motion if the buyer doesn't pay within a specified period of time.

State-controlled trading company: foreign government-sanctioned and controlled trade agency; often deals in raw materials, agricultural machinery, manufacturing equipment, and technical instruments.

Straight bill of lading: a non-negotiable bill that prohibits release of the goods to any-one but the person specified on the shipping documents.

Strategic alliance: an agreement between domestic and foreign companies to work toward a common goal.

Tariff: trade barrier in the form of a tax.

Tariff-rate quota: a time period during which a specific product can be imported at a reduced tariff rate.

Temporary entry under bond (TIB): customs bond posted for goods, such as product samples, temporarily entering the country.

Terminal receiving charges (TRC): fees charged by the shipping line to load the goods.

Three-level channel of distribution: a trade channel that uses a middleman who resells to the consumer.

Through bill of lading: used when several carriers are involved.

TIB: see Temporary entry under bond.

▲

Time draft: draft payable within a specified time period after the importer has received the merchandise.

To order of shipper: shipping term meaning the goods are consigned to the steamship line rather than the importer; also called a negotiable bill of lading.

TOP: Trade Opportunities Program; a trade leads program available from the U.S. Commercial Service.

Trade barrier: checks or hindrances on international trade set up by national governments to protect domestic industries from foreign competition.

Trade channel: the means by which merchandise travels from manufacturer to end user.

Trade preferences: privileges of being a trading partner or having normal trade relations with the United States and therefore paying standard duty rates.

Trading partner: favorable trading relationship with another country.

Tramp vessel: cargo ship that doesn't operate on a fixed schedule.

Transship: to ship a product into one trade region or country, offload it, and then reload and ship it on to another.

TRC: see terminal receiving charges.

United States-Israel Free Trade Area (FTA): an agreement that provides duty-free entry for certain Israeli products.

USD: U.S. dollars.

US & FCS: the U.S. Foreign and Commercial Service, also called the Commercial Service, a division of the U.S. Department of Commerce.

Validated export license: license required to export U.S. goods on the Department of Commerce's Commodity Control List, such as articles of war, advanced technology, and products in short supply.

Value-added tax (VAT): a tax tacked onto domestic and imported products in European Union countries.

VAT: see Value-added tax.

Warehouse entry: customs entry for goods to be stored in a bonded warehouse and then withdrawn in portions.

Wholesale distributor: see Distributor.

Wire transfer: procedure in which funds from the importer's bank are wired to the exporter's bank account.

Index